# THE VALLEY OF FLOWERS

Also available in the Plant Hunters series:

THE DOLOMITES by Reginald Farrer
Introduction by Geoffrey Smith

PLANT HUNTING ON THE EDGE OF THE WORLD
by F. Kingdon Ward
Introduction by Geoffrey Smith

ANEMONE OBTUSILOBA

# THE
# VALLEY OF
# FLOWERS

## BY F·S SMYTHE
### INTRODUCTION BY
### GEOFFREY SMITH

CADOGAN BOOKS
LONDON

First published in Great Britain in 1938
by Hodder and Stoughton

This edition published 1985 by
Cadogan Books Ltd
16 Lower Marsh, London SE1 7RJ

British Library Cataloguing in Publication Data

Smythe, F
    The valley of flowers.—(Plant hunters)
    1. Himalaya Mountains—Description and travel
    I. Title
    915.4'04359        DS485.H6

    ISBN 0-946313-18-0

Printed and bound in Great Britain by
Biddles Ltd, Guildford and King's Lynn

# INTRODUCTION TO THIS EDITION

Fortunately F. S. Smythe became interested in gardening a year or two before returning to the Bhyundar Valley, otherwise he might not have achieved that total identification and unity with his environment that for four months brought him the contentment which is so clearly expressed in this book. The Bhyundar Valley, as Smythe described it, is 'a valley of peace and perfect beauty where the human spirit may find repose'. The author's happiness permeates the whole book, particularly in the last summarising paragraph of each chapter; 'I ate my supper in peace beneath the accumulating stars', or, 'happiness is best achieved by adapting ourselves to the standards of our environment'.

My introduction to F. S. Smythe came when I read 'The Kangchenjunga Adventure', which so stimulated my interest that I searched for, and then read, 'The Spirit of the Hills'. Both books deal almost exclusively with climbing adventures, for Smythe was first and always a mountaineer.

Francis Sydney Smythe was born in Ivythorne, Maidstone, on the 6th July 1900. He was only two years old when his father died. After leaving Berkhamsted School he trained as an electrical engineer. In 1922, after qualifying, Smythe went to work in Austria where he spent his holidays walking and, of course, climbing. Then, rather curiously, he joined the R.A.F. in 1926, only to be invalided out after 12 months. The cautionary advice given by the service doctor that he 'be careful even walking upstairs'—which to many would have sounded like a death sentence —only drove Smythe to great feats of endurance. Work as a free-lance writer and lecturer on mountaineering and allied subjects enabled him to spend summers climbing and winters ski-ing.

Reading the various tributes to his achievements and skill in mountaineering, mention is usually made of Smythe's slight physique and even in childhood his frailty caused concern. Yet the strength and endurance needed to accomplish, for example, the route Smythe pioneered on the Brenva face of Mt. Blanc suggest a remarkable constitution. In addition, he led the successful expedition to Kamet, the first peak over 25,000ft to be climbed, and took part in three Everest expeditions. Contradiction is added to contradiction: according to one commentator the sense of inferiority obvious in Smythe at low altitudes gradually changed to sublime self confidence as a climb progressed, until at heights over 20,000ft his strength and endurance were phenomenal.

The picture which emerges, both from Smythe's own writings and those of his contemporaries, is, I think, a true reflection of the man—and one to be envied. A modest man almost to the point of self effacement, he nevertheless enjoyed argument on favoured topics. Discussion and debate on mountains and mountaineering were the breath of life to him. A contemporary writes of Smythe as a man incapable of malice and unable to understand harboured resentment in others. This probably offers the best explanation of why his descriptions are as crisp, clean, and refreshing as alpine air. Take, for example, his reflections on a rain wet woodland—'On such a morning the gloomiest forest seems charged with laughter, the whisper of falling water drops, the breeze in the treetops, and the cadence of a small stream; the pipes of Pan sound sweet-noted down the dim sun flecked aisles'. To anyone who has known such a morning that description evokes memories of happy occasions.

Smythe was also a master mountain photographer. His eye for a picture is, perhaps, best expressed in the photograph I have in front of me, taken from the Base Camp of autumn tents in the 'Valley of Flowers'. Smythe was fortunate in that he could make a living doing those things he most enjoyed—climbing and ski-ing amongst the mountains he loved. Had circumstances been otherwise he would, no doubt, have pursued these with equal zest as hobbies.

His interest in gardening must, surely, have been generated from the flowers encountered during mountaineering expeditions. Who, indeed, could fail to be moved by flower decked Alpine meadows or valleys blue with Meconopsis or Gentian? Even the sheer rock faces over which he climbed to reach the mountain summit would offer flower encrusted crevices to delight the eye.

Later in life an interest in art and history broadened his perspective still further. Smythe was not initially a plant collector; his intention on the expedition was merely to do a little desultory seed collecting. Dr. Cowan of the Royal Botanic Gardens in Edinburgh persuaded him otherwise by providing plant presses, drying papers, and seed envelopes. Smythe expresses regret—'I now realise' he writes 'what I have missed in the past . . . Merely to travel in the Himalayas without some additional interest, whether it is surveying, geology, anthropology, or botany is to miss one of the vital interests of a region that abounds in beauty and interest'. If he had met Dr. Cowan on his first expedition to the Himalaya, instead of virtually his last, the gardening public might have gained another writer plant hunter in the mould of Farrer or Kingdon Ward.

My third copy of 'Valley of Flowers', like the first two, is well used and will not be loaned out, or lost. Towards the end of the book Smythe writes—'Beauty, health, good comradeship, peace, all these had been mine in the "Valley of Flowers". For a while I had lived simply and happily, and I like to think, indeed, I know that those about me had been happy too'. Add to that all those who have derived pleasure from reading the book and the sum total of happiness increases considerably.

Happy indeed is the man who, like Francis Sydney Smythe, makes business a puppet to play with and, as Goethe writes, 'amuses himself with what his situation makes his duty'.

*GEOFFREY SMITH*
*1985*

TO ALL
WHO ENJOY
HILLS
AND THE FLOWERS
THAT GROW
ON HILLS

# CONTENTS

# CONTENTS

# CONTENTS

# AUTHOR'S NOTE

I wish here to thank many kind friends for their help and generosity, and especially my wife who was indefatigable in assisting me with the preparations for the expedition. Some I have mentioned in the text; of others, I must especially mention Messrs. Huntley & Palmer, who supplied and shipped 80 lbs. of their excellent biscuits; Kodak Ltd., who supplied photographic materials; Messrs. A. Wander Ltd., who supplied " Ovaltine " and " Ovaltine " chocolate. In India, I am indebted to Mr. Temple, the Purser of the S.S. " Corfu," for the preservation of my botanical specimens; to Mr. C. E. Boreham of the Army and Navy Stores, Bombay, the generous, efficient friend of previous Himalayan expeditions; to Mr. Wears Taylor, the Superintendent of Posts and Telegraphs at Naini Tal; to the Forestry Department, who kindly allowed me to use the Forest Bungalow at Ranikhet; to the Cawnpore Woollen Mills, who supplied porters' clothing at a generous discount; and to Messrs. Spencer & Co. of Calcutta, who supplied a quantity of excellent food at a very moderate price.

# CHAPTER I

## THE VALLEY OF FLOWERS

THIS is the story of four happy months spent amidst some of the noblest and most beautiful mountains of the world. Its inception dates back to 1931. In that year Kamet, a mountain 25,447 feet high, situated in the Garhwal Himalayas, was climbed by a small expedition of six British mountaineers of whom I was one. After the climb we descended to the village of Gamsali in the Dhauli Valley, then crossed the Zaskar Range, which separates the upper Dhauli and Alaknanda Valleys, by the Bhyundar Pass, 16,688 feet, with the intention of exploring the mountainous region at the sources of the two principal tributaries of the Ganges, the Alaknanda and Gangotri Rivers.

The monsoon had broken and the day we crossed the pass was wet, cold and miserable. Below 16,000 feet rain was falling, but above that height there was sleet or snow. A bitter wind drove at us, sheeting our clothing with wet snow and chilling us to the bone, and as quickly as possible we descended into the Bhyundar Valley, which bifurcates with the Alaknanda Valley.

Within a few minutes we were out of the wind and in rain which became gradually warmer as we lost height. Dense mist shrouded the mountainside and we had paused, uncertain as to the route, when I heard R. L. Holdsworth, who was a botanist as well as a climbing member of the expedition, exclaim : " Look ! " I followed the direction of his outstretched hand. At

first I could see nothing but rocks, then suddenly my
wandering gaze was arrested by a little splash of blue,
and beyond it were other splashes of blue, a blue so
intense it seemed to light the hillside. As Holdsworth
wrote : " All of a sudden I realised that I was simply
surrounded by *primulas*. At once the day seemed to
brighten perceptibly. Forgotten were all pains and
cold and lost porters. And what a *primula* it was !
Its leek-like habit proclaimed it a member of the *nivalis*
section. All over the little shelves and terraces it grew,
often with its roots in running water. At the most it
stood six inches high, but its flowers were enormous for
its stature, and ample in number—sometimes as many
as thirty to the beautifully proportioned umbel, and
in colour of the most heavenly French blue, sweetly
scented."

In all my mountain wanderings I had not seen a
more beautiful flower than this *primula* ; the fine rain-
drops clung to its soft petals like galaxies of seed-pearls
and frosted its leaves with silver.

Lower, where we camped near a moraine, were
*androsaces, saxifrages, sedums,* yellow and red *potentillas,
geums, geraniums,* asters, gentians, to mention but a few
plants, and it was impossible to take a step without
crushing a flower.

Next day we descended to lush meadows. Here our
camp was embowered amidst flowers : snow-white drifts
of *anemones,* golden, lily-like *nomocharis,* marigolds,
globe flowers, *delphiniums,* violets, *eritrichiums,* blue
*corydalis,* wild roses, flowering shrubs and rhododendrons, many of them flowers with homely sounding
English names. The Bhyundar Valley was the most
beautiful valley that any of us had seen. We camped
in it for two days and we remembered it afterwards as
the Valley of Flowers.

Often, in dark winter days, I wandered in spirit to these flowerful pastures with their clear-running streams set against a frieze of silver birches and shining snow peaks. Then once again I saw the slow passage of the breeze through the flowers, and heard the eternal note of the glacier torrent coming to the camp fire through the star-filled night.

After many years in London I went to live in the country, where I set to work to make a garden out of a field of thistles, ragwort and dandelions. I had looked on gardening as an old man's hobby, and a dull and unremunerative labour, but I came upon something that Karel Capek had written :

" You must have a garden before you know what you are treading on. Then, dear friend, you will see that not even clouds are so diverse, so beautiful and terrible as the soil under your feet . . . I tell you that to tame a couple of rods of soil is a great victory. Now it lies there, workable, crumbly and humid. . . . You are almost jealous of the vegetation which will take hold of this noble and humane work which is called the soil."

So I became a gardener. But I was profoundly ignorant. Two and a half years ago I did not know the difference between a biennial and a perennial. I am still ignorant, for there is no limit to ignorance or knowledge in gardening. But I discovered one thing ; that there is a freemasonry among gardeners which places gardening on a pinnacle above jealousy and suspicion. Perhaps this is because it is essentially a creative task and brings out a fine quality of patience. You may hasten the growth of a constitution but you cannot hasten the growth of an Alpine plant.

In 1937 the opportunity came to return to the Bhyundar Valley. I travelled alone for several reasons, but it was arranged that Captain P. R. Oliver of the South Waziristan Scouts should join me towards the end of July and that he and I should spend two months mountaineering in the Garhwal Himalayas, after which I should return to the valley to collect seeds, bulbs, tubers and plants. Thus, I should have six weeks on my own before and during the monsoon season, and to help me I engaged, through the kind offices of Mr. W. J. Kydd of Darjeeling, four Tibetan porters of whom the Sirdar, Wangdi Nurbu (or Ondi), was an old friend of mine.

One reason for this small party was that, after four large and elaborately organised Himalayan expeditions, I welcomed the opportunity of taking a Himalayan holiday, a very different affair from an attempt to climb one of the major peaks of the world and involving an entirely different scale of values both human and material. The ascent of Mount Everest has become a duty, perhaps a national duty, comparable with attempts to reach the Poles, and is far removed from pleasurable mountaineering. Mountaineering in the Garhwal and Kumaon Himalayas more nearly resembles mountaineering in Switzerland, for here are mountains and valleys like Swiss mountains and valleys but built on a greater scale. But, unlike parts of Switzerland, the country is unspoilt by commercialism. There are no railways, power lines, roads and hotels to offend the eye and detract from the primitive beauty and grandeur of the vistas, and there are peaks innumerable, unnamed and unclimbed, of all shades of difficulty, and valleys that have never seen a European, where a simple, kindly peasant folk graze their flocks in the summer months.

Then the flowers. From the hot valleys in the south, moist and humid during the monsoon season, to the golden hills of Tibet with their dry, cold winds, there is much to tempt the imagination of the gardener and the botanist, yet, strangely enough, little collecting has been done since the years between 1846 and 1849 when Sir Richard Strachey and J. E. Winterbottom made their famous collection of specimens. It was left to R. L. Holdsworth in 1931 to point out the potentialities of this floral storehouse and in " Kamet Conquered " he wrote : " There are many enthusiastic gardeners who, I feel sure, would welcome these Himalayan high-alpines, and I write this in the hope that some enter-prising philanthropist will go and get us seed or plants, not merely of the easier, bigger species from compara-tively low down, but of many a shy *primula* and gentian which haunts the more austere heights of that wonderful world."

It was my privilege to undertake this work and the reader, while remembering, and I hope generously, my ignorance, must judge for himself whether the Bhyundar Valley deserves its title the Valley of Flowers. Others will visit it, analyse it and probe it but, whatever their opinions, to me it will remain the Valley of Flowers, a valley of peace and perfect beauty where the human spirit may find repose.

. . . . . . .

On June 1st I arrived at Ranikhet from Naini Tal where I had stayed with Sir Harry Haig, the Governor of the United Provinces, and Lady Haig. Sir Harry was then President of the Himalayan Club and he very kindly promised to do everything in his power to help me, whilst Lady Haig, who is an enthusiastic gardener, has done much to beautify the already beautiful sur-roundings of Government House at Naini Tal.

Ranikhet is a hill station situated at about 5,000 feet on a foothill ridge which commands a view of the Cen-tral Himalayas, from the peaks of western Nepal to the snows of Badrinath and Tehri Garhwal, comparable in beauty, grandeur and extent to the celebrated view of Kangchenjunga from Darjeeling. In a single sweep the eye ranges from east to west past Nanda Kot, 22,530 feet, climbed in 1936 by a Japanese expedition ; Nanda Devi, 25,645 feet, the highest peak in British administered territory and thus strictly speaking in the British Empire, which was climbed in 1936 by the Anglo-American Expedition ; Trisul, 23,360 feet, climbed by Dr. T. G. Longstaff in 1907, and which remained the highest summit to have been reached until 1930 when the Jonsong Peak, 24,344 feet, was climbed by the International Kangchenjunga Expedition ; then the great massif of Hathi Parbat, 22,070 feet, and Gauri Parbat, 22,027 feet, with Nilgiri Parbat, 21,264 feet, behind and slightly to the west ; the Mana Peak, 23,860 feet, and Kamet, 25,447 feet, nearly 100 miles distant ; and so westwards to the snows of Badrinath, 23,420 feet, with Nilkanta, 21,640 feet, one of the most beautiful peaks in the Himalayas, standing alone, and the far snows of Tehri Garhwal, where much interesting exploration remains to be done.

This vast wall of mountains is best seen in the clear atmosphere of morning before the clouds, formed by the hot, moist air currents from the valleys, have obscured it, and many a time I have risen early to look over the foothills, dim and shadowy in the twilight, to the snows, hung like a glowing curtain across the whole width of the northern sky, yet so remote it seemed no human foot could tread their auroral steeps.

It is in these moments of awakening, when not a bird twits from the forest and the sun steps from peak to peak slowly and in splendid strides, that the sage's words ring true : " In a hundred ages of the Gods I could not tell thee of the glories of Himachal."

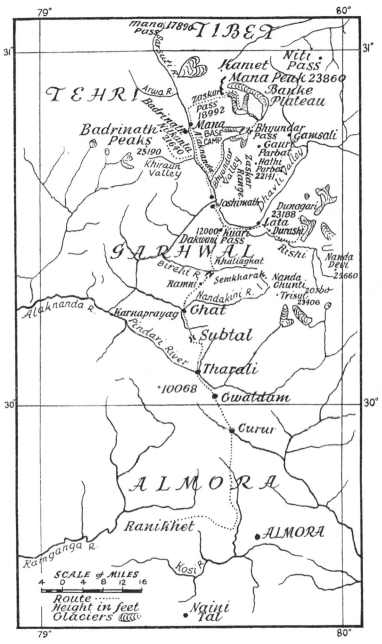

79°
80°

Mana Pass 17890
TIBET
Niti Pass
31°
Kamet
Mana Peak 23860
Banke Plateau
TEHRI
Arwa R.
Zaskar Pass 18992
Sarsuti R.
Badrinath R.
Badrinath Peaks
23190
Nilkanta 21640
Mana BASE CAMP
Alaknanda R.
Bhyundar Pass
Gamsali
Khiraun Valley
Bhyundar Valley
Gauri Parbat
Hathi Parbat 22141
Zaskar Range
Dhavli Valley
Joshimath
Dunagari 23188
Lata
Durashi
Kuari Pass
Dakwani
12000
Rishi
Nanda Devi 25660
GARHWAL
Khaliaghat
Birehi R.
Semkharak
Ramni
Nanda Chunti
Norbo
Nandakini R.
Trisul 23406
Alaknanda R.
Karnaprayag
Ghat
Pindari River
Subtal
Tharali
30°
10068
Gwaldam
Curur
ALMORA
Ranikhet
Ramganga R.
ALMORA
Kosi R.
SCALE of MILES
4 0 4 8 12 16
Route ........
Height in feet
Glaciers
Naini Tal

79°
80°

At Ranikhet I was joined by the four Tibetans from Darjeeling. I have already mentioned Wangdi Nurbu. He will be familiar to some readers as the man who fell into a crevasse on Kangchenjunga and remained in it for three hours before he was found. He was badly knocked about and was sent down to the base camp to be cared for by the doctor, but two days later insisted on returning to the highest camp. Then, on Everest in 1933, he was taken ill with double pneumonia and was sent down to a lower valley in an apparently dying condition, only to reappear at the base camp one month later carrying a heavy load on his back and clamouring for work on the mountain. Such is the spirit of the man. He is a little fellow, all bone and wiriness, who does not carry an ounce of superfluous flesh and has one of the hardest countenances I have seen ; he looks a " tough," but in point of fact he is sober and law abiding. He has less pronounced cheek-bones than many Tibetans and his lips are thinner and firmer. His eyes are usually slightly bloodshot in the whites, which gives them a ferocious, almost cruel look, but Wangdi is not cruel ; he is merely hard, one of the hardest men I know, and fit to enter a select coterie of Bhotia and Sherpa porters which includes men such as " Satan " Chettan, who was killed on Kangchenjunga, and Lewa, the Sirdar of the Kamet Expedition, not to mention that pockmarked piece of granite, Lobsang, who distinguished himself on Everest and Kangchenjunga, but who has, unhappily, since died.

Wangdi is illiterate, but in addition to his native language he can speak fluent Urdu and Nepali. He is quick and jerky in action and in speech ; it is as though some fire burns within him which can never properly find a vent. Like many of his race he is an excellent handy-man but failing his kukri (curved Gurkha knife) prefers to use his teeth, and I have seen him place the recalcitrant screw of a camera tripod between them and turn the tripod with the screw as an axis until the latter was loosened, then calmly spit out such pieces of his teeth as had been ground off in the process. Last, but by no means least, he is a fine climber. On Everest in 1936 he jumped automatically into the lead of the porter columns on the North Col and was never so happy as when exercising his magnificent strength and undoubted skill.

Pasang, with his high cheek-bones and slanting eyes, is a true Tibetan type. A tall stringy man with thin spindly legs, he somehow suggested clumsiness, and undoubtedly he was clumsy on a mountain, particularly on snow, so that when climbing with him I had always to be on my guard against a slip. I think he must have been something of a fatalist, for whenever he did slip the first thing he did was to let go of his ice axe, the one thing by which he might have stopped himself, and leave it to God or his companions to decide whether or not he should continue to slide into the next world. But though this passivity was exasperating at times I liked Pasang. He might give the impression of being a lout, but there was plenty of common sense packed away behind his ungainly exterior, and he was to be trusted on any other matter but climbing. His naïve awkwardness, and I can think of no better way of putting it, betokened a nature free from all guile and he was ever ready and willing to do his best, however uncomfortable the conditions in a rain-soaked camp or on a storm-lashed mountainside. He was no leader and had none of the fire, vivaciousness or conscious toughness of Wangdi—where others went he was prepared to follow—but there was some-

thing solid and enduring about his character, and the
quick smile that unexpectedly illumined his normally
solemn countenance was a sure indication of kindliness.

Tewang was an old stager and one of the men who
climbed to Camp V on Everest in 1924. Hugh Ruttledge wrote of him in " Everest 1933 " that : " Efficient,
completely reliable, and never idle, he performed every
office from porter messman to nurse, in a manner beyond praise." Undoubtedly he was ageing, for he had
become heavy, and it was apparent that he would be
of little use in difficult mountaineering and would have
to be relegated to the base camp as sheet-anchor of the
party. Age tells quickly on Tibetans, perhaps because
they wear themselves out when they are young, or it
may be that the height at which they live has something
to do with a rapid deterioration in their physique at a
period when a European is in his prime. He was of
an even quieter disposition than Pasang and in all ways
slower than his companions ; you could see this in his
heavy face and lumbering gait. I scarcely ever saw
him smile, but there was a natural fatherliness about
him which would have chosen him automatically as a
nurse, as it did in 1933, had there been any nursing
to do.

Nurbu was the youngster of the party. He had been
Major C. J. Morris's servant on Everest in 1936, and
the training he had then received had stood him in
good stead, for he was the most efficient servant I have
ever had. A good-looking lad, with a round, boyish
and remarkably smooth-skinned face, he was invariably
cheerful and quick to seize upon and remember anything to do with his job. He had had little or no
mountaineering experience and came to me as a raw
novice at the craft, but he was a natural climber, neat
and careful, particularly on rocks, on which he was cat-

like in his agility and, unlike many of his type, quick to learn the finer points of mountaineering, such as handling the rope and cutting steps in snow and ice. Himalayan mountaineering will hear more of him in the future and I venture the prophecy that he puts up a good showing on Everest in 1938.

Such were my companions—I cannot think of them as porters—and I could scarcely have wished for better. They contributed generously and in full measure to the pleasure and success of the happiest holiday of my life. Three days at Ranikhet sufficed to complete my preparations, but I might not have got away so expeditiously had it not been for the help given me by Mrs. Evelyn Browne, whom many Himalayan mountaineers will remember with gratitude, whilst my short stay was rendered additionally pleasant by the kindness of Major Browne, the Secretary of the Club.

On June 4th my arrangements were completed and eleven Dotial porters, of a race indigenous to southern Nepal, had arrived to carry my heavy luggage to the base camp. So at last the dream of several years was on the verge of practical fulfilment.

# CHAPTER II

## THE LOW FOOTHILLS

EVERYTHING was ready on the morning of June 5th and the lorry which was to convey me the first part of my journey was packed to capacity with fifteen porters and some 1,000 lbs. of luggage. This journey, of some fifty-five miles from Ranikhet to the village of Garur, was along narrow roads, the hairpin bends in which were innumerable and acute, and the driver drove on the principle that no obstacle was to be encountered on the corners, and if it was, Providence must decide the issue. Fortunately Providence was well disposed and, apart from some hectic encounters with stray cows and bullock carts, the drive was uneventful.

The foothills of the Himalayas provide the perfect introduction to the " Snows " and their gentle forest-clad undulations lead the eye forwards to the background of gigantic peaks which distance serves to increase, not diminish in beauty.

After following for some miles the clear-running Kosi River and passing numerous villages and Government resin-collecting stations, the road climbed over a high ridge, where I saw several tree rhododendrons and the distant snows of Trisul and Nanda Devi, then wound sinuously down to the level floor of the wide Sarju Valley.

Garur, the terminus of the motor road, is a sordid little place, like any native place to which " civilisation " has penetrated disguised in the form of motor-cars. Flies swarmed over the offal in the street, beggars whined for alms, and from one of the single-storey hovels a cheap gramophone wheezed drearily. There is no doubt that the farthest-flung tentacles of civilisation debase, not improve human conditions. However, like Mr. Gandhi, I might damn motor-cars, but I had not hesitated to employ one. I turned my back gladly on the place with its smells, the immemorial and " romantic " smells of the East, which are compounded quite simply of the effluvium from an inadequate drainage system and unwashed human bodies, mingling in the present instance with a reek of oil and petrol, and set off on the first stage of my march. For the next few months I should neither see, hear, nor smell a motor-car or aeroplane ; it was a stimulating thought.

Beyond Garur, the path crosses the Sarju River by a well-built suspension bridge, then, after sundry ups and downs, begins a long climb to the Gwaldam dak bungalow.

It was a hot march—the temperature cannot have been much less than 100 degrees in the shade—and the Dotials poured with sweat. How they managed to carry their 80-lb. loads I do not know. I felt a slave-driver, but it is possible I estimated their efforts by my own incapacities, for I had left Ranikhet with a temperature of 101 degrees and a feverish chill. This may have been unwise, but I am convinced that the best way of ridding myself of a chill is to walk it off and sweat it out ; I certainly must have accomplished the latter as I was fat and flabby after many months of sedentary living.

The foothills of the Central Himalayas are poor in flowers owing to forests of chir (*Pinus longifolia*), which cover the ground in a carpet of needles, thus preventing the growth of plants or the germination of seed.

Yet these forests have a charm of their own, for the chir is a fine tree and, though it has few branches and casts little shade, grows straight and true to a considerable height.   Furthermore, trees are well spaced and owing to the absence of clogging undergrowth or lank grass, the country resembles a well-kept parkland. Lastly, the chir is highly resinous and the air is fragrant in its neighbourhood.

In normal circumstances it is an enjoyable walk to Gwaldam, but that day it was a matter of setting my teeth and plugging on with a bursting head, aching limbs and a thirst which I satisfied recklessly at every spring.

So, at last, after a ten miles' walk and an ascent of some 4,000 feet I emerged from the forest on to the ridge where the bungalow stands overlooking the haze-filled depths of the Pindar Valley to the remote gleam of the Himalayan snows.

Two Englishmen were encamped near the bungalow, Mr. G. W. H. Davidson, the Headmaster of Colvin Taluqdars College, Lucknow, who had with him one of his Indian pupils, and Major Matthews of the Royal Engineers, and their kindness and hospitality had much to do with my rapid recovery from my chill, for I went to bed with an excellent dinner and a considerable quantity of whisky inside me and woke miraculously better next morning.

From Gwaldam a forest path descends steeply into the Pindar Valley.  We were away early, soon after the sun had fired the snows, and an hour later had descended 3,000 feet to the Pindar River.

About half-way to the village of Tharali I met with another Englishman, Corporal Hamilton, a member of a party of soldiers of the East Surrey Regiment who were at this time attempting the ascent of Kamet.

Unfortunately, he had damaged his arm, which had become poisoned. As I had with me a comprehensive medical kit I was able to disinfect and bind up the wound, which had already been treated by an Indian doctor.

The expedition in which he took part is one of the most remarkable in the annals of Himalayan mountaineering. The soldiers, who were led by Corporal Ralph Ridley, after an expedition the previous summer to the Arwa Valley glacier system, boldly decided to attempt Kamet in 1937. Their organisation was admirable and they failed primarily through lack of sufficient porterage after overcoming the greatest difficulties of the route and reaching a height of 23,700 feet. At the same time to attempt a major peak, even though it has been climbed before, is unwise without adequate mountaineering experience ; there are peaks of all heights and shades of difficulty in the Himalayas where the novice may learn the craft. Nature is intolerant of ignorance, and he who attempts the greater peaks of the Himalayas without having acquired that delicacy and acuteness of perception, that instinctive *feeling* for his task, will sooner or later blunder to disaster. This is not meant to detract from the merit of an expedition which was conspicuous for the initiative and self-reliance displayed, but merely to point out the advisability of preliminary preparation in mountaineering. It is to be hoped that future mountaineering expeditions will receive the encouragement of the High Command.

Tharali huddles at the foot of a knoll thrusting forwards into the Pindar River, which narrows considerably at this point. The village was devastated by a flood in the summer of 1936. Twenty inches of rain fell in one day and the Pindar River, unable to discharge its surplus waters through the narrow portion of the valley, rose and flooded the village, destroying a number of houses and drowning forty of the inhabitants.

The usual camping ground is a strip of sun-scorched turf by the river, but I preferred the partial shade of some pines on the knoll near the village school, which sports large notices over every approach to the effect that all are welcome ; ineffective propaganda to judge from the absence of pupils, but perhaps it was a holiday.

The afternoon was the hottest I ever remember. My tent, which was only six and a half feet long by four feet wide, was intolerable, so I lay outside it on a mattress in the scanty shade of the pines, plagued by innumerable flies.

Evening brought little relief, and the sun set in a furnace-like glare. The night was breathless but I managed to sleep, only to be awakened shortly before midnight by flickering lightning and reverberating concussions of thunder. The storm was confined to the hills and passed after an hour, leaving a dull red glow in the sky, presumably the reflection of a forest fired by lightning.

I breakfasted early and was away at five o'clock, anxious to break the back of the long march to Subtal, which entails some twelve miles of walking and 5,000 feet of ascent.

The storm had done nothing to clear the air and the forests were charged with damp enervating heat, so that it was a relief to emerge from them after two hours' uphill walking on to more open slopes, where the village of Dungri perches below a basin-like rim of hills. The air here was cooler and men and women were working energetically in the terraced fields or scratching shallow furrows with primitive wooden ploughs drawn by oxen or buffaloes. The men greeted me in a friendly way, and the children gazed at me curiously, impudently or shyly in the manner of children the world over, but the nose-beringed women I met with on the path hastened by with averted faces. At one hamlet a man ran out of a house, saluted with military precision and offered to carry my rucksack. Doubtless, like many another in this country, he had served with the Garhwal or Kumaon Rifles.

Forests of chir, open country artificially deforested, then rhododendrons, deciduous trees, spruces and firs is the natural upward order of growth in the lower foothills, where crops flourish best in the temperate zone from 4,000 to 8,000 feet. I entered the cool forest above Dungri and seating myself on a mossy bank ate my lunch of biscuits and potatoes. I was far ahead of the porters ; the forest was profoundly silent, and great clouds were slowly building up in a sky of steely oxidised blue. Not even in the Sikkim forests have I seen finer tree rhododendrons, and there was one moss-clad giant which cannot have been less than five feet in diameter. For how many centuries had these trees endured ? Long before the wooden ships of " The Company " sailed to India they must have established themselves on the knees of the Himalayas.

Beyond my luncheon place I had a glimpse of a brown bear as it leapt from the path—a little fellow who was gone in a flash. After this the path mounted at a restful angle and passing over a brow descended to a stream issuing from a rocky rift. There was a deep pool and I stripped and bathed, gasping at first in the ice-cold water, then dried myself on a flat rock in the sun. While I was engaged in this a small boy passed and catching sight of me bolted precipitately up the path ; then halted to eye me with fearful curiosity. Probably he had never seen a European before, and at all events anyone who bathed, and in ice-cold water, was indubitably mad.

The camping ground at Subtal, the name given to an extensive pasture, is a sparsely wooded ridge which rises on either hand to hills densely forested in spruce and the Himalayan oak, which is a narrow spreading tree as compared with the English oak. To the north the ridge falls away into a branch valley of the Nandakini Valley, through which the western glaciers of Trisul pour their waters into the Alaknanda River.

It was not yet midday, but the sky was thick with gathering stormclouds and the earth lay still and silent beneath a weight of lurid haze. The porters were long in arriving, but it was a marvel that they should arrive at all considering the weight of their loads, the distance and the climb. If my mathematics are not too rusty, the energy required to lift a human body plus an extra 80 lbs. of weight through nearly a mile of height comes to well over 1,000,000 foot pounds, of which the load amounts to about 400,000 foot pounds. In terms of the load alone it is equivalent to shovelling about 75 tons of coal into a furnace.

Meanwhile, a party of traders with a dozen ponies had halted close by and lit a fire after carefully stacking their merchandise under a tarpaulin. Presently one of them, seeing that I was alone, asked me if I would care for some food. It was a generous thought, but I had no need to deplete their probably slender supplies. This was only one instance of the kindliness of the people of this country and it seemed to me that the human atmosphere of Garhwal and Kumaon was very different to what it had been in 1931. Is Mr. Gandhi's creed of non-violence bearing the fruits of sympathy, tolerance and understanding or is a more positive and less vacillating British rule responsible? Whatever it is, one thing is certain : only through co-operation, friendship and mutual respect between the British and Indian races is any real and lasting benefit for either to be achieved in India in that distant future when education and evolution will have emancipated the Indian peoples from their strangling social and religious prejudices.

The early afternoon darkened gradually and in the close sultry atmosphere flies attacked me venomously. The haze deepened until it was difficult to perceive where the hills ended and the clouds began. A rust-coloured light invested the forest, then faded as the last oases of blue sky were swallowed up by chaotic and enormous thunderclouds, and the far north where the Himalayas lay began to shudder with long muffled reverberations of thunder.

At two o'clock the porters straggled into camp, soaked with sweat and very tired. As the Darjeeling men pitched the tents, one for me and one for themselves, heavy drops of rain were splashing into the forest and the thunder was rumbling continuously as though a column of tanks and guns was crossing a hollow-sounding bridge.

Soon lightning was flickering and stabbing through a blue wall of advancing rain, smeared dull white with hail, and the thunder was tearing overhead like a giant rending endless strips of calico. Then above the thunder I heard a dull roar, rising in strength and pitch every instant, and almost before I had time to realise its meaning the thin-topped spruces a hundred yards distant bent like whip-lashes and a terrific squall of wind and hail, rifted by mauve swords of lightning and fearful explosions of thunder, burst in wild fury on the camp.

This first blast of the storm did not last long, and

half an hour later the rain stopped and the wind died into a damp calm, smelling of wet earth and vegetation. Though the storm had retreated from the immediate vicinity of Subtal the thunder continued, coming from every direction and without pause in a single tremendous sound that grew and ebbed and grew again in concussions that seemed to shake the hills to their foundations.

The storm was working up for another climax when Nurbu brought me my supper, which Tewang had artfully cooked in the shelter of a hollow tree. Afterwards I lay in my sleeping-bag and watched through the entrance of the tent the finest display of lightning I have ever seen. The whole sky was continuously blazing with mauve fire and it was possible to read uninterruptedly from a book. Slowly the lightning grew in brilliance, if that were possible, and the thunder in volume. This was no ordinary storm, even in a district where storms are frequent, and I wished I had moved the tents after the first storm, though with the ridges on either side of the camp there did not seem any likelihood of danger. There was no time to do anything now and at nine o'clock the storm was upon us in a hurricane of wind, hail and rain, punctuated every second by blinding lightning and terrible explosions of thunder.

Lightning when it strikes close to the observer does not make the noise we conventionally term " thunder," or even the rending, tearing noise already mentioned, but a single violent explosion, a BANG like a powerful bomb. I have no hesitation in admitting that I was thoroughly scared, and as I lay in my sleeping-bag I could have sworn that streams of fire flickered along the ridge of the tent and down the lateral guy-rope.

The worst was over within half an hour and I went

outside to see how the Dotials had fared, for I half feared that one or other of the trees beneath which they were sheltering had been struck. To my great relief they were all safe, though even the irrepressible Wangdi, who together with Pasang, Nurbu and Tewang had been in the other tent, seemed a trifle shaken by the experience.

This was the last of the storm so far as it concerned us, but long afterwards the sky flamed with lightning and thunder serenaded the ranges. I am not exaggerating when I state that I do not remember a second's pause in the sound of the thunder during a total period of eight hours.

The sky next morning was cloudless, but dense haze concealed the view I had hoped to obtain of the snows. We were away as the sun touched the camp and descended through cool and fragrant forests, alive with the song of birds, to cultivated slopes and small villages ; then into a wooded valley with a stream of clear-running water. Here at about 7,000 feet on an open slope I saw the first of a little *iris* (*I. kumaonensis*), which I knew I would meet with later on the Kuari Pass and in the Bhyundar Valley. I also came upon hundreds of the largest cobwebs I have ever seen. For a mile, the trees and shrubs had suspended between them vast nets, wet and shining after the rain, with the spider waiting for his breakfast in the centre of each. So strong were the webs that stout twigs to which they were affixed were bent at right angles, whilst the largest was stretched between two trees fully twelve feet apart and had as its spinner a spider about six inches in width from tip to tip of its hairy legs.

At the village of Ghat which is situated in the deep Nandakini Valley, a single-room dak bungalow destitute of furniture did not attract me and I preferred to camp by the river.   The tent had scarcely been pitched when thunder began to growl again and a mass of inky clouds advanced quickly down the valley.   A few minutes later I was astonished to see a writhing column of spray appear round a bend of the river and descend on the camp.   Next moment up went my tent, wrenching the metal tent-pegs away as though they were matches, and swept along the ground towards the river. Yelling to the men I threw myself on it and a few moments later was joined by Wangdi, Nurbu and Pasang, all shouting with laughter, evidently convinced that a whirlwind was a huge joke.

Later the weather improved and I supped in the calm of a perfect evening.   I had no official cook. Experience has taught me that official cooks are to be avoided in the Himalayas as they are almost invariably dirty and are born " twisters " and " scroungers " ; worst of all they are impervious to insult, sarcasm, or righteous anger, and like their European prototypes, resent the best intentioned suggestions and advice. Furthermore, they are set in their habits, and their habits are vile, and, lastly, they are invariably bad cooks, or so my experience goes, and are largely responsible for the stomach troubles that beset Himalayan expeditions.

Therefore, I had left it to the men to decide between themselves as to which of them should cook for me, and Tewang had elected himself or been elected to the post.   To write that he was a good cook, which implies the exercise of imagination and a fertility of invention, would be to overstate his abilities.   He was simply a plain cook, so plain that his cooking would have palled at an early date on an appetite less voracious than mine.   His most artistic culinary flight was rissoles, and he would produce these with one of his

THE LOW FOOTHILLS 23

rare smiles creasing his broad face and an exaggerated
pride worthy of a conjurer who has out-Maskelyned his
own professors. But he cooked what he did cook well
and I seldom had cause to reproach him on this score.
So having seen that he was clean, that doubtful water
was boiled, and that dish-cloths were used in preference
to the tail of a shirt, I left him to his own devices.

The Dotials were averse to proceeding to Joshimath
via the Kuari Pass. As they justly pointed out the route
from Ghat via Nanda Prayag and the Alaknanda Valley
is considerably easier. I had, however, no intention of
proceeding by that route, which is very hot and at times
fever-ridden, in preference to the cool, healthful and
beautiful high-level route via the Kuari Pass, and when
I pointed out the disadvantages of the former route,
their objections soon resolved themselves into good-
humoured grumblings.

From Ghat the path crosses the Nandakini River by
a strongly built suspension bridge, then zig-zags up a
steep and arid hillside. Some 2,500 feet up this, perched
on a grassy spur, is a small village, the inhabitants of
which greeted me cheerfully. Their lives are spent, like
the lives of most people of this country, in agricultural
pursuits. A spring and summer of intense activity,
devoted to the task of levelling their little fields on the
steep hillsides, removing innumerable stones and building them into walls so that the monsoon rains do not
wash the precious soil into the valley, turning the thin
soil with wooden ox-drawn ploughs, sowing, reaping
and threshing, is followed by a winter of comparative
inactivity. Scarcely less strenuous is the work of the
shepherds deputed to drive the flocks to the upper
pastures, which are so few and scanty that owners must
take it in turns to graze them. Theirs is the life of the
mountain peasant the world over ; a struggle against

adverse forces, yet forces that once tamed will yield, if
not bountifully, at least enough to maintain a fit and
hardy race. A dull, monotonous life perhaps, a minute
cycle of work and rest, but running through it all the
never-ending thread of human propagation and con-
tinuity. These dour peasants may be outwardly in-
sensible to their tremendous environment, but the vast
hills that everlastingly mock their puny efforts, the deep
valleys with their rush of glacial waters bearing onwards
to the far-distant plains, the remote glimmer of the high
snows have become a part of them, and deep in their
inmost selves must rest a love, respect and reverence
for their unrelenting taskmasters, the Himalayas.

From the village, the path mounted an open hillside
to a ridge clothed with oaks and tree rhododendrons.
I lunched in a glade which commanded a view between
the trees of Trisul, a vast barrier of shining snow at
the head of the deeply-cut Nandakini Valley, whose
ribbon-like stream thousands of feet beneath me twisted
and turned between bare shoulders of the hills. The
air was fresh, and only the whirring and humming of
insects fell on a profound stillness. All around me grew
a pale mauve daisy, whilst on the slope below was a
catmint with rosette-like silvery foliage and blue flowers,
some of which were already in seed.

Presently the porters appeared. They were singing,
and their simple little song, echoing through the silent
glades of the forest, somehow partook of the beauty
and majesty of the surroundings ; complicated music
would be out of place where everything is simple and
sublime.

Beyond the glade, the path traversed a forest-clad
hillside, then emerged on to open slopes terraced with
fields where the little village of Ramni perches. Our
camping place was on turf close-cropped by the village

animals, but not eaten so short as to destroy the brilliant blue flowers of a tiny gentian (*G. capitata*). In 1931 we had been pestered by flies at Ramni, but on this occasion a mosquito net over the entrance of my tent enabled me to escape their hateful attentions.

It was a hot afternoon, but the evening was delightfully cool; the flies disappeared and, with no midges or mosquitoes to take their place, I ate my supper in peace beneath the accumulating stars.

# CHAPTER III

## THE HIGH FOOTHILLS

THE following morning was cloudy, but the clouds soon dissolved in the sun.  As I walked up the forest path to the next ridge I felt myself to be nearing the threshold of the high hills.  The *anemones* increased in number as I climbed, whilst hosts of buttercups spread a golden carpet over the dew-drenched turf.

Many sheep and goats laden with grain were following the same path on their way to the upper valleys of Garhwal, where the grain is transferred to yaks and jhobus (half-breed yaks), then taken over the high passes into Tibet.  Ponies are sometimes employed for load-carrying, but the bulk of the grain is carried in little bags, reinforced with leather, on the backs of sheep and goats, the sheep carrying some 20 to 25 lbs. and the goats as much as 30 lbs.  The drivers are ragged, picturesque, friendly fellows, some with long curly hair.  They walk with a shambling flat-footed gait something like that of the Alpine guide, and two or three of them will share a long water-pipe with a wide, shallow bowl, which they fill with villainous tobacco, mixed with charcoal, or when no tobacco is available, charcoal alone.  Smoking one of these pipes is something of a ritual.  A man takes two or three rapid puffs, then hands on the pipe to his neighbour, so that the pipe soon goes the round of a dozen men.  In this way asphyxiation or carbon monoxide poisoning is avoided.

Thunder was rumbling in the west as I breasted the

ridge above Ramni, but the north and east were clear and Nanda Ghunti stood revealed in all its beauty. This peak is 20,700 feet high, and is so beautifully proportioned that it appears almost as high as its greater neighbour, Trisul.

On the far side of the ridge the path descended through forests, crossing occasional glades. I remembered that Holdsworth found *Paeonia Emodii* hereabouts, and I kept my eyes open. But I did not see one until I was within half a mile of the camping ground ; then, suddenly, in a shady place, and close to the path, I saw a clump of them. The day was dark now, for a storm was brewing, but even in the gloom of the forest, their cream-coloured blooms shone out as though retaining the recent sunlight in their petals. The clump was the only one in bloom, as the rest were already seeding. This place must be a marvellous sight in April and the first weeks of May, for this paeony blooms early, pushing its way, like the Alpine crocus, through the edge of the retreating snows.

I remembered Semkharak as one of the most delightful camping grounds we had seen during the march to Kamet, but now hills and forest were burdened with impending storm, and the little alp seemed dreary and forlorn. Thunder was growling about the hills when I arrived, but I did not have to wait long for the men, who were just in time to pitch the tents before rain fell in torrents.

For the next two hours lightning darted viciously at the forest-clad ridges and the thunder reverberated from lip to lip of the cup-shaped hills, then, towards evening, with that suddenness peculiar to mountainous countries, the rain and the thunder ceased, and the clouds vanished as though absorbed by some invisible vacuum-cleaner.

The men collected wood from the forest and soon a
great fire was blazing.  It was my first camp fire, and
I sat by it contentedly while the golden sunlight died
on the nearer heights, then fired the distant snows of
Nanda Ghunti.  Nothing had altered since we camped
here in 1931 and there was even the same half-burnt
tree-stump where our fire had been lit.  Possibly the
slender oaks and conifers had added a few inches to
their stature, but for the rest Semkharak was the same.
Things do not change quickly in the East.

Raymond Greene, a born raconteur, had kept us
amused with stories throughout the evening.  Six years
had passed, but I could not regret them, for the peace
and beauty of the hills was mine that evening.  The
last cloud vanished, the last glow faded from Nanda
Ghunti, and the sky lit up with stars.  Not a breath
of wind stirred in the treetops.  Darkness fell.  I ate
my supper, then smoked my pipe and dreamed, until
the fire had died down to a heap of glowing embers
and the dew lay hoary on the grass.

Next morning I descended into the Bireh Valley,
passing through hundreds of acres of paeonies in seed.
The seed was unripe, but I gathered some, hoping to
ripen it later ;  I know now that this is difficult if not
impossible in the case of the paeony, for the seed shrivels,
and becomes valueless.  It must be gathered when it
is perfectly ripe and ready to fall out of the pod.

The path crossed a small log bridge over the river
near a vertical crag of crumbling rock, beneath which
some drovers, disregarding the law of gravity, had
camped for the night.  We exchanged greetings and,
as is customary in this country, they inquired as to
where I was going and from whence I came.

From the river the path zig-zagged steeply upwards,
then traversed the hillside almost levelly, through forests

of tree rhododendrons, roses and a white sweet-scented flowering shrub to the camping ground at Kaliaghat, which is in an open grassy place, sprinkled with large boulders. Adjoining it are cultivated fields, beyond which rises a vast wall of forest, broken high up by gigantic crags. Many queer noises came from this forest, including the whistle-like cries of a bird, and once I heard a coughing sound which was probably made by a bear or panther.

The afternoon was hot and fly-ridden. It was impossible to sit outside my tent without being pestered by innumerable flies, whilst inside it was like an oven, so I occupied myself with collecting flowers for my press. It was a beautiful evening, but the flies, as is usual in Garhwal, were replaced by midges, which although small seemed capable of biting through the toughest skin, to judge from the exasperated scratchings of the porters.

From Kaliaghat a pleasant path across meadows, then through rhododendron and oak forest, led to a wide alp gay with white and blue *anemones* (*A. obtusiloba*) within view of the Kuari Pass, which cuts a notch in a ridge. Thenceforward the route lies across steep craggy hillsides, then past an impressive gorge, where a stream spurts out of a narrow cleft to form a perfect bathing-pool, and finally, after sundry ups and downs, mounts towards the pass.

As I was well ahead of the porters I seated myself with my back to a mossy bank, where grew the delicate sprays of a beautiful little *androsace* (probably *A. rotundifolia*), and ate the lunch provided by Tewang. I had not been there long before I heard a footfall, and looking up saw a wild-looking fellow with a long-handled axe over his shoulder regarding me with the greatest curiosity. As soon as he saw that I was disposed to be friendly he squatted on the ground and burst into an unintelligible gabble. Probably he had seen no one to talk to for some time and was making the best of his opportunity. My very limited stock of Urdu elicited that he was there with his flock for the summer and that he lived at Kaliaghat. Apart from this, our "conversation" was limited to gestures and smiles which, however, are very good substitutes for speech in the wilds. I gave him some tobacco and he departed beaming.

Presently along came the Dotials. As usual, in spite of their heavy loads, they were happy, and were singing their rhythmical little songs. We lunched at Dakwani, a fertile alp 1,000 feet below the Kuari Pass. There I saw many *Iris kumaonensis* in bloom. This little *iris*, a miniature edition of the English garden *iris*, grows on hot, well-drained sunny slopes. All it asks for is a cool root run. Then, when the winter snow melts, it pushes out its thin leaves and a little later its spire of purple blooms which partake in colour of cold shadowed snow and rich blue sky. It grows well in England and I have one in my own garden which brings to me every spring a memory of the Himalayas.

Dakwani is the usual camping ground, but I determined to push on and camp on the pass, for this is a renowned view-point and commands a prospect extending from the Nanda Devi group to the peaks of Badrinath. Accordingly, I left the main transport at Dakwani and with three Darjeeling men and four Dotials climbed a zig-zag stony track to the pass. The crest is not the best view-point, and I camped on a rocky ridge some distance to the east, where there are no near hills to interfere with the panorama. Unfortunately clouds and haze concealed most of the peaks, but I hoped that the following morning would afford a clear view particularly of the Zaskar Range, into

which the Bhyundar Valley cuts, and the peaks I hoped
to climb during the next few weeks.

The evening was dark and dense clouds massed along
the haze-filled Alaknanda Valley. We hoped that no
thunderstorm was brewing as the camp was in an
exposed position and we had no wish to repeat the
experience of Subtal. The men had carried up some
wood from Dakwani, but there was plenty of dwarf
rhododendron available, the sight of which delighted
the Tibetans as it reminded them of their native land,
in many parts of which it is the only fuel, apart from
dried yak-dung.

Winter snow still covered large areas of the hillsides,
but already a tiny gentian with daintily frilled petals
carpeted the ground.

At sunset the dark clouds delivered a sharp hailstorm but later the sky cleared somewhat, revealing
scattered stars. After the hot marches across the foothills, it was good to feel the need of a sweater and the
warmth of an eiderdown sleeping-bag. Better still,
there were no flies or midges and I could sleep with
the tent-flaps wide open.

The tonic of the high places was in the air. So far,
I had lived with little thought of the future, my thoughts
circumscribed by the day's march, but now for the first
time I experienced that feeling of expectancy which every
mountaineer has when approaching high mountains.

A restful sleep, and I awoke as usual with the first
light. But there was no view; above and below, sluggish vapours concealed the glorious panorama which I
had seen in 1931 from the same place. The Tibetans
were as disappointed as I, for they were anxious for a
glimpse of the peaks we hoped to climb.

Presently the main party joined us and we descended
towards the Dhauli Valley, at first over open slopes,

then into pine forest; and there at the upper limit of the trees I came upon an old friend, which I had photographed in 1931, a solitary sentinel gnarled and weather-beaten by countless storms. It was decaying, for to judge from its appearance it had been mal-treated by lightning, but it still stretched gaunt, hard branches against the sky, an embodiment of that endur-ing force which epitomises, in material form, the spirit of the hills.

As we came out of the upper forest on to a wide alp, the clouds parted, revealing the great massif of Gauri Parbat and Hathi Parbat; then almost before I had time to take in the grandeur of this sudden revelation, a terrific icy spire, shining and immeasurably remote, thrust itself through the clouds, Dunagiri.

The Dotials said they were certain of the path to Joshimath. It is true there was a path at first, but it soon petered out in the forest. We kept on for some distance through a tangle of vegetation; then it was brought home to us that we were lost. I was well ahead of the men and stopped. The forest was very quiet; not a sound, not a breath disturbed the serene silence. Above, the great trees formed a canopy with their interlacing branches, and at my feet the deep shadows were accentuated by pools of sunlight.

Wangdi joined me and we yelled lustily until all the men were assembled; then we struck straight down the hillside, forcing our way through undergrowth, and at length, to our relief, came to a path leading in the direction of Joshimath.

I halted for lunch by a leisurely little stream, fringed with marigolds, that wandered into a sun-drenched glade. After this the path wound sinuously across the hillside, descending gradually as it did so into a forest of chir, hot and resinous in the nearly vertical noonday sun. Thenceforward it was a somewhat weary march, but enlivened at one place by a number of lemurs playing about on a boulder. They allowed me to approach within a few yards of them, but looked so hostile that I felt glad of my ice-axe. Beyond were numerous hamlets whose inhabitants were working industriously on their small terraced fields of grain and vegetables. I asked one of them how far it was to Joshimath, and he replied two miles, but it was more like four or five ; these people have small regard for distance, and measure it in time rather than mileage.

The path divided, and not sure as to which branch to take, I waited until a small woman driving some oxen appeared. She seemed terrified when I questioned her and hastened by with averted eyes. How many decades will there be before the Indian woman is emancipated from the mental, moral and physical slavery she has endured for countless generations ?

Joshimath is perched on a hillside some 1,500 feet above the junction of the Alaknanda and Dhauli Rivers. It is a halting-place of pilgrims who journey to Badrinath during the summer months to pay their respects to Mother Ganges, and worship at the shrines of deities associated with the sacred snows of Himachal (Himalaya). Unhappily, they bring with them many diseases from the plains, and cholera, dysentery, typhoid and malaria exact their toll from the devout, whose notions as to sanitation, cleanliness and hygiene are at constant variance with the well-intentioned preventive and remedial efforts of the Indian Government. All along the road infection is spread by hordes of flies and he is a wise traveller who boils every cup of his drinking water.

The village is an ugly little place with slate- or corrugated iron-covered, two-storeyed houses, straggling unbeautifully over the hillside. Primitive little shops displaying sweetmeats, vegetables and other commodities line the main street, which is roughly paved in places and in others has been deeply channelled by the monsoon rains. The pilgrims spend the night in single-storeyed rest-houses, not unlike the hovels provided for the Kentish hop-pickers of former days, some of which are situated in narrow passages running off the main street, and are filthy, and evil-smelling. Such pestilential conditions have little effect on the pilgrims and scores were to be seen, many being naked save for a loincloth, seated in meditation, their thoughts fixed on the shrine at Badrinath, their sacred destination.

There are numerous temples dedicated to various gods, principal among them being Vishnu, who is represented by an idol carved from black stone. Joshimath was at one time the capital of the Katyuris, the rulers of western Kumaon and Garhwal, and the successors of the Buddhists, who were driven out of Nepal, Kumaon and Garhwal by Sankara, the indefatigable destroyer of Buddhism in India, who is thought to have lived in the seventh or eighth centuries. It was he who advocated pilgrimage to the shrines of Shiva and Vishnu at Kedarnath and Badrinath. His disciples were established in these ancient shrines and the consequent influx of pilgrims prevented a reversion to Buddhism. Owing to religious quarrels between the followers of the two deities, Joshimath was abandoned by the Katyuris, whose kingdom was broken up, forcing them to establish themselves as independent rajahs. Since it was first instituted, the pilgrimage to Badrinath and Kedarnath has increased in importance and nowadays some 50,000 or 60,000 pilgrims from all parts of India, including the remote south, make their way every year up the Alaknanda Valley. Even the pilgrimage to Benares is not so beneficial to the soul as that to the snows of the Himalayas, which bestow so bountifully their sanctity and bliss to the heart of man. It is written in the Skanda Purana :

" He who thinks of Himachal though he should not behold him is greater than he who performs all worship in Kashi (Benares). In a hundred ages of the gods, I could not tell thee of the glories of Himachal. As the dew is dried up by the morning sun, so are the sins of mankind by the sight of Himachal."

Doubtless some of the old Buddhist demonolatry is responsible for the veneration in which the snows are held. It may be that the European mountaineer has something of the same superstitious instinct handed down from the days of sun and moon worship, when the hilltops were the abiding places of gods and devils ; and not long ago Mount Pilatus was reputed to be haunted by the uneasy ghost of Pontius Pilate. Understanding has replaced fear, but it may be that the shadows of ancient mysteries remain, so that the sight of high mountains rekindles in a different guise the same feelings of awe which our remote ancestors had in their presence. That Kumaon and Garhwal should be especially consecrated to the gods of Indian religious mysticism, is easily understandable. Is there any region of the Himalayas, or even of the world, to excel this region in beauty and grandeur ? Where else are there to be found such narrow and precipitous valleys and gorges, such serene vistas of alp, forest, snow-field and peak ? This " abode of snow " is rightly the goal of the heat-enervated people of the plains. Never was a pilgrimage of finer accomplishment. It is the perfect antidote to a static life, and it cannot fail to inspire in the dullest a nobler conception of the universe.

Below Joshimath, sins are purified by the swift-running

waters of the Alaknanda River. From the shrine at Vishnu Prayag the pilgrims descend a flight of steps and dip themselves in the ice-cold torrent ; they ascend rejuvenated in mind, and it must be in body, ready to tread the stony path that leads through the gorges to Badrinath, along the " great way " to final liberation of spirit.

There is a bungalow at Joshimath perched on the hillside above the village, and containing one living-room and a bathroom with the usual zinc hip-bath, the servants quarters and kitchen being in a separate building. In the living-room are some book-shelves, the last resting-place of a number of volumes of great antiquity, among them Blackwood's Magazines, the Christian Science Monitor, and works of Victorian and Edwardian novelists, all of which form a restful home for small beetles, " silver-fish " and numerous unidentifiable insects. In these respects the bungalow is similar to others in the district, but in one other respect it is remarkable, as being the home and breeding-place of the largest spiders I have ever seen, not excluding the tarantula of South America. The bathroom is their happy hunting-ground, and I bathed that evening with one eye on the dilapidated ceiling lest some huge brute, six or seven inches across, should descend upon me.

The men had marched well, so I rested them for a day which I devoted to letter-writing. Joshimath boasts a post-office, a curious ramshackle little building, with a doorway so low I had to stoop to enter. In this lair, surrounded by the usual appurtenances of his craft, a morse key, ledgers, pigeon-holes and official notices innumerable, I found the Postmaster and his assistant.

In 1936, during the Mount Everest Expedition, the letters sent back by members mysteriously disappeared, to reappear some six or eight months later in England bearing the following typewritten notice :

" Suffered detention in Gangtok post office owing to the postmaster's failure to affix stamps and to forward them in time. The Postmaster has been sent to jail for his offence."

But any doubts I may have entertained as to the efficiency of the Indian Posts were dispelled by the Postmaster of Joshimath, who proved not only courteous, but helpful and efficient.

Later, the local Bunnia (storekeeper), a comfortable-looking person who beamed amiably through thick spectacles, put in an appearance and I ordered sattoo (parched barley, a staple food in the Central and Eastern Himalayas), rice, gur (native sugar, which is purchased in lumps resembling solid glue), tea, curry ingredients, atta (flour), spices, potatoes and onions. I bought enough to keep the four Darjeeling men for a fortnight, allowing two pounds of food per man per day, and the cost worked out at roughly 6 annas per man per day. Eggs I failed to secure, although a man was sent to scour the country for them.

Late in the afternoon there was a thunderstorm, but towards sundown the clouds melted away, and with my work done and arrangements completed for the morrow's march, I reclined in an easy chair on the verandah, while a gentle breeze stirred an apricot tree above me, then fell gradually to a complete calm. A rosy glow invested the great rock faces opposite and dusk gathered in the deep Alaknanda Valley. The last mist vanished in a sky of profound green, and the first star shone out.

Little did I know, but this was the evening before the great tragedy on Nanga Parbat, 400 miles to the north-west, where seven German mountaineers and nine

Sherpa porters were settling down to a sleep from which they were destined never to awake.

At Joshimath the evening was supremely peaceful, and there came to me, for the first time since leaving Ranikhet, an indescribable exaltation of spirit, which most travellers experience at one time or another in the Himalayas. For days past I had walked over the foot-hills, rejoicing in the scenery ; yet never for one moment had I escaped civilisation ; it had been always at my heels, and I had walked with one eye on time and another on distance, my mind occupied with futile matters. Now I had in some way escaped from this slavery to schedule and was free to enjoy some of the grandest country of the world.

# CHAPTER IV

## THE BHYUNDAR VALLEY

WE were away at 6 next morning. One of the porters was leading a goat which I had purchased at the last moment for the exorbitant sum of 9 rupees, a fine beast with a long clean shaggy coat which reminded me vaguely of those curious little doormat-like dogs that trail behind amply-proportioned females in Hyde Park and Kensington Gardens. I dubbed him Montmorency, but why I cannot for the life of me recollect. I liked Montmorency, and had not known him above an hour before I regretted his fate ; he was very intelligent, very affectionate, very fond of human society, very docile at the end of his lead, and he had a most pathetic expression, as much as to say, " Please don't kill me yet. Let me enjoy for a little longer the sun, the air and the luscious grass."

From Joshimath a steep path, a preferable alternative to the long tedious zig-zags of the pilgrim route, descends 1,500 feet to Vishnu Prayag, the junction of the Alaknanda and Dhauli Rivers. Perched on a spur between these rivers is a hamlet and a little square-walled temple whence a flight of stone steps descends to the Alaknanda River, here known as the Vishnu Ganga, for the benefit of the pilgrims who wish to immerse themselves in the sacred waters.

Above Vishnu Prayag, the pilgrim path enters a gorge with sheer precipices on either side which echo the thunder of the Alaknanda River as it rages furiously over

39

its steep rock-strewn bed. It was a cool still morning and already the path was thronged with pilgrims. They were an amazing assortment of men and women : fakirs, with wild, haggard, sunken faces and unkempt beards, clad only in a loin-cloth, their bodies smeared with ashes, and fat bunnias, squatting like bloated bull-frogs on charpoys borne by sweating coolies, their women-folk plodding dutifully in the rear, carrying the family bedding, cooking-pots and food ; and, queerest sight of all, little old men and women, so old it seemed impossible that life could persist within their fragile shrunken bodies, hunched uncomfortably in wicker baskets on the backs of coolies. But most were on foot : first father, striding unencumbered along, and wrapt in meditation, then mother, often as not a poor weak little creature perhaps 15 years of age, bowed down beneath an enormous burden, sometimes with a baby in addition on her shoulder.

So they venture on their pilgrimage, these pilgrims, some borne magnificently by coolies, some toiling along in rags, some almost crawling, preyed on by disease and distorted by dreadful deformities. And the stench ! Fifty thousand pilgrims for whom sanitation and hygiene have no place in the dictionary. And not least the flies, millions upon millions of flies. Small wonder that cholera, dysentery and typhoid are rife along the route.

Something sustains these pilgrims ; few seem to enjoy their pilgrimage, yet their faces are intent, their minds set on their goal. They are over-awed, too, by their stupendous environment ; you can see this in their faces. Europeans who have read and travelled cannot conceive what goes on in the minds of these simple folk, many of them from the agricultural parts of India. Wonderment and fear must be the prime ingredients. So the pilgrimage becomes an adventure. Unknown dangers threaten the broad well-made path ; at any moment the gods, who hold the rocks in leash, may unloose their wrath upon the hapless passer-by. To the European it is a walk to Badrinath ; to the Hindu pilgrim it is far, far more.

The path, after crossing the Alaknanda River by a well-built suspension bridge, traversed a craggy hillside to a small village where the porters halted to refresh themselves. A mile beyond this village, a rocky bluff marked the entrance to the Bhyundar Valley. Except for the size of its stream, which suggested an extensive glacier system, there was little to distinguish the valley from other side valleys of the Alaknanda Valley. A disreputable little suspension bridge spans the Alaknanda above the confluence of the two rivers, and near it I waited for the porters. The sun stood high, and the heat filled the valley like faintly simmering liquid. Pilgrims were plodding along the path. Most were clad in white, but here and there were splashes of vivid colour. Old and young, feeble and infirm, plod, plod, plod. They passed in their hundreds.

I smoked my pipe in the shade of a boulder and ruminated. Why ? What was the force that impelled them from their homes on the far-off plains to the Himalayas ? What was the force that had impelled me ? No concrete religious motive, but something far more complex and indefinable. Perhaps the answer lay in this upward bending valley with its dark forests and the distant glimmer of the high snows.

The porters appeared and one by one crossed the shuddering little bridge, then halted on the green slope beyond. A rough track passed a small hamlet at the entrance of the valley, a filthy little place with ankle-deep mire like an Irish farmyard, then mounted through woods by the side of the sun-wickered torrent which rushes impetuously over great boulders under a lacery of spreading trees. Soon the Alaknanda Valley was well behind and the air partook of a new freshness.

After a steep climb the path emerged from the forest on to cultivated fields, presided over by a small village. Here a stinging nettle introduced itself to my bare knees. I do not know its botanical name but it springs up in Garhwal wherever cultivation upsets the natural order of things. It defends itself with light-coloured stiletto-like spines, sharper than the sharpest needle, and is altogether more vicious than the English species.

This village is typical of many in Garhwal. The houses for the most part are single-storeyed, and their rough stone-tiled roofs are strengthened by additional stones placed upon them, so that with their wide eaves they resemble in a remarkable degree the chalets of the upper Alpine pastures. They are fronted by roughly paved yards in which much of the work of the household is carried out, such as threshing, weaving and wool-spinning. Most of the population were working in the fields, but here and there women squatted engaged in weaving on a simple hand frame helped by their children who, when they had overcome their fear of the white-skinned stranger with his stubbly red beard, were all agog with that excitement and curiosity which is the prerogative of children the world over.

These Garhwalis affect dark-coloured workaday cos-tumes, which, on occasion, are brightened with coloured shawls, aprons and bandeaux. Like the Tibetans they are fond of ornaments and trinkets and there is a distinct similarity in the costumes of the two peoples, a similarity which becomes more marked as the Tibetan frontier is approached. As might be supposed, ex-tensive trading between Garhwal and Tibet over the

Niti and Mana Passes has resulted in a fusion of blood, and the people of the upper valleys of Garhwal, though Hindus by religion, are partly Tibetan in origin. Unlike some half-breeds the Marcha Bhotias, as they are called, combine many of the best qualities of the two races. Some of them are shepherds and are used to scrambling about on steep hillsides, so that they make excellent porters, and with mountaineering training should rival the Bhotias and Sherpas, who have done so well on Mount Everest and other high peaks.

Beyond the village the path entered dense deciduous forests, and the valley narrowed into a gorge with vast sheets and curtains of rock on either hand, shimmering here and there with gauzy waterfalls. The heat-tempering breeze died away as the afternoon lengthened, the sun disappeared behind the hills and not a leaf stirred in the shadowed forests.

We camped in the river-bed on a sandy place which is only covered when the snows are melting fast or the monsoon rains are torrential. It was my first camp in the high mountains and I could hardly have chosen a better site. A few yards away the river hastened through a shallow channel and beyond it was forest, riven in places by gullies littered with stones and broken trees brought down by avalanches ending in terrific crags stained black with seeping water whilst far up the valley a snow-robed peak shone between the dark precipices of a distant gorge.

It had been a long hot march, but the porters were in great fettle, and busied themselves collecting driftwood and building a large fire of which the core was a tree-trunk weighing the best part of a ton, deposited near the camp by some flood. Dusk fell. The sunlight died on the far peak, and between the precipices the stars shone out one by one. Nothing moved except the river. Then, in this profound calm, a small bird in a tree above my tent broke suddenly into song, a queer little song, plaintive, very sad and very sweet. It had none of the throaty luxuriance of the nightingale, or the optimistic pipings of a song-thrush ; it was an unhurried little song, a tweet-tweet or two, then silence, then a sudden trill, then a slow sad note. For a full half-hour this bird sang its evening hymn, until darkness had thickened in the valley and the sky filled with stars.

I dined off soup and vegetable curry by the fire ; afterwards the men threw log after log into the blaze until the flames stood high and the tents and nearby forest were illumined. Presently the moon appeared and transmuted to the purest silver the torrent and the far snow peak at the head of the valley. Long after the men had wrapped themselves in their blankets I sat by the glowing embers in a great peacefulness of spirit.

# CHAPTER V

## THE BASE CAMP

NEXT morning, as usual, I breakfasted luxuriously in my sleeping-bag. There is no better preliminary to a day's marching than a plateful of porridge. For the rest, biscuits, butter, jam or marmalade with plenty of tea or coffee made up my normal repast. Eggs and bacon were lacking, but so also was my craving for this peculiarly English dish at five in the morning.

The weather was cloudless and the air deliciously cool. This march, I hoped, would take me to my base camp. The path lay through dense jungle and as I walked several pheasants flew up in front of me and twice I heard crashing sounds as of some large beasts making off. Then the path descended to the river-bed, where to my astonishment we met with a snake. It was curled on a flat stone and at first sight I took it for a strip of cloth dropped by a villager. I was about to step on it when it moved and raised an ugly little head in readiness to strike. It was a brown snake, perhaps fifteen inches long, with banded markings. The men said it was poisonous and one of them killed it, but probably it was harmless for, contrary to popular opinion, harmless snakes form by far the larger percentage in the Himalayas and, for that matter, on the plains of India.

Some two miles above the camp was a side valley ascending towards Hathi Parbat. Seen against the brilliant morning light this great mountain appeared

45

magnificent, and its massive, wall-sided precipices support a remote little snow-field tapering languidly into a snowy summit. If the col between it and Gauri Parbat could be reached both mountains should prove accessible, but it appears totally inaccessible from the west owing to steep icefalls exposed to ice avalanches from hanging glaciers.

Having passed a small village at the junction of the two valleys, populated by cheerful peasants and shepherds, the path crossed the river by a bridge consisting of two tree-trunks held in position by cross-pieces, the interstices of which were filled with stones. Here I was met by a Sikh surveyor, who was camped in the side valley, a fine-looking man attached to Major Gordon Osmaston's party which was engaged in resurveying Garhwal and Kumaon. He showed me some of his work, which seemed to me to be careful and well-drawn, but I am no judge of draughtsmanship. He had discovered that the side valley, instead of ending under Hathi Parbat, as delineated in the old maps, bends southwards, parallel to the watershed of the Zaskar Range, and continues for several miles. I asked him whether he thought that Hathi Parbat could be attacked from the west, but he did not think it was possible from this side though, as he told me with a smile, he was as yet no mountaineer, and was only a beginner in the art—a very necessary art when surveying such rough steep country as this.

The junction of the two valleys is only about 7,500 feet, and beyond it is a forest of oaks, tree rhododendrons, chestnuts, bamboos and willows, to mention but a few trees, densely undergrown with shrubs and briers. Abundant proof of a moist climate is afforded by epiphytic ferns suspended in delicate tendrils from the trees, but of flowers there were few, though here and there I noticed an arum (*Arisaema Wallichianum*), which I had seen already on the foothill ridges, a plant which is more striking than beautiful, with an evil-looking, cobra-like head, whilst in open places were many strawberries, daisies and buttercups. Yet there was so little of floral interest or beauty in the lower and middle sections of the Bhyundar Valley that I began to wonder whether my memory had tricked me and coloured falsely something that was dull and uninteresting. However, I could scarcely grumble : there was no carpet of flowers to beautify my way, but there were forests, cool and shadowed, and above the forests remote hills, and higher still a sky of gentian blue untenanted by a single wisp of vapour.

The path climbed steeply, and presently the deciduous trees gave way to conifers and the cold smell of dank vegetation and decaying leaves was replaced by the warm incense of resin. Then it came to a wide sloping alp. The grass here was less lank and had grown little since the winter snow left it, but already it was being grazed upon by sheep and goats, whose shepherds had quartered themselves in stone huts. The height must have been nearly 10,000 feet, and from peaks on either hand, tongues of snow descended far into the valley.

Beyond the alp was a forest of firs growing between enormous boulders, the debris of a great rock-fall. The difference between the lower and upper forests of the Himalayas must be experienced to be appreciated. The lower forests, jungles that extend upwards to some 7,000 feet, are full of insect and animal life, the upper forests are characterised by their silence. My footfalls were hushed by a carpet of needles, and as I walked I became gradually aware of this silence, so that when I seated myself on a moss-clad boulder, I was already accustomed to it. There was no wind, not a whisper in the pine-tops, and the only sounds were my heart pumping audibly in my ears and the steady thunder of the valley torrent.   Here and there the sunlight had slipped between the tree-tops, and cast brilliant pools amid the shadow, revealing moss-plastered boulders and a delicate tracery of ferns.   These pools of sunlight and the shadows of the trees were the only things that moved, and that very slowly, as the day lengthened.

The path emerged from the forest on to another alp, a favourite haunt of shepherds to judge from the well-built huts.   Here were innumerable blue and white *anemones* (*A. obtusiloba*) and in between them *Primula denticulata*, many of which were already in seed.

I crossed two streams and on a high bank beyond the second came on a monkshood (*Aconitum heterophyllum*) with dark green-purple blooms, and a host of pink rock jasmine (*Androsace primuloides*), lovely little flowers which never ceased to fascinate me.   This *androsace* is a common enough plant.   You can buy it in England for nine-pence and it is described in nurserymen's catalogues as " pretty and easy," but to appreciate its true worth, you must see it tumbling over grey boulders in a rosy cascade under the deep blue of the Himalayan sky, revelling ecstatically in the beauty and grandeur of its home, eager to perpetuate itself, and sending out its runners in all directions, each with a little rosette of leaves ready to root in any scrap of soil or earthy crack.

As I walked across this last alp, I saw that beyond it the valley narrowed into a gorge finer than any I had yet seen.   The forest was compressed between immense walls of rock, of which one was nearly vertical and the other, that to the east, actually overhung and was fully 1,500 feet high.   Even the noonday sun, only a degree or so from the vertical at this time of the year, could not relieve this gorge of its austerity or impart kindliness into the stern-visaged crags.

Through the gorge loomed a wall of high rock peaks, and had it not been for my previous visit to the Bhyundar Valley, I might have concluded that the valley ended abruptly at the base of these peaks.

At the entrance to the gorge the path zig-zagged steeply downwards to a log bridge spanning the river between two large boulders. Over this frail structure, which is prevented from falling to pieces by bamboo thongs, the shepherds drive their flocks to the upper pastures of the valley. Any domestic animal save a hardy Garhwali sheep or goat would be appalled by such a passage, for the river issues with savage force from the jaws of the gorge and to fall into it would mean for man or beast instant destruction.

With the thunder of the torrent in my ears, I ascended steeply through a pine-forest, and presently came to open slopes where the gorge widens. Here were two gullies filled with hard snow in which I had to cut steps with my ice axe ; I cut large ones for the benefit of the porters as a slip would have precipitated a man into the torrent several hundred feet lower. Beyond the second gully I regained the path, which traversed a steep grassy hillside where the valley widens out and bends eastwards almost at right-angles under the wall of peaks that from below the gorge seems to form an impasse.

Since leaving the village I had been alone, having outstripped the porters. For weeks and months past I had visualised the Bhyundar Valley as I had seen it in 1931, but so far I had come upon few flowers. Beauty and grandeur I had seen in plenty ; valleys, rivers, mountains and vistas such as only the Himalayas can show, but of floral beauty comparatively little, but now,

as I turned a corner of the path, I saw out of the corner
of my eye a sheet of blue on the hillside. It was
a blue fumatory, the *Corydalis cashemiriana*. I had
seen it once before in Sikkim, or a flower like it, growing
here and there between boulders, but here was a whole
slope of it, a colony of thousands. It is a small plant
with a stem six inches high, and flowers an inch long,
narrow, pipe-like and tipped in dark-blue, and so
delicate and beautiful they might have been made for
the lips of Pan.

A great avalanche, thousands of tons of snow, had
fallen into the valley just above the gorge and covered
the stream bed a hundred feet deep for several hundred
yards. I have never seen the debris of a bigger avalanche and as it had descended from a peak of not more
than 16,000 feet, it was the proof of an abundant winter
snow-fall. Passing it and keeping to the west of the
main torrent, I presently crossed a steep little subsidiary torrent, after an awkward jump between two
boulders, and continued round the bend until I reached
a point where there was a view up the valley to its
end. It was the same view as in 1931, but with a
difference. In that year, we had visited the valley
during the monsoon season, when the peaks for the
most part were concealed by clouds and the atmosphere
was moist and warm by comparison with the dry, cold
Tibetan winds we had experienced on Kamet; but this
was a pre-monsoon day—the sun shone from a moisture-
less sky, only the lightest of fleecy clouds rested on the
peaks, and the air was imbued with the vigour of spring.

In this part of the valley there were camping places
innumerable, yet none of them satisfied me completely.
I had several weeks to spend in the valley and desired
perfection. My camping site must be so beautiful that
I could never tire of it, a site where the march of light

and shadow would charm me the day through, where there was shade from the noonday sun, and fuel unlimited for my camp fires. My eye was caught and arrested by a shelf on the far side of the valley, an alp that sloped green and smooth, with birch forests above and below, ending in an almost level lawn. Here if anywhere was the perfect place. I retraced my steps to the avalanche, crossed the torrent, and ascending to the lower end of the shelf sat down to await the porters.

The base camp was pitched at the uppermost end of the shelf, and within a few minutes the men, with that peculiar facility of Tibetans for digging themselves in, had converted a nearby hollow into a kitchen, and collected firewood and water ; so that within a quarter of an hour I was comfortably ensconced in my rickety folding chair drinking a cup of tea.

There was no doubt about it ; here was the ideal camping site. On three sides it was bounded by silver birches with a lower frieze of purple- and white-flowered rhododendrons. Never have I seen finer birches. In the westering sun their brilliant foliage and silver bark seemed to partake of the purity of earth and sky, whilst their leaves, rippling in a light breeze, suggested some pebble-floored pool of shimmering water. The valley meadows were 500 feet beneath, and beyond them stood the great wall of rock peaks now revealed in all its magnificence, a wild uprush of giant crags biting into the slow pacing clouds.

After this dizzy climb the eye turned almost with relief to the soberer peaks at the head of the valley, past a torn glacier and subsidiary buttresses, to the snow-crowned crest of Rataban. Of the gorge there was no sign, it lay concealed round the bend of the valley, so that to all intents we might have been cut off from the lower world in some exitless valley inaccessible to men.

Immediately above the camp lay masses of avalanche snow, that had swept through channels in the birch forest and strewn timber upon the alp, enough to keep our fires lighted for weeks, without the necessity of cutting down a single living branch. Spring had only recently come to the alp, but already the moist turf was pulsing with life. Between the lank dead herbage of the previous summer innumerable shoots were pushing upwards, some fat and stumpy, others thin and spearlike, some uncurling as they rose—countless plants anxious to perpetuate themselves before the summer was done and winter's grip closed in once more.

A few plants were already in bloom. A minute blue gentian spread its tiny frilled blooms over the turf, just above the camp were hundreds of purple *Primula denticulata*, and here and there a white *allium* was clustered —a graceful plant with a bulb which, as I soon discovered, was excellent to eat.

One of my first jobs was to pay off the Dotials. It is usual in such cases for the native to assume at the outset that his employer is out to do him down and the foreman, having been summoned, squatted before me with such an expression of mingled distrust, cunning and relief (at being paid at all !) on his wizened pippin-like face that it was all I could do not to laugh. However, the business was settled amicably and without the usual corrosive and entirely unprofitable arguments which result from the payee's primitive knowledge of arithmetic. One rupee per man for each day's outward march, half-pay for the return journey and some " baksheesh," minus such advances of pay as had already been made. It was perfectly simple but it took an hour of noisy argument between the Dotials to convince themselves that they had not been swindled ; then the pippin-faced foreman, doubt and suspicion removed from his beaming countenance, returned and expressed himself as satisfied and more than satisfied; if the sahib wanted him and his men for the return journey, well, he had only to send word to Ranikhet.

By the time these financial details had been settled and the stores unpacked and arranged in a spare tent it was evening. A warm light filled the valley and the lengthening shadows revealed unsuspected grandeurs. and beauties in the great rock walls opposite. The light breeze had fallen to a complete calm and not a leaf of the birches quivered. Quickly the sun dipped behind the Khanta Khal pass which we had crossed in 1931 from the Bhyundar Valley to the Alaknanda Valley. Best of all the men were contented. Wangdi came up to me with a happy grin on his hard face. He swept his arm in a single comprehensive gesture over the birches and across the valley, past the glowing snows of Rataban. "Ramro, sahib!" He was right; it was beautiful. While Tewang cooked the supper, Pasang, Wangdi and Nurbu collected wood, so that by the time the sun had set and a chill crept into the air I was comfortably seated by a roaring log fire.

Let me confess at once that I am an incurable romantic. Since the days when I devoured G. A. Henty and Fennimore Cooper I have looked upon the camp fire as a necessary adjunct of enjoyable travel. What is the charm of it? Is it because it panders to deep-seated hereditary instincts? Are we for all our central-heated homes and "no draught" ventilation system essentially primitive at heart? Have our cavemen ancestors handed on to us an animal-like love of its warmth and light, and safety from bestial marauders? And has such love been transmuted to something purely romantic? Will civilisation grind out of man all his ancient qualities, his fierce unreasoning passions, his hopes and fears, his love of nature and primitive things ? Does peace and security spell effeminacy and deterioration of the virile qualities ?   What will we become when the need to struggle for our existence is banished from the perfect world promised us by philosophers, economists and pacifists ?   Perhaps in this a reason is to be found for all forms of physical adventure.   The qualities that have given us domination over the beast, that demand safety not as a dead level of existence but in opposition to danger continue to find an outlet for their activity in sports labelled dangerous, useless or unjustifiable.   Peace between men is not incompatible with maintenance of physical virility when so many adventures are possible in the open air.   Whether it be the cricket or rugger field or the heights of the Himalayas there is enough to satisfy this adventurous spirit of ours without resort to the soul-deadening work of killing our fellow men.   It remains to be seen how our inherited instincts are to be adapted to our need of peace and happiness, the two things which men crave most.   I am sure myself that they are to be found in the open air, and that the present movement in this direction, not only in Britain but in many other countries, is an unconscious revolt against the primæval desire to kill in order to maintain physical safety and virility and represents the growth of the human intelligence towards a new and happier conception of the universe and human relationships.   Most of all does it indicate a Divine desire for the physical, mental and spiritual progress of mankind.   Who are we to talk of degeneration and retrogression in a God-made world ?

It was the first time I had travelled alone in the Himalayas and the experience after the last two caravanserais to Mount Everest was more than refreshing.   For the first time in my life I was able to think.   I do not mean to think objectively or analytically, but rather to surrender thought to my surroundings. This is a power of which we know little in the west but which is a basic of abstract thought in the east. It is allowing the mind to receive rather than to seek impressions, and it is gained by expurgating extraneous thought. It is then that the Eternal speaks ; that the mutations of the universe are apparent : the very atmosphere is filled with life and song ; the hills are resolved from mere masses of snow, ice and rock into something living. When this happens the human mind escapes from the bondage of its own feeble imaginings and becomes as one with its Creator.

My pen has run away with me ; it often did when recording my impressions in the Valley of Flowers, for it is impossible to continue along conventional channels when the country on either side is so fair, so even though I am not understood or at risk of being labelled " sentimental,"—a red rag this word to the bull of materialism —I must endeavour to record my impressions during my sojourn in this valley.

That first evening I sat long by the camp fire until the talk in the porters' tents had dwindled away and the silence was complete save for the light, almost imperceptible hiss of the burning logs. Presently even that died and the fire shrank to a heap of glowing embers. The cold stole up behind me ; suddenly I was chilly and my pipe was out. A few minutes later I was warm in my eiderdown sleeping-bag. The last thing I saw before closing my eyes was a bright star poised on a distant ridge looking at me through the door of the tent.

The sun rose above Rataban at 6.20 next morning. I awoke to birdsong—a great chorus from the surrounding birch forest and rhododendron brakes. Most prominent was a small undistinguished brown bird, of the corncrake family I should say. I dubbed it the zeederzee bird for this most nearly describes its song. It was a perfect morning, not a cloud, and the dew-soaked grass shone like a pavement of frosted glass in the brilliant sunlight.

Nurbu brought me my breakfast as I lay slothfully in my sleeping-bag. Occasionally Pasang officiated, but more often it was Nurbu, and his cheerful smile was a happy beginning to a day.

As I ate the usual porridge, biscuits and jam there seemed to be something missing, pleasantly missing. Then I remembered—the flies. Except for the camp on the Kuari Pass, flies had been with me all the way from Ranikhet; they had become a part of the natural order of things. And now there were no flies; it seemed almost too good to be true.

After breakfast the Dotials, who had bivouacked close by, left for Ranikhet. They seemed well contented and the pippin-faced foreman, for about the tenth time, announced his readiness to return with his men.

Leaving Tewang to mind the camp, Wangdi, Nurbu, Pasang and I set off on a tour of inspection.

Immediately below the camp we found a rough sheep track running downwards through the steep birch forest. It was partly overgrown with vegetation but some vigorous work with a kukri soon cleared a way. Here, as on the alp above, *Primula denticulata* was growing. This plant seems to like shade and sun almost equally well so long as it receives plenty of moisture at the roots, but a moist place in the sun is probably ideal.

Below us we could hear the roar of the torrent and soon we were slithering down a snow-slope between it and the lowermost edge of the forest. Immediately to the east of the camp was a wide gully, and a huge spring avalanche pouring down this had bridged the torrent so that we were able to cross without difficulty to the other side of the valley. Here on well-drained south-facing slopes many plants were already in bloom. As we scrambled up a steep grassy buttress between clumps of dark green juniper I saw growing on a skyline above the same dark purple monkshood I had seen below the gorge ; then the white umbels of *Anemone polyanthes* which is closely allied with *Anemone narcissiflora*, with *Corydalis cashemiriana* brilliantly blue in between.

A steep scramble and we stood on a wide shelf littered with boulders and there grew a plant which is one of the rarest and most beautiful of its family, the lily-like *Nomocharis oxypetela*. In colour this *nomocharis* is very different to the *Nomocharis nana* which also grows in the Bhyundar Valley ; the latter is blue, the former rich daffodil yellow. Obviously it revels in the sun on well-warmed, well-drained meadows and slopes where there is plenty of fibrous material and rocks to feed its roots with moisture.

I set the men to work to collect bulbs and presently they had dug up two or three dozen with their ice-axes. It was not easy work, for the *nomocharis* bulb grows a full six inches deep and its favourite habitat is a dense matting of bracken roots and sometimes juniper roots and between boulders and stones.

Another plant in bloom was a purple *orchis* one to two feet high, whilst the ubiquitous little *Iris kumaonensis* was approaching its best—thousands of blooms on the stony hillside. Then, over the rocks, the pink *Androsace primuloides* was fast spreading its silver-green rosettes and pink flowers.

A light breeze had sprung up and before it the *nomocharis* nodded and bowed their golden heads. In slow waves it rippled across the slopes, bringing an indescribable scent of plant life with now and then a breath of delightful thyme-like perfume which I soon found emanated from a purple-flowered plant that creeps over the sunny faces of boulders and dry slopes.

We returned to camp for lunch, after which I busied myself pressing the specimens collected during the morning. I had never pressed flowers prior to this expedition and I must confess I found it an irksome and finicking task. The remainder of the afternoon I spent collecting in the vicinity of the camp. Among the plants I discovered was a fleshy leafed *bergenia* (*B. Stracheyi*) growing between moss-clad boulders on a northern slope, and in the forest behind the camp a wood lily, *Trillium Govanianum*. Not far from the camp was a bank facing south already gay with flowers, including *Nomocharis oxypetela*, whilst on the edge of the gully east of the camp a creamy dwarf rhododendron common throughout the Himalayas and many parts of Tibet was in bloom together with the delicate little creamy bells of a *cassiope* (*C. fastigiata*).

At tea-time Tewang announced that he had a bad foot and that it was now hurting him up the leg to the groin. He had blistered it during the march and the sore had festered, but like any other happy-go-lucky Tibetan it had never occurred to him to mention it until his whole leg was poisoned. Before I could treat him I made him wash his foot. I do not suppose he had ever consciously washed in his life and he performed the ablution with a sort of pained surprise and indignant resignation. Needless to say his foot was filthy, the dirt of years being caked between the toes. It would seem an impossible task to make the Tibetan realise the connection between dirt and disease, the one is just dirt, the other an affliction meted out by the Gods. This done, I scraped and probed the wound with a scalpel until blood and pus flowed in generous quantities, afterwards bandaging it with lint. The sight of the blood heartened Tewang and his broad flat face broke into a beaming smile. "Now I shall be all right," he declared. And so indeed he was, for in a few days the trouble had cleared up completely.

That evening I supped again by a great fire. During the heat of the day a breeze flowed up the valley, but it dropped at sundown to a complete calm so that I could light my pipe with an unshielded match and the sound of the stream served only to emphasise the profound stillness. The clouds ebbed fast from the peaks and a silent rush of mist swept up through the gorge and passed across the opposite hillside. The sunlight died and the night came swiftly ; in less than half an hour from the time the sun set it was dark except for the coldest and faintest of afterglows on the high peaks, a light matching the pale brilliance of the stars.

The fire of birch logs burned perfectly, red and blue flames with scarcely any smoke, and in its light the faces of the men stood out from the darkness against a still darker background of forest.

The moon became apparent, a brilliant crescent riding high overhead ; it silvered the snows and glaciers and lit the gathering dew with a cold fire.

Slowly, as the air required equilibrium, the low valley mists dissolved until by 8.30 not one vestige remained.

A bird sang during the first hour of darkness, a curious song that I had not heard before ; chuck, chuck, chuck, chuck, eee, chuck, chuck chuck, chuck, eee ; something between that of a nightjar and a corncrake, but presently it stopped and all that remained of sound was the steady rumbling of the glacier torrent.

# CHAPTER VI

## A MINOR CLIMB

IMMEDIATELY above the camp the birch forest swept up in an unbroken sheet for some 500 feet. Above it were open slopes still snow-covered, whence rose the steep ridges of a peak about 17,000 feet high. This peak I decided to climb, for not only would it provide an admirable training expedition, but it should command a panorama of the Bhyundar Valley and its surroundings. So on June 19th, after an early but leisurely breakfast, Wangdi, Nurbu, Pasang and I set off to exercise our climbing machinery. We avoided the fatigue of forcing our way through the forest by ascending a grassy ridge bounding the gully to the east of the camp. Two hundred feet higher, this ridge tailed out into snow-slopes broken only by occasional rocky outcrops and incipient ridges. The snow was hard frozen and we made rapid progress. We were passing one of the rocky outcrops when a flare of imperial purple caught my eye and I halted to admire a superb *primula*. Fully ten inches high, it rose in regal dignity from a centre of thin mealy leaves, rooted in a moist crack generously fed by snow water, which oozed over a slab in convulsive jerks beneath a film of ice. I think it was the dark blue form of *Primula nivalis macrophylla*.

Above this point the slope steepened and presently we were forced to kick, and sometimes to cut, steps. Here, for the first time, I was able to observe the different climbing styles of my companions. Wangdi was the most experienced of the trio, but he had not learnt to move rhythmically, and put a great deal of unnecessary effort into his climbing, kicking his steps with a restless, untiring vigour and so viciously he might have had a grudge against the snow. Nurbu followed docilely, obviously intent on learning all he could about the finer points of mountaineering. Pasang, on the other hand, had not the remotest idea of rhythm or co-ordinated movement. He moved jerkily and in rushes, breathing heavily the while, and appeared incapable of transferring his weight gradually from one foot to the other so that it seemed he might slip at any moment. After a while I made him lead in the hope of teaching him the art of walking up a snow-slope, but it was all in vain ; he was wedded to his own method, or lack of method. So I left him to his own devices and he went rushing on ahead, kicking steps as though his life depended on reaching the summit in the least possible time, and of course soon had to stop for a rest. It is indeed curious that these Tibetans, and the same applies to the Sherpas, who spend their lives among the hills, have never learned to walk uphill easily ; they have to be taught this art by Europeans with not half their experience of hill-walking.

As we mounted, making height at the rate of nearly 1,500 feet an hour, the green valley fell away, shrinking as it did so, and the wall of rock peaks opposite increased in apparent stature and grandeur. Presently a peak well to the north-east came into view, an isolated, pyramidal, wall-sided mountain rising head and shoulders above its neighbours that reminded me of photographs of Mount Robson in the Canadian Rockies. Later, I learned that Lieutenant Gardiner, who had been surveying the district, had named it Nilgiri Parbat, and had placed its height at 21,264 feet. Could it be climbed ? Certainly not from the Bhyundar Valley, though to judge from the general angle of its ridges, the north face was probably less formidable. At all events it would be well worth reconnoitring, though to approach it from the north would mean forsaking the Bhyundar Valley in favour of a parallel valley, to reach which it would be necessary to force a pass over the wall of rock peaks, separating the two valleys.

Without any difficulty we gained the crest of a minor spur. Barhal (wild sheep) had been there before us, and their tracks zig-zagged aimlessly about the snow-slopes. Kicking steps, we advanced steadily, and within three hours of leaving the camp had gained the east ridge of our peak at a point about 500 feet below the summit.

A brisk little wind was blowing across the ridge, but we sheltered from it under some sun-warmed rocks a few feet below the crest and ate a meal. It was a beautiful morning, and the sky in our vicinity was un-clouded. In the south, dense pillars of cumulus were rising from the valleys, and between them we discerned the snow-fields of Trisul and the massive spire of Nanda Devi. Separating us from these two great mountains were the subsidiary spurs and ridges of the main Zaskar Range, a bewildering labyrinth of rocky edges, and up-tilted strata over which the eye wandered restlessly, seeking lodgment but finding none until, wearied of sheer savagery, it passed to the west where Nilkanta stood solitary and serene, the undisputed queen of the Badrinath Peaks. The mists were slowly embracing it, but before they concealed it I examined the final pyramid through my monocular glass. The only route that seemed to offer the remotest chance of success was the south-east ridge. The lower part of this was hidden behind nearer mountains, but if in the upper part a rock step several hundred feet high could be surmounted, the upper slopes of snow and ice should prove feasible.

After a halt of half an hour in the sun, we continued on our way. From the point at which we gained the ridge, the peak springs up steeply in a serrated edge of reddish rock. It was possible to avoid this obviously difficult crest by scrambling up the disagreeably loose south face, but for the sake of exercise and training I determined to attempt it. To begin with, there was little difficulty, but presently we came to a steep slab. Here I had a further opportunity of observing the methods of my companions. Wangdi made light of it but did not scruple to use the rope as a hand-hold, although the holds, if small, were sufficient. Pasang, though more at home on rocks than on snow, was very ungainly, and inclined to pull himself up by strength of arm. Nurbu was the best of all, and his swift effort-less agility convinced me then and there that in him were the makings of a first-rate mountaineer.

Above this preliminary slab was a wall which I found distinctly trying. Furthermore, a tightness in my head, that had accrued during the past hour or so, was rapidly developing into one of those jarring headaches which result from lack of acclimatisation to altitude.

From the top of this second pitch, the ridge rose in an overhanging tower culminating in a fang-like point and was completely inaccessible. The alternative, as already mentioned, was the south face. To reach it, we had to descend an unpleasantly loose chimney where Pasang, now the last man down, managed to dislodge an angular block of rock weighing a fair hundredweight, which flew close to those below before shattering itself into fragments. Then tongues wagged and hard things were said, and it was a very abashed and painfully careful Pasang who descended the remainder of the chimney.

A traverse across some rickety ledges, and a scramble up the decaying face brought us to the summit. Mists were forming, but between them the nearer mountains showed and, more distantly, the buttresses of Gauri Parbat and Hathi Parbat. The day was now windless and warm, but I was in no mood to appreciate this or the grandeur of my surroundings, for my headache had become worse and every movement sent a thrill of pain from the base of the skull to a point just above the eyes. The descent was a purgatory. I could scarcely see straight and vomiting supervened, but this did not relieve the headache—it increased it, if that were possible. After what seemed an age, owing to the clumsiness of Pasang and the consequent necessity to move one at a time, we got off the rocks and began the descent of the snow-slopes. Had it not been for my mountain sickness I should have enjoyed the longest glissade of my experience, as it was possible to descend about 4,000 feet of snow-slopes to a point within two minutes' walk of the camp. Wangdi glissaded expertly, and Nurbu was a trier, but Pasang was hopeless and it was not long before he slipped and descended ungracefully on his back for some hundreds of feet, dropping his ice-axe, which the good-natured Nurbu recovered. Except for Wangdi, who was soon out of sight, it was a melancholy procession. First of all myself, able to glissade only a few yards at a time owing to the pain in my head, then Nurbu, and lastly the unfortunate Pasang, scrabbling about like a beetle on a sheet of glass. And so at length to the camp, where Wangdi and Tewang greeted me with broad, unsympathetic grins and a mugful of steaming hot tea. My first peak had not been enjoyable.

# CHAPTER VII

## THE SNOW COL

THE two days following the ascent of the minor peak I devoted to flower collecting. The weather was already appreciably warmer, and at night lightning flickered in the south. The monsoon was approaching, and as though in anticipation of its warm, life-giving breath, plants sprang up everywhere with astonishing rapidity. Already the green bells of a fritillary (*F. Roylei*) surrounded the camp. This is an unobtrusive flower, but it has a charm of its own, a delicacy surpassing that of many more showy flowers. As the green bells on their springy stems nodded and dipped vivaciously in the light breezes, I half expected to hear the tinkling of fairy chimes over the alp. Maybe they sounded, but not to mortal ears.

By the stream I came on a bank blue with *cynoglossum* (*C. glochidiatum*), a blue that matched the midday sky. Then there was a moist place on the opposite side of the valley, yellow and purple with marigolds and *Primula denticulata*. It was an incongruous combination of colours which would look out of place, perhaps ugly, in a garden, yet if Nature is sometimes reckless, her taste is unerring. Picture a golden carpet quivering ceaselessly in the wind, with violet splashes between and the clear waters of a stream lapping over the grey boulders, in little collars of foam, or reposed in deep quiet pools that mirror the peaks and sky. In the middle distance the valley-sides sweep upwards, green at first,

65

then blue, breaking on high in bleak and desolate crags, and beyond, the massive buttresses of Rataban, their harsher details softened by distance, supporting snow-fields and silver-edged ridges etched against the intensely blue sky.

In Britain the atmosphere subtly deceives our estimation of height and distance, but in the moisture-free atmosphere of the Himalayas the peaks look high because they are high. At midday they gleam like polished steel under a nearly vertical sun and the eye sinks with relief to the green valley floor. Yet, if in the matter of detail and height little or nothing is left to the imagination, the colourings compensate ; in this brilliant atmosphere they are celestial. Possibly the ultra-violet in the light at high altitudes has something to do with this. Take a knot weed, the little *Polygonum affine*, one of the representative plants of the Central Himalayas : it colours the hillside in millions upon millions of rosy blooms, and the glow of it may be seen a mile away, lighting the slopes. Yet in England, it is a poor, dull-coloured flower, and becomes lank and attenuated in our soft climate. Even such an un-pretentious flower as a yellow violet (*Viola biflora*) imparts to itself some quality of sun and atmosphere, for it shines like a star from the coarser herbage.

The second day saw the death of Montmorency. I was loath indeed to kill him, for he had become an institution, but fresh meat was necessary. For nearly three weeks I had lived on a vegetarian diet, and though it suited me admirably in some ways I discovered that I was not going as strongly on hills as I should have done, whilst my craving for meat, which had remained temporarily in abeyance, had returned with twofold force. I was tired of vegetable curries, so I cast hungry, predatory eyes on poor Montmorency and ordered his execution. It was a grisly business. The men, unwilling to lose any of his blood, scraped and cleaned a large rock slab, then trussing Montmorency's legs together, they laid him on the slab like a sacrifice and a moment later a razor-edged kukri had severed his head from his body. But if goats have souls, then perhaps Montmorency looked down with a certain complacency on the subsequent proceedings, for his meat, having been buried in a snow-drift, lasted for more than a fortnight, whilst his skin, after being well scraped, afforded an excellent carpet for the floor of the porters' tent. For the remainder of the day the men scraped and flogged it, and even put it in their tent with them at night. But here Montmorency got something of his own back. Even the Tibetans have a power of smell, though it is seldom obvious, and in the night I woke to hear a chorus of oaths, then the sound of something being hurled into outer darkness. It was the skin of Montmorency.

One of my memories of 1931 was of a col at the head of the Bhyundar Valley. It is a col that no mountaineer could look at without wanting to ascend ; a parabola of pure snow, between Rataban and a minor unnamed peak to the north. I determined, therefore, to pitch a camp on it and, if possible, attempt the ascent of Rataban, via its steep north ridge.

After a night of distant lightning, midsummer day dawned with a murky, watery sky. We were off at 6.30, leaving Tewang at the base camp, carrying five days' food, and light equipment. The men were lightly laden, but soon they began to make heavy weather of the march up the valley. It was obvious that they had been over-eating themselves with the innards of Montmorency. The Tibetan is perforce normally a vegetarian, but when he can get meat he stuffs himself until he is scarcely able to move. I was not exactly comfortable myself, having dined very heartily off Montmorency's liver, and this heavy meat meal, after nearly three weeks' abstinence from meat, had put a strain on the digestive organs ; so our progress was slow and subject to many halts.

Having crossed the snow-bridge below the camp, we ascended along the northern side of the valley. It was easy going, at first between boulders, then along the wide, dry stream-bed, which was littered with the remains of avalanches fallen during the spring. I was surprised to notice that the northernmost slopes of the valley had been extensively burned. Wangdi explained that this had been done by shepherds the previous summer, presumably with the object of improving the fertility of the ground, and of destroying numerous juniper bushes which encumbered the slopes. This burning could only have been accomplished some time after the end of the monsoon season or during a spell of very dry weather.

On the way up the valley we passed two shepherds' huts. It is the practice in these mountains for the shepherds to let their flocks wander over the hillsides during the daytime, but to round them up at night in a space near their huts to prevent them from straying or being attacked by bears. These rounding-up places are distinguishable by the weeds that grow on them. It was also very noticeable in Garhwal that where extensive grazing is permitted, the smaller and tenderer plants are soon eliminated and in their place spring up a tall knot weed (*Polygonum polystachyum*) and an even taller balsam (*Impatiens Roylei*). Once these two plants have got a hold of the ground, pastureland is permanently ruined and I noticed a number of places in the Bhyundar Valley where this had occurred.

Beyond the second shepherds' hut, the flowers were abundant. In a marshy place where a stream seeped between cushions of bright green moss, grew a tall white *primula (P. involucrata)*, and near by was a small dank alcove in the rocks, padded with moss, where a trickle of water fell like liquid silver into a pool girt around with rosy knot weed. This pool emptied in its turn into a larger stream with rocky banks, already gay with white *anaphalis*, an everlasting flower with a golden centre, whilst on higher, drier places, yet with their roots well down in moist fissures, *Androsace primuloides* grew in thousands of pink blooms, exuding a sweet, almost musky scent impossible to analyse or describe.

We next crossed a hillside and there on a corner I came on the bright blue *Eritrichium strictum* which, in my ignorance, I mistook at first for a forget-me-not. It is a cousin of that Alpine king of flowers, the *Eritrichium nanum*, but unlike the latter is comparatively easy to cultivate in England. Its colour reminded me of an *eritrichium* I had seen in Tibet during the 1936 Mount Everest Expedition. We were crossing the Doya La, a pass of about 16,000 feet, into the Kharta Valley when we came upon a cushion-like plant covered in almost stalkless brilliant blue forget-me-not-like flowers. I have never been able to discover its name, nor is there any mention of it in any list of plants collected during the Mount Everest expeditions.

Our route was the same as that followed by shepherds who cross the Bhyundar Pass, and presently we came to the place where the Kamet Expedition had camped in 1931. The tent platforms in the grass-slope were still visible, and though the flowers were not as advanced as they had been then, there were enough to remind me of what Holdsworth had written, " Where we pitched our tents it was impossible to cut a sod of turf from the ground without destroying a *primula* or a fritillary."

To gaze upon an old camping site years after is like returning to the scenes of one's youth. It inspires a sadness as well as an interest. Six years had passed since we camped there and now we were scattered about the world. Life is too short, its memories too evanescent ; I was the only one to return to the Valley of Flowers.

Above this camping place the glacier forked into two glaciers, one of which originates on Gauri Parbat, the other on Rataban and Nilgiri Parbat. Both are extensively moraine-covered, and with the winter's snow half-melted presented a dreary appearance. The fast-melting snow on the peaks was bringing down many stone-falls ; a steep rock buttress at the junction of the glaciers grumbled ceaselessly and although half a mile from the base of it, I could distinctly hear the hum and whine of falling rocks. But the most impressive rock-fall came from a peak to the south of the main glacier, and must have weighed hundreds of tons. Not content to follow any prescribed route the stones leapt furiously down the mountainside and across the lower grass-slopes, leaving long scars in their wake. Among them was a block the size of a house, which took the side moraine of the glacier in its stride and rushed a full hundred yards out on to the ice.

Where the rough shepherds' track passed beneath a crag, I saw a small yellow flower which I dug up with my ice axe and discovered to be bulbous. It proved to be the yellow star of Bethlehem (*Gagea lutea*). Beyond this crag the track mounted a gully, then climbed steeply to a turfy shoulder. There were juniper bushes here, so we were able to collect some fuel. The men were in better form now, having to some extent walked off the effects of Montmorency, and while they occupied themselves with the juniper, I wandered about the hillside collecting specimens. I had not to look far before I saw a minute and almost stemless *primula* with a pink star-shaped flower, peeping up from densely clustered masses of foliage. This was *Primula minutissima*, one of the smallest of *primulas*. Then there was a cinquefoil, the yellow variety of *Potentilla argyrophylla*, which at this height is considerably smaller than its wine-red brother. I also found a cross between it and the red variety, and this is perhaps the most beautiful of all, for in colour it reminded me of a yellow sunset splashed with scarlet, the whole uniting to form a superb deep orange.

Having loaded ourselves with wood, we followed the crest of a side moraine. Here, growing among the grit and stones, were numerous rock plants, among them *sedums* and what I knew from Holdsworth's description must be *Androsace poissonii*, a little white flower that grows from cushions of silver wool-like foliage. But as Holdsworth wrote, " It spreads into big masses in open peaty places and seems to need no stone," and I found it later covering such ground.

Presently we left the moraine in favour of the snow-covered glacier. This glacier, like the main Bhyundar Glacier, bifurcates in its turn. The easternmost branch, which has its origin under Rataban and the snow col, forms in its lowermost portion an impressive ice-fall, bisected horizontally by a belt of cliffs over which the ice is precipitated every minute or two, recompacting itself on the glacier beneath. This ice-fall is inaccessible to direct attack, but can be outflanked by following the route towards the Bhyundar Pass almost to the pass, then traversing to the south-east on to the snow-field above it.

A prominent buttress to the west of the ice-fall affords

a good approach to a steeply sloping snow-covered shelf, which I knew must be traversed before a direct ascent could be made to the Bhyundar Pass. As I scrambled up it, well ahead of the men, I came once again upon the dark blue *Primula nivalis macrophylla.* Every moist place held its quota of these glorious flowers which charged the still afternoon air with their subtle fragrance, whilst a little higher grew the light blue variety, which seems to combine the colours of earth and sky, the blue of the Himalayan sky and the duskier blue of the valley.

We camped on a shelf formed by an overhanging crag. All around, between clumps of dwarf rhododendrons, the turf was starred with *Primula minutissima,* and close by was a small cave whence a rivulet trickled down a mossy gully gay with *androsaces.* The ice-fall was close at hand and every minute or so there was a harsh roar of falling debris, with now and then the thunderous crash of a larger avalanche.

Mist had formed during the afternoon, but at sundown it melted away at our level and we looked across a sea of vapour, its topmost waves reddened by the declining sun, to a snow-peak south of the Bhyundar Valley. The base of this peak was mist-shrouded, but the summit stood out sharply against a green sky. It was of pure snow, and there was a beautifully moulded ridge that ran straight as a die to the crest. The map does not indicate its presence, but that was not surprising. Was it climbable ? If so, from which valley ? It would be necessary to reconnoitre the approaches to it. Mountaineering difficulties in the Himalayas are two-fold : that of climbing a mountain, and that of finding a route to one or other of the ridges of that mountain ; and the second difficulty is sometimes greater than the first.

As the sun sank it lit Rataban, which I examined with interest through my monocular glass. The north ridge rising from the snow col looked formidable, if not impossible, in its lowermost portion, and about 800 feet above the col was an overhanging nose that appeared entirely inaccessible to direct attack. The east face of the mountain was not visible and failing a route on it the most hopeful alternative was a route up the northwest face. There were two or three minor rock-ridges and though the face as a whole looked steep and complicated, there seemed reason to suppose that with good conditions it could be ascended to a point on the north ridge above the overhanging nose. Once on the snow-covered uppermost portion of the ridge, the summit should prove accessible. Even as I gazed at the great mountain the sunlight moved quickly up it to be superseded quickly by the cold night shadow.

The men cooked a tasteful supper, but I had scarcely time to eat it before a violent wind rose. To sleep afterwards was impossible owing to the wildly flapping canvas of my tent, but the rising moon came as a signal and with that incalculable suddenness peculiar to atmospheric conditions in high mountains this ephemeral wrath of the elements ended as abruptly as it began.

Pasang awakened me soon after five next morning. I wish I could muster the vim and cheerfulness of a Tibetan at this drear, cold hour. When he attended to me he always did so clumsily and with a take-it-or-leave-it manner, but this last was only a mannerism.

Our way lay diagonally upwards across snow-slopes and two wide gullies. The snow was frozen and a slip would have precipitated a man over the cliffs below ; so we roped up at the camp. So hard was the snow that in many places it was necessary to cut steps, but apart from this there was no difficulty and presently, when we came to a ridge of broken rocks, we advanced unroped.   The rock-ridge ended a short distance below the Bhyundar Pass and we roped up again for the traverse which took us across the snow-field above the ice-fall.   In a very short time we were at the foot of the final slopes leading to the col.   The weather was now uncertain and mists had already formed.   We were unable to see clearly and because of this I disliked the look of a snowy corridor between some *séracs* (ice pinnacles) and the slopes of the minor unnamed peak to the north-west of the col, as the debris of avalanches was lying there and I could not tell whether it was of snow or ice ; if the latter, we would be well advised to avoid it.

The alternative route, which I decided was the safer, went straight up through the *séracs*, and provided us with some pretty ice-work.   In one place we had to descend into and climb out of a wide crevasse well bridged with snow, with a steep upper lip 40 feet high. It was fatiguing work, especially for laden men, and we were glad to reach unbroken slopes above.   Thenceforwards, it was a monotonous plug up steep slopes in thick mist to the crest of the col, where the two tents were pitched, partly on stones and partly on snow and ice.

It had been a short and, in the main, easy ascent, and after lunch clearer weather tempted me to work off my superfluous energy in scaling the minor unnamed peak of about 19,000 feet to the north-west of the col. A ridge, at first of broken rock, then of snow, leads to the summit, and as there was no difficulty or danger about the climb I decided to go alone and was on the summit within an hour of leaving the camp.

The view of Rataban across the col confirmed the con-

clusions I had already reached. It was useless to attempt
the north ridge directly from the col, whilst the east
face was entirely impracticable owing to sheer precipices
swept by avalanches from a hanging glacier perched on
the uppermost slopes of the mountain. The north-west
face, however, was more hopeful, and provided that a
belt of steep rocks about two-thirds of the way up it
could be climbed, it should be possible to reach the
north ridge and follow it over snow to the summit.

In other directions the view was partially obscured
by clouds, but I could see the Banke Glacier 5,000 feet
beneath to the north-east, and beyond it a complicated
muddle of rock peaks. The view to the north and north-
west was totally obscured and I was disappointed at
not seeing the Mana Peak and Kamet. It was pleasantly
warm on the summit, but there was something about
the atmosphere I did not like, an indefinable feeling of
impending storm.

I descended leisurely to the camp where Wangdi
welcomed me with a cup of tea. The remainder of the
day passed uneventfully, except that now and then an
ice avalanche thundered down the eastern precipice
from the hanging glacier already mentioned. Towards
sunset a chill wind rose and it was apparent from the
sky that a storm was about to break. The west was
filled with boiling clouds, but to the north-east I could
see the distant rust-coloured plateau of Tibet beyond
ranges of snow-streaked peaks. More to the east, a
storm was centred on the Nepalese border, and a vast
anvil-shaped cloud was linked with the earth by steel-
blue rain streaked grey with hail and snow, whilst
other clouds were scattered like glowing embers along
the Himalayas.

It was a magnificent but desolate scene, and a biting
wind soon hustled us into our sleeping-bags. I slept

lightly but moderately well, only to wake at 3 a.m. with a sense of impending danger. There seemed no reason to suspect danger of any kind, but presently I noticed a curious feeling as though a cobweb covered my face. At first, in my drowsy condition, I thought it *was* a cobweb, and several times put up my hand in an attempt to brush it away, but presently, when I was fully awake, I realised that it was an effect of electrical tension, for I had experienced the same sensation on several occasions in the Alps. It is not a happy situation lying in a tent pitched on the very crest of a ridge knowing that an electrical storm is brewing, and ever since I was struck on the Schreckhorn I have dreaded lightning, for it is the least combatable of all Nature's forces on a mountain.

During the next minute or two, the feeling of tension increased rapidly, then, suddenly, there was a mauve glare, a pause of less than one second and a muffled roar of thunder that seemed to come from every direction like some subterranean explosion. Then came the wind, blasting across the ridge with such force that it threatened to tear away the camp and hurl it down the precipice. But the tents had been well pitched, for with memories of what Himalayan gales may accomplish on Everest such an important detail was not to be overlooked.

Happily there were no more lightning discharges, but snow fell so heavily that by five o'clock it was clear that not only must our attempt on Rataban be postponed, but that we would be well advised to retreat, before it accumulated to such a depth as to render the slopes below the col dangerous from avalanches. So I shouted to the men and eventually succeeded in waking them. They must have thought me a fool not to wait until the blizzard abated, for the Tibetan, though he

may be a good climber, has little or no conception of
the finer points of mountaineering and cannot appreciate
danger until it occurs.  However, after I had done my
best to explain the position, they showed alacrity in
packing up the camp.

In the matter of sheer unpleasantness breaking camp
on an exposed Himalayan ridge in a howling blizzard
at 5 in the morning must be hard to equal.  Such an
occasion always discovers Wangdi at his best.  He seems
everywhere at once, lion-like in strength and active like
a cheetah.  His grim little face becomes even grimmer.
There is a job to be done, an unpleasant job ; no use
fiddling with it, get it done and quickly.  So it came
about that within a very short time the frozen, wildly
flapping tents were smothered and subdued, and sleeping-bags, cooking utensils and food rammed into rucksacks.

It was impossible to see more than a yard or two in
the blizzard ; our upward track had vanished beneath
six inches of snow, and it was more by luck than judg-
ment that we steered a course which avoided awkward
crevasses.  Visibility improved as we descended, so
abandoning our upward route in favour of the suspected corridor which we now knew to be perfectly
safe we slid pell-mell down easy slopes to the snow-field.

Henceforward the descent was uneventful, except that
Pasang slipped twice on the snow-slope above the lower
camping place.  The second time this happened I was
nearing a boulder projecting through the snow, so
jumped forward to get the rope round it, in doing
which I caught my shin violently against a projecting
flake of rock.  This inspired me to such a flight
of oratory that the unfortunate Pasang moved with
unexampled care for the remainder of the descent.

We breakfasted in rain at the lower camp ; higher,

however, it was still snowing hard, and I wondered whether the storm heralded the monsoon.

With most of the day before us, we descended leisurely, and I took the opportunity to collect further plants. When we left the snow-covered glacier in favour of the moraine, and came a little later to flower-covered slopes it was brought home to me how supremely delightful mountaineering in Garhwal can be. On Everest, a climber may be for weeks above the plant-level, and he longs for a sight of grass and trees until even the Rongbuk Valley with its dwarfed herbage and wilderness of stones becomes desirable. Climbing in Garhwal is altogether different. There the climber is never far from green valleys, indeed little or no farther than he is when climbing in the High Alps. Thus he is able to spend the morning on the snows and the afternoon amid the flowers. In such contrast lies the spiritual essence of mountaineering. The fierce tussle with ice-slope and precipice and complete relaxation of taut muscles on a flower-clad pasture ; the keen, biting air of the heights and the soft, scented air of the valleys. Everest, Kangchenjunga and Nanga Parbat are " duties," but mountaineering in Garhwal is a pleasure —thank God.

Ere we reached the uppermost shepherds' hut, the scowling cloud roof broke up, and the sun poured into the valley, lighting the rain-soaked pastures, so that every flower and blade of grass shone with a marvellous purity.

So unsuccessfully, but delightfully, we returned to the base camp.

# CHAPTER VIII

## ON DOING NOTHING

THE day following our unsuccessful attempts to climb Rataban was brilliantly fine. I did nothing, not because I was tired, but because I was lazy. By nature I am a lazy person, but, unhappily, I seldom have the opportunity of being lazy, in which I do not differ from any other father of a family who has to earn his living. And now there were heaven-sent opportunities. Why had I sweated up to the col on Rataban, when I might have been lazy? I could see its serene and shining curve against the deep blue sky, distant and remote above the silver birches. In that answer lay the answer to " Why do you climb ? " Mountaineering madness no doubt, but assuming that this madness (call it sublimation of sex or atavism or anything you like) is impossible to eradicate, how is mountaineering to be enjoyed best ?

Amid a welter of conflicting philosophies, I have always clung to one idea—that to get a kick out of life, a man must sample the contrasts of life. And so it is with mountaineering. The positive ceases to exist when there is no negative. Activity can only be measured against inactivity ; therefore, to appreciate the joys of activity it is necessary to practise passivity. Hence the off-day. Now an off-day is not something to be indulged in grudgingly ; it is a necessary and integral part of mountaineering, the essential complement of the " on-day." I can sympathise with the man who with only a short holiday scales all the peaks he can in the time ; yet, if he neglects inactivity, he neglects contemplation and we cannot appreciate Nature otherwise.

There are many who climb and enjoy climbing for exercise, fresh air, good health and relaxation from a sedentary life, yet Nature is discernible in part only through the medium of physical exercise. A superman may be able to divorce his spiritual consciousness from his physical make-up at all times, but there are few supermen, and most of us must strive physically and mentally to discern the verities of creation.

The West assumes its superiority over the East primarily because it is further advanced in mechanical matters, but woe betide it should it continue to associate mechanisms with spiritual progress. In Garhwal I met a true civilisation, for I found contentment and happiness. I saw a life that is not enslaved by the time-factor, that is not obsessed by the idea that happiness is dependent on money and materials. I had never before realised until I camped in the Valley of Flowers how much happiness there is in simple living and simple things.

By the standards of the West I led a life of discomfort, and I frankly admit that I should not be content to lead such a life in England, for it is necessary to conform to the standards of one's environment. A large majority of people do not realise how necessary it is to conform to these standards and for this reason look aghast on the " discomforts " endured by explorers. Genuine discomforts of fatigue, heat and cold are common enough in mountaineering and exploration, but the largest part of so-called " discomfort " is not discomfort at all except when measured against a different standard and a different environment.

To my mind, the acme of mental and spiritual discomfort would be to live in some super-luxury hotel in the Valley of Flowers. Happiness is best achieved by adapting ourselves to the standards of our environment. For this reason, I suspect that cranks and extremists are essentially unhappy persons and symptomatic of a life that has become socially and mechanically too complex for its environment. In Garhwal I found no red, green or black shirts, no flags or emblems, no mechanisms, no motor-cars or aeroplanes, but I did find a happy and contented people. I think the attitude of Himalayan peoples to western progress is best summed up in the words of a Tibetan, and Tibetans consider themselves superior to Europeans in spiritual culture. He said : " We do not want your civilisation in Tibet, for wherever it is established it brings unhappiness and war." It is a terrible indictment and it is true.

During the morning I lounged about the camp. It was a morning like other mornings, quiet and seeming scarcely to breathe. Dew lay thick on the flowers ; birds sang in the forest and the air was sweet and charged with pleasant smells.

I reclined on a bank below the camp. Presently a gentle breeze began to blow, touching the flowers with light fingers. Smaller flowers such as the blue *corydalis* quivered a little but the taller flowers, the white *anemones* and golden *nomocharis*, nodded in slow undulations, as though conscious of their grace and dignity.

During the afternoon clouds gathered ; building up slowly, column by column and mass by mass. There was a wild sunset with fingers of lurid light but, as usual, evening established equilibrium in the atmosphere, and the stars shone out in their thousands as night spread from behind the ashen snows of Rataban.

We were very content. I knew the men were content because they used often to sing their simple Tibetan melodies. This is one, a great favourite with Wangdi

when he was climbing a hillside, as well as I can
remember it.

**Lento.**

In immeasurable contentment I sat by the fire.

# CHAPTER IX

## THE SNOW-PEAK

DURING our attempt to climb Rataban, I had been much impressed by the beautifully proportioned snow-peak to the south of the Bhyundar Valley, and had decided to attempt the ascent. It might prove accessible from the southernmost branch of the main valley glacier, but this route would involve at least two camps, and at the moment I had no intention of making lengthy expeditions. Could it be approached from the Bhyundar Valley? It should be possible to examine it by climbing some distance up the northern side of the valley, and such a reconnaissance had the advantage of including botanical work. So two days after our retreat from Rataban, Nurbu and I crossed the valley and after mounting grass-slopes scrambled up a steep craggy buttress on which our hand-holds consisted for the most part of juniper roots.

We did not pause until we were nearly 2,000 feet above the floor of the valley, when we seated ourselves and I examined the mountain through my monocular glass. From this direction it appears as a rock-peak rather than a snow-peak, built up of striated cliffs dipping sharply from south to north. The snow-ridge we had seen consists of *névé* resting on the uppermost of these striations. Between the peak and a minor rock-peak to the north overlooking the Bhyundar Valley is a wide gully ; if this could be entered from a little valley branching off at right angles from the Bhyundar Valley it seemed as though the ridge could be approached over one or other of a series of sloping snow-covered shelves. The lowermost portion of the gully was concealed behind the shoulder of the minor rock-peak we had already climbed, but I came to the conclusion that serious difficulty was unlikely.

These points settled, Nurbu and I spent two or three hours scrambling about for flowers. We were climbing a steep ridge when I came on the first blue poppy (*Meconopsis aculeata*) I had seen in bloom. It was growing solitary in a rocky sentry-box, its roots and foliage protected from the sun, yet adequately nourished by a slow seep of water.

Holdsworth described this flower as being the colour of the sky at dawn, and so, indeed, it is. As I pulled up on to a ledge out of breath after a stiff scramble, it confronted me not more than a yard away, lighting the dark-shadowed rocks behind it. Like most poppies, it is open and wide, droops slightly, has a centre of many golden stamens, and is so fragile that its petals are detached merely by brushing against them. It protects itself with sharp spines arranged on the stem and buds, which penetrate the skin like so many minute spears.

We were crossing a gully, when my companion pointed upwards, and I saw not more than 400 feet higher, on a snow-bed in the gully, a herd of about a dozen barhal. For a few moments they did not see us, then the leader, a grand old beast with a splendid head, gave a shrill whistle, and away they went, helter-skelter over the snow and in an incredibly fast rush across the steep wall of the gully.

When they penetrated the Nanda Devi basin, Messrs. Shipton and Tilman found herds of comparatively tame barhal. It is possible that the absence of bears as well as of humans accounted for this. In the Bhyundar Valley there are bears and the barhal are very wary ; this is the only explanation I can give for their timidity in a district which, as far as I know, has never been visited by sportsmen. In Tibet I have seen almost tame barhal, and during the 1933 Mount Everest Expedition they grazed near the base camp. No bears have been observed in the Rongbuk Valley and the Tibetans take no wild life.* Tameness and timidity in wild life is a study of considerable interest. Where small beasts are hunted or preyed upon by larger or fiercer beasts, they must of necessity become timid and wary, but in districts where no hunting occurs and there are no ferocious beasts, it is reasonable to suppose that creatures should be less timid.

June 26th dawned with an evil sky. Far above the highest peaks lay a roof of slate-coloured cloud, and in the valley livid mists had already congregated. I was doubtful whether it was worth while setting off to climb the snow-peak, particularly as a drizzle of rain was falling, but the men settled matters by pulling down my tent and packing it up. As I had sent Pasang down to Joshimath for my mail I took with me only Wangdi and Nurbu, which meant that I had to travel with light equipment.

Descending into the valley we walked along the south bank of the stream and, after forcing our way through some dense vegetation, entered the side valley already mentioned. The weather improved visibly as we ascended this and we were trudging up the terminal moraine of the small glacier which fills most of it, when the mists parted and the snowy summit of our peak

---

* It is possible, however, that snow leopards are to be found and these would prey on barhal and other wild life. There are also wolves in Tibet.

stood out full in the sun. As quickly as possible I climbed the moraine, arriving on top as the last mists were vanishing. Now I could see what I had not seen before, that the base of the gully could be approached without difficulty over a level and un-crevassed glacier.

I had already noted a possible camping site on a ridge between the gully and another gully to the south of it, which formed a channel for ice avalanches from a conspicuous hanging glacier far up on the face of the mountain. As the main gully was exposed to falling stones we mounted for some distance by the side of it, then crossed it quickly where it was comparatively narrow. Although the crossing only took a minute or two, we did not care for it, as now and then stones came skidding down the hard snow.

Our camping site was by a large overhanging boulder, perched on the crest of the ridge, which formed an excellent kitchen. It had cracked above and appeared insecurely poised, but Wangdi laughed away my faint protests and proceeded to pitch the porters' tent under the overhang, after levelling a platform for my tent immediately above the boulder.

The cooking fuel was dwarf rhododendron collected on the way up. It was necessary first of all to construct a little trench of stones ; in this an empty cigarette box and sundry pieces of dried grass were placed to provide the nucleus of the conflagration. Pieces of dwarf rhodo-dendron were then arranged on top, after which Wangdi and Nurbu lay flat on their stomachs at either end of the trench and, taking it in turns, blew energetically at the smouldering wood. It was an exhausting process and soon their eyes were streaming from the acrid smoke which issued in suffocating clouds from the " kitchen," but they were undaunted and an hour later with a grin of triumph Wangdi brought me a cup of tea. It was wellnigh undrinkable, but so much hard work had gone to the making of it that I could not in decency refuse it or even surreptitiously throw it away, so summoning up all the fortitude of which I was capable I gulped down what was virtually liquid rhododendron smoke.

A hundred feet above the camp was a steep crag forming a projecting buttress, which would deflect down the gully to the south of us any ice avalanches falling from the hanging glacier. I had already seen *Primula nivalis* on the way up, so to work off the baleful effects of the tea, which promised to be both peculiar and distressing, I climbed up, ostensibly to look for flowers. I had not gone far when I saw, spreading from a thin crack above me, a little clump of densely clustered light blue flowers, still shining with the morning rain. I had an awkward climb, as the rocks were nearly vertical at this point, but when at length I succeeded in reaching the plant I recognised it as a *paraquilegia* (*P. grandiflora*) which I had seen once before during the 1936 Mount Everest Expedition. It would be difficult to find a more genuine rock plant than this, or a more delightful contrast to the stern crags. One blast of cold wind should suffice to wither and shrivel it, a single frost to burn its tender foliage, yet it grows ; a miracle of growth, battered by storm, scorched by sun, the prey of hail, storm and blizzard. Heaven knows how it grows, and that I think is the correct answer.

The weather, having cleared up to a point, remained undecided until sunset, when there was a further turn for the better, and in the west, Nilkanta appeared, cutting sharply through long thin lines of mist. Ours was an impressive situation. On the one hand was the wide gully by which we must commence the ascent on the morrow, with an icy channel down the middle, cut

by falling stones ; on the other hand, the ice-swept
gully ending beneath a precipice, crowned by a great
mass of shattered ice, fully 300 feet thick. No ice fell,
but there were numerous rock-falls, among them a
block weighing at least a ton, which tore down the
gully, hit a projecting crag, and flew far out into
the air, disappearing from sight with a deep droning
hum.

Just before dark, our boulder gave two or three such
ominous creaks that Wangdi and Nurbu thought better
of camping immediately beneath it, and hastily exca-
vated a platform to one side. For supper I had the
cold remains of Montmorency, a couple of potatoes,
biscuits, jam, and a cup of " Ovaltine." This last-
named beverage, which in happier circumstances makes
an excellent night-cap, had been ruined by the all-
pervading smoke of dwarf rhododendron. I threw it
away, when the men were not looking, but did not fail
to compliment Wangdi ; poor man, it had cost him and
Nurbu fully an hour's energetic blowing to produce it.

The night was calm and warm, too warm for the
height, which cannot have been less than 14,500 feet.
We breakfasted at the late hour of 5.30 instead of 4.30
as planned, everyone having over-slept. The tea was
undrinkable and the porridge barely edible. However,
this had the effect of hastening us on our way, and we
were off at six o'clock.

The snow, although only slightly frozen, was hard,
and step-cutting or kicking was necessary all the way.
To avoid falling stones we kept to the edge of the gully,
and there was only one place, where we had to turn
a projecting corner of rock, that was in the least dangerous. It was a calm morning, but there was a certain amount of cloud about, whilst the southern sky
was heavy with dense masses of cumulus, backed by

tall anvils of false cirrus ; in all probability the monsoon was already drenching the plains and foothills.

Having passed a precipitous belt of rock above the camp, we abandoned the gully in favour of a snow-shelf, which slanted steeply towards the upper *névé*. In gaining this shelf we came upon a glorious display of *Primula nivalis*, growing in thousands on ledges watered by the melting snows. There can be little or no earth in such a situation and there is no doubt that this is the hardiest of all *primulas*, rejoicing as it does in barren rocks, running water, and coarse grit.

Without pause we climbed up and along the shelf, presently passing above the hanging glacier. I was now reaching my best mountaineering form, and it was no longer a fatigue but a joy to climb. This stage is reached when muscles are entirely under control, and rhythm, without which it is impossible to enjoy mountaineering, has been acquired. Wangdi was also fit, else he could not have sung without pause a monotonous little ditty, which lasted him only two or three steps before it had to be repeated.

Presently the slope steepened into an ice-bulge, to avoid which we mounted close to the rock-wall bounding the uppermost edge of the shelf. Above the bulge we saw that in order to gain the snow-slopes leading to the upper *névé*, we must either work through an ice-fall, up slopes which would almost certainly become dangerous later in the day, or climb the rock-wall immediately above us to the crest of a ridge. I decided upon the latter course as the wall was breached at one place by a gully of no particular difficulty. At its base the gully was defended by a *bergschrund* (marginal crevasse), but this was well bridged with avalanche debris and we crossed without difficulty to the snow-slope above. The snow was in good order, and we

mounted quickly to where the gully ended under some
rocks. These proved loose but not difficult, and within
a few minutes we had climbed them and were seated
in the sun on the ridge.

We had been going hard and it was time for a rest
and a meal. From our position we looked along an
easy, almost horizontal ridge, ending in the glacier-clad
face of the mountain, which we must scale before gaining the upper snow-crest. It was a straightforward
climb, except at the point where the ridge abutted
against the face. Here a wall of ice about fifty feet
high would have to be surmounted in order to gain the
easy-looking slopes running up to the summit ridge.

Twenty minutes later we set off again and scrambled
along the broken rocks of the ridge where I had to
tell Wangdi, who was at the end of the rope, that he
must not attempt fancy routes of his own. He was an
independent fellow and always imagined that he knew
best; occasionally he did, but generally he did not,
and he would waste valuable time in climbing up a
bit of rock by a different route simply because it was
a different route.

The ice-wall was not as formidable as it looked, but
it presented a pretty problem in step-cutting up a
broken corner. I enjoy ice-work and solving this alone
made the climb worth while. Furthermore, it was a
sensational place, as the corner overhung a sheer drop
of two or three hundred feet where the glacier broke
away to the left. To a lover of ice-craft there is something peculiarly satisfying in the hard clean thump of
an ice-axe pick meeting ice, and step-cutting brings
the same sort of satisfaction that a sculptor experiences when working with his chisel. Cutting steps is
not a matter of brute force but an art to be performed
with the minimum expenditure of effort and the maxi-

mum of enjoyment. A good ice-axe is not merely a shaft of wood with a steel head at the end of it, but something that lives, and is for the time being an essential part of the mountaineer. The feel of it, and the balance of it, contribute in some subtle way to enjoyment : to get the best out of it, you must treat it gently, deliberately and rhythmically, not blindly and forcefully. To the layman this may seem unnecessarily lyrical and even ridiculous. What is there, he asks, in cutting a step in ice ? If you would answer this, watch one of the Oberland guides at work. " Easy," you say —then try it for yourself. There is Sonja Henie's skating—easy, but . . .

Presently we were on the slope above. At first we had to steer a devious course between crevasses, but once these were passed the slope stretched unbroken before us to the summit ridge. The climbing now was the antithesis of the work on the ice-wall ; dull, slogging work, of no interest whatsoever. Light mists had formed and the sun shone through them with a hot suffocating power that sapped our energy. I was not altogether happy about the snow, for that fallen during the recent bad weather had not consolidated perfectly as yet, and the general formation of the slope made it an avalanche trap ; so at intervals I kicked and prodded it with my axe in order to determine its consistency. The surface layer of new snow was about eight inches thick ; beneath this was a breakable crust, and beneath that granular snow. It was in the surface layer that danger lay, if any. At present it was adhering firmly to the old crust beneath, but later, when the sun grew hotter, it might slide. It was essential, therefore, to reach the summit and return as quickly as possible.

Our pace was very slow on the last part of the slope, for the sun was wellnigh intolerable and the snow very soft, and it was with considerable relief that we reached the ridge leading towards the summit. The summit was not far distant, or so we thought, and was separated from us by a sharp snow-edge. After the slogging work of the snow-slope, this edge was delightful to tread. With renewed energy we pressed on, and some twenty minutes later trod the point we had seen. It was not the summit ; beyond, stretched the ridge, at first almost horizontally, then steeply, disappearing into the mist. I heard a groan of disappointment from Nurbu. I could echo his protest, as we had climbed fully 4,000 feet in three and a half hours and I was now very tired. It was a pity to be so tired, otherwise we might better have enjoyed this splendid ridge. When I had first seen it from our camp under the Bhyundar Pass it had looked magnificent, and it *was* magnificent, the beau ideal of snow-ridges, not too soft and not too hard, with an edge moulded by wind and storm into a perfect blade.

We had not advanced far when a strong cold wind forced us to halt to put on our spare clothing and Balaclava helmets. This wind had only one thing to be said in its favour : it would prevent the lower snow-slopes from becoming dangerous ; for the rest it was bitterly cold and though it had little effect on the grim-visaged Wangdi, it was fast knocking the stuffing out of Nurbu.

The ridge seemed interminable, for mist always adds to the apparent length of a ridge. I had assumed that it stretched unbroken to the summit, but such was not the case. There was a break in it, a curious rift where the lowermost part had separated from the uppermost and sunk, leaving an almost vertical wall about twenty feet high. No doubt the mist and our fatigue magnified this wall out of proportion to its true size ; at all events, the sight of it was too much for Nurbu. " Tik nay, Sahib ! Tik nay ! " (" No good, Sir ! No good ! ") he ejaculated. But strangely enough this unexpected difficulty had the opposite effect on Wangdi and myself; it stimulated our flagging energy. I shouted at Nurbu through the rush of the wind, a villainous mixture of English and Urdu—we were not going to lose the peak now. At the same moment I saw through the ice-rimmed oval of Wangdi's Balaclava a sudden grin ; the next moment, like the mountaineer he is, he had driven in his axe, and given the rope a turn round it, prepared for my advance.

The wall was composed of hard *névé*, not pure ice, and a few slashes with the adze end of the ice-axe were sufficient for a step. In a few minutes we were up. The summit could not be far off. Of a sudden the mists swirled asunder. Ahead of us, the snow-ridge swept up in a perfect curve, to end in a perfect point, sunlit and infinitely beautiful, against a pool of blue sky.

Ten minutes later, at 10.50, we were there. Strangely enough the air was calm although the wind was tearing across the crest a few feet below : not an unusual phenomenon on mountains. My principal memory is of my feet, which were very cold. On the lower slopes my boots had leaked in the wet snow and the cold wind on the summit ridge had completed my discomfiture. Thus, much of my time on the summit was spent in waggling my toes about in my wet half-frozen socks in an attempt to restore circulation. Apart from this, I mustered up sufficient energy to take a photograph, or rather to set the delay-action release in the shutter so that all three of us could be included, as a memento of the occasion. This, when printed, showed Wangdi posed in the manner of some Grecian athlete about to do his stuff, looking his very toughest and

grimmest, with a long, bamboo cigarette-holder projecting defiantly from his lips. Nurbu, also, had so far
forgotten his tiredness as to smoke a cigarette, whilst I
am chiefly remarkable for my head-gear which consisted
of a Balaclava helmet to protect my ears and face from
the cold wind, and on top of that a double Terai felt-
hat put on during our stay on the summit to protect
my head from the sun. Such are the peculiar conditions at high altitudes.

The peak we had climbed must be about 19,500 feet.
As our camp was between 14,500 and 15,000 feet,
we had climbed between 4,500 and 5,000 feet. The
climb had taken, including halts, four hours and fifty
minutes, which must be accounted fast going at this
height.

With the possibility, ever present in my mind, of the
lower snow-slopes becoming dangerous, I gave the order
to descend after a stay of ten minutes. Even at great
altitudes in the Himalayas, it is possible to descend at
an Alpine speed and within half an hour we were off
the snow-ridge. The slopes below had not changed
appreciably, and were still safe, and we raced down
them to the ice-wall. Here an unpleasant incident
occurred. Wangdi was first down, then came Nurbu,
and lastly myself. I was reasonably well placed to
check a slip, but when Nurbu decided to jump down
the last six or eight feet without saying anything to me
as to his intention, he nearly pulled me after him. I
should be very surprised if he ever did such a thing
again, for what I had to say about it at the time must
have impressed itself indelibly on his memory. We
regained the camp at one o'clock, having descended in
two hours, and after drinking some dwarf rhododendron
tea, set off an hour later to the base camp.

As we passed along the river-bed, we came on a

bird's nest in a hollow between two stones, containing four eggs of a greyish-blue colour. It was a foolish place for a nest as it was only an inch or two above the stream level and would certainly be inundated when the monsoon broke. And there was every sign that the monsoon was about to break, for the sky was dark with impending storm and heavy drops of warm rain began to fall shortly before we reached the base camp.

At 6 p.m. it rained heavily, and soon after nightfall there was a fall little short of a cloud-burst. As I lay in my sleeping-bag, writing up my diary by the light of a candle, lightning began to flicker, and above the bombardment of the rain on the tent I heard the thunder growling on the peaks. The sound of the torrent rose to a roar, and I thought of the bird's nest ; by now it must have been destroyed. Finally I slept, drummed into oblivion by torrential rain.

# CHAPTER X

## THE SECOND BASE CAMP

THE monsoon had broken. It was still raining when I awoke on the morning of June 28th. Yet breakfast appeared as usual. With that aptitude for overcoming apparently insuperable difficulties, Wangdi and Co. had rigged a rough canopy of sacking over the hollow forming the kitchen; some wood, kept dry in their tent overnight, had done the rest. Further to assist them, I gave them the jaconet outer cover of my sleeping-bag and this, when cut up and spread out, made an excellent waterproof canopy some six feet square beneath which and the other pieces of sacking, culinary operations were carried out.

I had decided, before climbing the snow-peak, to shift my base camp to the floor of the valley. There were two reasons for this: firstly, it would be central for botanical work and, secondly, the snow-bridge beneath the camp was rapidly disintegrating. True, there was another snow-bridge near the new camping site, which would last a fortnight at least, but on the whole the north side of the stream was more convenient.

At ten o'clock the rain stopped and a watery sun appeared. I decided, however, to postpone moving the camp until the morrow in order to search the neighbouring woods for plants. This work was delayed by the arrival of Pasang with the mail, and a local coolie carrying a maund (80 lbs.) of coolie food. Among the mail was " The Times " Special Coronation Supplement. The men were vastly intrigued with the pictures.

" That I suppose is your Potala ? " said Wangdi, pointing to a drawing of Westminster Abbey. " And that is the King and the Grand Lama about to crown him ? "

I agreed that the Archbishop of Canterbury was in fact our Grand Lama.

Wangdi had already spoken to me about the abdication of Edward VIII. In spite of my very limited knowledge of Urdu, I could follow him when he said that if a King was indeed king, how is it that he cannot marry the woman of his choice ? Either he does his work well or badly. And whom he marries is his own affair and his own choice. And what has woman to do with kingship ? I think this may be said to sum up the feeling of the Indian peoples towards the abdication.

Later in the morning, the men spotted a black bear on an alp across the valley. At first, in spite of Wangdi's pointing finger, I could not see it, and when I did I needed my monocular glass to confirm that a tiny black spot was indeed a bear. These Tibetans have eyes like hawks.

It was only twelve days since I had arrived in the Bhyundar Valley, but time and the warm breath of the monsoon had wrought marvels to the flora. All around my tent were the nodding bells of *Fritillaria Roylei* and hosts of a white-flowered onion (*Allium humile*), whilst on a rocky slope above the camp was a huge *megacarpaea* (*M. polyandra*) with stately spires of yellow flowers that exuded a sweet musky smell. In the woods were many white *herminiums* and I found another *primula* with a mealy purple flower which seemed to like the shade in a cool mossy place under rocks. Then there was a *clematis* (*C. grata*) not yet in flower, rambling over the bush rhododendrons, and on a bank near the tents a small shrub with charming bell-like, pink-white flowers, which I learned later was a *gaultheria,* and another shrub with long spikes of bloom which I could not for the life of me identify, not even its family. Indeed, my ignorance was pitiable. I was like a Cockney in a museum of precious things, only too eager and willing to acquire knowledge, but so confused and dazzled by the splendours about him as not to know how and where to start his quest. My sheet anchor was Dr. Ethelbert Blatter's book "Beautiful Flowers of Kashmir." It had been given to me by that great gardener, Mr. G. P. Baker, and was invaluable in helping me to identify specimens, but even so there were many occasions when I was not even able to relegate a flower to its family. However, when the worst came to the worst I could always collect a specimen for my press and leave it to be named by the experts.

The afternoon I spent wandering about the woods where I found various ferns, including such homely species as the maidenhair and oak ferns. There is something blithesome and gay about a birch forest; it is not jealous of the sun or dank with rotting vegetation. I well remember a little glade in which I spent some time reclining on a bank with my back to a moss-clad boulder. It was an absolutely still afternoon, for the warm breath of the monsoon seemed to have stifled the usual breeze. Above the tree-tops the peaks showed, dusted with freshly fallen snow between woolly masses of cloud, and from all around came bird-song. Close at hand the notes of individual birds were discernible, and I heard from the alp the grating trill of the "Zeederzee bird," but the songs of more distant birds were indistinguishable from a chorus that resembled music played very softly in a vast cathedral.

When I came out of the forest I saw the lower slopes of the shelf dotted black and white. The sheep and goats, which I had been expecting for the past few days, had arrived. I did not welcome them, for they would eat the flowers, but I comforted myself with the reflection that there was plenty of room in the Bhyundar Valley and that they could do comparatively little damage.

Two of the shepherds called on us that evening and were entertained by the Tibetans. They were dressed in some dingy woollen material, with a plaid of sackcloth over their shoulders. Their features were of a Semitic cast with well formed aquiline noses and, like most Garhwalis, they had allowed their hair to grow long and had bobbed it in a becoming manner.

Rain fell during the night, and did not stop until after breakfast the next morning, when we packed up and moved the camp to the new site, a level meadow immediately above the stream, which had carved for itself a deep channel at this point. A short distance from the camp a huge avalanche, composed partly of ice, had fallen from the wall of peaks to the north of the valley, and after pouring through a gully in the gently sloping floor of the valley, had spread itself across the stream to a depth of fully fifty feet. It had shrunk considerably during the past few weeks, for it had originally extended 300 yards down the stream, after being bent at right angles from its original direction. This avalanche must have weighed many tens of thousands of tons, and the wind of it had snapped off short a number of birches along the edge of the meadow.

There was an abundance of birch and juniper for fuel, whilst a few paces from the camp a stream of crystal-clear water meandered down a gentle slope, then splashed over some rocks into a little flower-filled valley.

It was a beautiful camping place and from a floral point of view more interesting than the original base camp. The tents were pitched in the midst of flowers, prominent among which was the *Anemone polyanthes.* In between grew thousands of yellow *Nomocharis oxypetala* and here and there the blue *Nomocharis nana.* There were two kinds of *geraniums* and a blue *delphinium* (*D. brunnianum*). One of the loveliest of the taller plants was the *Polemonium caeruleum*, with wide flattish flowers of amethyst blue. The fritillaries were short-lived and in their place *potentillas* were springing up in their millions. It was remarkable how one plant replaced another as the summer wore on. When the fritillaries were in bloom, it seemed impossible that anything else could grow, so closely packed were they, yet here were *potentillas* equally closely packed. Only an uninterrupted cycle of growth can maintain such perfect balance. Would it were possible to perfect this cycle in our gardens. It is not possible in a cultivated garden where the balance is artificially maintained by constant weeding and thinning, but it may be possible in a wild garden provided that the cycle of growth and relationship of plants one to the other are made a scientific study. I believe that Rudolph Steiner has approached nearer to the problem than anyone. He has devoted his life to the study of rhythm in nature, and it is only through rhythm that harmony and beauty are achieved in the garden of flowers or in the garden of the human mind.

I spent the afternoon pottering about the camp. The little valley and a knoll close by the camp were rich in plants, though it would be a fortnight or more before many of them bloomed. Close to the stream was a

drift of blue *cynoglossum* and on the slope above the
tall spires of a stately pink-flowered, thistle-like plant,
subsequently identified as *Morina longifolia*.   At the head
of the little valley, to one side of the tumbling stream,
was a overhanging rock and under it glowed a single
blue poppy, whilst on the steep bank above the river
were many shrubs, including a pink rose and a bush
rhododendron not more than five feet high which edged
the meadow with crimson flowers.    Scarcely less colourful was a mass of *Androsace primuloides*, falling over a large
boulder perched near the edge of a dry and sunny bank,
where various rock plants grew, including a yellow-
flowered *saxifrage* (*S. flagellaris*), which sends out long
questing tendrils in all directions, and a little yellow
*potentilla* (*P. eriocarpa*).

That evening the men collected an abundance of
firewood, which Nurbu arranged with loving care ; he
is a connoisseur of camp fires.   Before the monsoon I
had need of an eiderdown jacket in the evening but now
is was unnecessary, for the air was warm and mild like
an English July.   I sat in my rickety camp chair, which
had been artfully and ingeniously repaired by Wangdi
to prevent it falling to pieces, and read Shakespeare's
sonnets.   What would he have written had he been
there that evening ?   What message would he have
carried from the flowerful meadows and dim forests ?
What language would he have garnered from the paling
snows ?

When night fell I continued to sit without reading and
the pale faces of the *anemones* looked at me without
moving, out of the darkness.

Rain fell in the night, but next morning was fine.
I was off at eight, taking with me Nurbu, who usually
accompanied me on my botanical expeditions, and who
had become expert at pressing flowers and rigging the

camera ; furthermore, he took a genuine interest in the proceedings and often pointed out a flower which he thought might interest me.

The lush vegetation was wet and soon we were soaked to the hips. On the floor of the valley I saw nothing I had not seen before, except a *ranunculus*, but it was a different tale on a buttress. We had mounted perhaps 500 feet without seeing anything of special interest, when we came on a beautiful rose-coloured *cypripedium*, which could be none other than the *Cypripedium himalaicum* mentioned by Holdsworth. This little flower fully earns its popular title of lady's slipper, but it would be a very small lady who could fit it to her foot. It is not more than six inches high, but there were so many that the slope was imbued with a rosy glow. Nearby I saw a white flower with a golden centre at the end of a single stem. I identified it as a *lloydia* (*L. serotina*), also found by Holdsworth. This was an advance guard of millions which later covered the ground at the base camp. The red *potentillas* were now at their best, huge flowers the size of half crowns, and in between them was a purple *orchis*, which almost always grew in association with thistles. Higher up, we had a stiff scramble on some rocks where a neat little *draba* ornamented the crevices and ledges, whilst a creeping knot weed was spreading over a weathered slab. Only a few sprays of this (*Polygonum vacciniifolium*) were in bloom, but I saw it later in many places, and came to the conclusion that it is one of the most beautiful of Himalayan flowers. When fully in bloom it cascades over the rocks in a rose-coloured flood and is visible from afar.

We ate our lunch on a juniper-clad ledge. Fifteen hundred feet beneath was the camp, a cluster of minute tents and beyond it the ragged shining line of the stream. It was a typical monsoon day ; damp clouds were clinging to the peaks, or suspended in a sky of watery blue, their shadows almost stationary on the green valley floor ; slate-coloured nimbus was gathering in the south and, as we ate, a dense mist oozed through the gorge into the upper part of the valley and congregated on the hillsides above and below.

We retired but not in time to escape the rain which fell with drenching force. It persisted until 8.30 p.m. when the stars shone out through an atmosphere sweet with wet turf and flowers, but this was only a temporary fine spell and rain set in again later and fell without pause until the late afternoon of the following day.

There was nothing for me to do but lie in my sleeping-bag, write up my botanical notes, read, and in between whiles eat chocolate. This chocolate was remarkable, inasmuch as the makers presented with each packet half a dozen pictures of film stars. Presumably this was intended to increase sales, but unhappily the Indian hot weather had caused the chocolate to sweat, and beauties such as Greta Garbo, Bette Davis, Charles Laughton and Al Jolson presented a sadly debauched appearance.

Among the papers I had received by mail were copies of the " Spectator " and " The Times." The news of the day was, as usual, depressing, but I got a certain amount of kick out of literary reviews, especially as regards one book which " The Times " praised highly, and the " Spectator " damned to perdition. Such contentiousness seemed to me symbolical of the distant combative world. Another paper, an illustrated weekly, told me with a wealth of detail and many diagrammatic drawings how to make my house gas-proof, but it said nothing about tents. It all seemed utterly fantastic viewed from the Valley of Flowers. It was as though I were looking down on an ant-heap that had gone completely crazy. That men and women should have to know how they can make their houses gas-proof before they can live at peace and charity with their neighbours is something so fantastic that the perpetrators of the joke should be locked up in an asylum. I tried to explain the idea to Wangdi but he looked at me so strangely that I desisted.

# CHAPTER XI

## THE BELVEDERE

THE morning of July 2nd was overcast and grey but I decided, more for the sake of exercise than anything else, to take a camp up towards the Khanta Khal Pass. From this pass, over which a route lies to the village of Hanuman Chatti in the Alaknanda Valley, a gentle sloping valley extends some distance before falling sharply into the Bhyundar Valley. There is excellent grazing for sheep and goats and a well-defined track zig-zags up a steep lower pitch in the valley by the side of a waterfall. I remembered the valley well as Holdsworth had found many flowers there in 1931.

There was little of floral interest to begin with except that the edges of the birch forest were blue with *cynoglossum*, but higher up, where the path emerged into the open upper part of the valley, the slopes were brilliant with flowers and I found a *geum* (*G. elatum*), and the first *campanula* (*C. cashmiriana*) I had seen, a small flower like the English harebell. Then there was a collection of large boulders where I came upon a fine display of blue poppies ; each boulder affording shelter for one and in rare cases, two plants. Even on that dull morning they seemed to shine as though capable of retaining the sunlight and blue skies of two days ago. At the back of my mind was the possibility of attempting a peak of about 20,000 feet, to the north of the Khanta Khal Pass, but new snow had fallen during the recent bad weather and I now realised that an attempt would have to be postponed until conditions improved. The alternative was to camp on a ridge to the south of the valley, and on the morrow attempt the ascent of a rock peak of about 17,000 feet, which overlooks the gorge of the Bhyundar Valley. So we crossed the stream by a convenient snow-drift, and mounted slopes still bright with the blooms of a cream-white rhododendron, but had not got very far when rain fell heavily. The ridge for which we were making ends in a birch- and rhododendron-clad knoll, overlooking the Bhyundar Valley. It was a perfect belvedere and I decided to camp on it. There was snow close at hand and the men, miracle workers where fires are concerned, some-how contrived to light the wet dwarf rhododendron wood under a convenient overhanging boulder.

At tea-time we were able to get a larger fire going and dry our clothes, but the weather relapsed again later, and at six o'clock torrential rain fell and continued until after dark, when a perfect cloud-burst descended. Never in my life have I camped in such rain, and I lay in my sleeping-bag wondering whether the tent would be flattened beneath an apparently solid waterfall. To sleep was impossible, but shortly before midnight the rain ceased, leaving a calm atmosphere in which the roar of swollen torrents sounded a deep chorus, broken by a peculiar rushing and tearing sound, coming from a high waterfall on one of the rock peaks to the northern side of the valley.

No rain was falling when we awoke next morning, but the sky was packed with moisture-laden mist. The men had had an uncomfortable night. They are usually adepts in the art of selecting a tent site, but on this occasion had chosen a hollow for their tent, and had been flooded. It was some time before they could get a fire going, and breakfast was a scratch affair. In such weather a long or difficult climb was out of the question, and I decided to ascend the ridge from the camp in search of flowers and turn back if and when difficulties were encountered. We were away before seven, and scrambled up the ridge through dwarf rhododendrons and over big boulders. To judge from the amount of moss this portion of the Bhyundar Valley receives more rain than the upper portion. Doubtless its proximity to the Alaknanda Valley has something to do with this. At all events, there was a marked difference in the vegetation as compared with that of the upper end of the valley. Soon we came on a host of *primulas* of the dark blue *nivalis* section, looking wonderfully fresh and clean after the rain. I found also a *codonopsis* (*C. rotundifolia*), many *bergenias*, which like a moist situation among rocks and, here and there, *geums*.

Presently, after a scramble up some moss-covered slabs, we reached a minor summit. Beyond it, the ridge crest consisted of enormous boulders piled upon one another with formidable drops on either hand. We advanced cautiously, and a few minutes later reached a slightly higher point. This was the end of our climb, for further progress was barred by a gap fully 150 feet deep with vertical or overhanging, slimy, moss-covered walls. In any event there was little object in continuing farther as once again the weather was spoiling, and dense mists already enveloped us. On this minor summit I was interested to notice a round burnt patch of grass. Lightning alone could have done this ; indeed the rocks in the vicinity looked as though they had been frequently struck. Doubtless it was auto-suggestion, but I had a distinct feeling of electricity in my hair and beard and as it was not very dark, and we had no wish to offer ourselves as lightning-conductors, we descended to the camp.

Nothing was to be gained by staying in a particularly damp situation, so we packed up the sodden tents and descended ; and as we descended the weather, with that perverseness peculiar to mountain weather, suddenly mended ; the sun appeared, spilling brilliant light on the birch forest, and in less than half an hour the sky was almost unclouded and brilliantly blue.

It was a scene to make a photographer's mouth water. On high, the peaks dazzlingly white in freshly-fallen snow ; beneath, the emerald green valley, the green of an Irish landscape in springtime, and closer at hand the wet-leafed birch forest quivering and dancing with reflected light. Flowers are most beautiful after rain, and I strolled down the hill enchanted, through drifts of blue *cynoglossum* and regiments of pink knot weed, pausing every few minutes to photograph some new and intriguing composition of flower, forest, hillside and peak.

# CHAPTER XII

## THE WALL

As already mentioned, the Bhyundar Valley is bounded on the north by a wall of rock-peaks which rises to a maximum height of about 20,000 feet. I had often looked at this wall with the idea of ascending one of the peaks on its crest. The difficulties were obviously formidable, for the wall is steep and complicated, and consists of rock buttresses, with precipitous little glaciers perched on shelves in between, except to the east, where it is breached by a glacier pass of about 16,500 feet which Wangdi told me was sometimes crossed by shepherds *en route* to the village of Mana. It was a pretty mountaineering problem, and as such appealed to me enormously.

The day after our descent to the base camp, Nurbu left for Joshimath to collect my mail and some more coolie food ; the men took turns at this work which helped to relieve the monotony for them. Thus, I was left with Wangdi, Pasang and Tewang. The same day I took Pasang with me on a little expedition up the side of the valley which had as its objects flower-collecting and an examination of possible routes up the wall from the base camp. The former yielded nothing of especial interest. There seemed at this period to be a halt in floral growth, the earlier flowers having passed their best while many of the later flowers were not yet in bloom. During the ascent of a grassy buttress we disturbed a nestful of young pheasants which scattered in all directions.  They could barely fly, but had learned to glide with considerable skill, though their take-offs and landings were deplorable and reminded me of my own first solo efforts in the Air Force.  Pasang was unwilling to let them escape so easily, and after a horrible grimace at me, intended to convey the fact that they were good to eat, he went hurtling down the steep unbroken hillside.  He aimed a number of stones but not accurately enough, and with shrill derisive squawks the pheasants disappeared into the depths of the valley.

As regards the second object, the most likely route appeared to follow first a grassy ridge then a series of rock buttresses to a small glacier, whence it should be possible to mount to the crest of the wall by means of a slanting ridge and a snow-filled gully.

We commenced the ascent next day.  As it was high time Tewang had some exercise I took him in addition to Wangdi and Pasang.  He did not get very far. We had climbed less than a thousand feet, when I noticed that he was slipping about in a positively dangerous manner on the wet and slippery grass.  He had no nails in his boots !  In a laudable (to him) desire to take back his climbing boots new and unworn to Darjeeling, where they would doubtless command a good price, he had substituted a pair of boots so decrepit that a tramp would have scorned them.  I ordered him to descend to camp at once, put on his climbing boots and return, but when I saw him painfully and slowly descending the slope, obviously tired and perhaps still feeling the effects of his poisoned leg, I relented and told him to remain at the base camp.

We camped at the foot of the first rock buttress to one side of a narrow gully protected from falling stones by an overhanging rock.  On a wall of the gully was a bird's nest which Wangdi managed to reach after some sensational gymnastics, followed by a still more sensational, not to say dangerous, downward leap into the bed of the gully. He said that it contained young, but what manner of bird it was I could not tell as I did not see the mother.

While Wangdi and Pasang were pitching the tents, I scrambled up the gully over a couple of easy pitches on to the sloping crest of the buttress. This led to the foot of another buttress where the rocks were much steeper. At first sight it appeared as though a route might lie up the rocks to the east of this, but when I attempted to climb them I found that they were both smooth and steep.

An alternative was straight up the nose of the buttress, and here, entirely through my own fault, I got into trouble. By dint of an awkward bit of climbing, I reached a juniper-clad ledge, only to find that further progress was impossible, or at least desperately difficult. I had no option but to return and it was during this descent that I encountered an unexpected difficulty. On the ascent I had utilised an apparently firm hold in the middle of a slab, though being a staunch believer in the three points of attachment theory I had also utilised good hand-holds, but when I descended this hold broke away beneath my exploring foot. It was possible to descend the slab without it but very difficult, and it was half an hour before I succeeded in finding the right combination of finger-holds. Climbing alone in such circumstances is a trifle too exhilarating.

In safety once more at the foot of the buttress, I investigated the west side of the buttress, and here there appeared to be a route, although not an easy route. As a last alternative, I traversed across the mountain-side to determine whether or not the glacier was accessible to the east of the route originally planned. There may be a route here, but it is not a justifiable route, as the lowermost tongue of the glacier is loaded with stones and boulders of all sizes which it precipitates at intervals down the mountainside, and I soon decided against any further reconnaissance. I was returning when of a sudden there was a crash, and above a crag to my right, turning over and over against the blue, there appeared a block of rock the size of a grand piano. Without touching anything for several hundred feet, it descended with a noise like a shell, struck the rocks with another crash and burst into fragments which hummed and whistled through the air before plunging into the snow-slopes below.

After lunching in camp, Wangdi and I set out to scale the upper buttress. The climb began with a steep pitch with undercut holds ; then it was easy going to a wall about twenty feet high on which there was an awkward move diagonally upwards to the left. There was only one satisfactory hold, and getting on to it, while being pushed outwards at the same time by an overhanging rock, was not easy, so critical was the balance. I managed it with Wangdi waiting below to field me in the event of a slip. This wall was the only serious difficulty and above it a series of easier pitches and grassy ledges brought us to the crest of the buttress.

The usual afternoon mists had formed, so we waited in hopes of a temporary clearance. It came, and we saw before us a slabby ridge, running up to the left of the glacier. As we were merely reconnoitring we left the rope and followed the ridge as far as the slabby portion, then traversed off it on to a snow-slope which should afford an alternative route in the event of the slabs proving impracticable. Well satisfied with our reconnaissance we returned to camp.

There was plenty of juniper handy and to counteract the evening chill we built a large fire.  If the base camp life was remote from civilisation, this life of the bivouac camp was remoter still.  There was not a breath of wind and the smoke of the fire curled lazily up the cliff to vanish in the deepening blue of the evening sky. From our position, which must have been about 2,500 feet above the base camp, we gazed down the lowermost portion of the Bhyundar Valley to the hills of Joshimath and the Kuari Pass.  A vast range of cloud lay athwart the foothills, glowing so brilliantly that the shadowed hillsides in our vicinity reflected a faint opalescence. But the splendour of these cloudy citadels was short-lived, and half an hour after sunset night had fallen.

There is nothing that promotes an intimacy of spirit better than a camp fire.  He is dull and unimaginative who cannot sense the spirit of comradeship that persists within this warm circle of dancing light.  Wangdi talked to me of Nanga Parbat, and though my Urdu was execrable I could understand very well what he said, for there are occasions when language is no bar to understanding.  He had taken part in the 1934 Expedition, which ended disastrously when three Germans and six porters lost their lives in a blizzard.  After describing it he said :

" I have always felt that Nanga Parbat is different from other mountains.  There is something there that will kill you if it can.  It is a cursed mountain.  I was asked to go again this year, but I said no, I would rather come with you, because I am quite sure there will be another accident and that many lives will be lost."

I can see him now, cross-legged on the ground, the red firelight on his hard face, his lips clenching the inevitable cigarette-holder.

Pasang woke me next morning at 4.30 and at 5.15 Wangdi and I were away, leaving Pasang at the camp. Now that we knew the route we made rapid progress. The slabby ridge proved practicable and ended in a moraine where many *primulas* were growing, although the height cannot have been less than 16,000 feet.

A sloping shelf led without difficulty across the glacier to a snow-field whence the rocks rose sheer for fully 3,000 feet. Only at one point was there any hope of scaling them without excessive and, to judge from the amount of fallen stones on the glacier, unjustifiable difficulty, and that was where the ridge already mentioned slanted steeply upwards towards the crest of the wall.

Unfortunately the ridge ended in formidable cliffs. We tried at first to climb these but after wrestling with a loose gully and looser rocks above it, were forced to retreat and seek an alternative. This was by no means obvious until we discovered a snow-filled gully leading through the rocks to the crest of the ridge. The unpleasing feature of this gully was a wide crevasse at the foot of it, which had to be crossed by a snow-bridge. The crevasse was wide and abysmally deep and with two on a rope the fragile snow-bridge spanning it had to be treated with circumspection. Wangdi did not like it at all, but then he had spent three hours in a crevasse on Kangchenjunga, so some prejudice against crevasses in general must be allowed him.

Once on the crest of the ridge, the going was straightforward for a time up broken rocks and sharp snow edges, but the general angle increased gradually and with it the difficulties, whilst the weather was now brought to our attention by a drizzle of snow.

The crest of the wall was now not far above us, but the rocks leading to it were much steeper than I had supposed ; in fact, where the rib ended, they sprang upwards in an almost vertical wall on which the snow, fallen during the recent bad weather, had accumulated to a considerable depth.

Our objective was a conspicuous rock-peak immediately to the west of a snowy gap, whence falls the snow-filled gully previously noted, and our one chance of success lay in crossing this gully and climbing directly up the steep face of the peak. It was an impressive place and obviously extremely difficult. Wangdi did not like the look of it and was, like myself, unfavourably impressed by the snow-covered slabs we should have to traverse in entering the gully. Fortunately there was an excellent block of rock around which the rope could be placed to secure the party, and with this to hearten me I embarked on the traverse. It reminded me strongly of the slabs beyond the great gully on Everest. True, the angle was steeper and the snow, instead of being loose and powdery, was wet and heavy, but in the feeling of insecurity there was a remarkable affinity between the two places.

When at length I reached the gully, my doubts were resolved into certainty. The angle was steep, and the snow so soft that at every step I went in above the knees. True, there was a slight crust due to the over-night frost, but even if we succeeded in crossing safely, what would it be like when we returned? It would certainly avalanche. And there was no security; the gully was too wide to allow of enough rope to secure one man to the rocks while the other man crossed. To add to the jest, snow suddenly began to fall thickly and the wind rose, sending it scurrying across the already snow-plastered crags.

" This is no good. Let us go down." Wangdi's voice was urgent. He was right. Nothing was to be gained by reconnoitring further.

I rejoined him and we descended as quickly as possible through the snowstorm. Lower, it was raining and we arrived back at the camp soaked through. But we soon forgot our misery and sense of failure when some hot tea prepared by the thoughtful Pasang was inside us. Thus ended a climb which by Alpine standards would have been accounted a difficult expedition. Our highest point was about 18,500 feet, which meant that we had climbed 4,000 feet from our camp.

It was still raining when an hour later we descended to the base camp. I was first down and as I neared the camp, I saw Tewang, who was seated near the fire, suddenly dart into the porters' tent. He reappeared just before I reached the camp and came out a few yards to greet me. There was a smirk of righteousness on his broad face. He was wearing his climbing boots.

# CHAPTER XIII

## A ROCK CLIMB

THE morning following the unsuccessful attempt to climb the rock wall, Nurbu arrived with the mail, and news of the terrible disaster on Nanga Parbat—the worst disaster in the history of mountaineering. It occurred on the night of June 15th, when an avalanche overwhelmed the camp, killing seven Germans and nine Sherpa porters. The news cast a gloom over our small camp, for my men had all lost friends. I had known the leader, Dr. Karl Wien, and had felt confident that he would lead his party to success. From the first newspaper reports it appeared that he had escaped, but these were false ; he had died like Willy Merkl, the leader of the 1934 expedition, amid the snows of that most terrible and death-dealing of Himalayan peaks.

The weather was in poor shape, but not bad enough to prevent flower-hunting. The abundant rain and warmth of the past few days had had the effect of bringing many plants into bloom. The wide stony river-bed a mile above the camp was coloured a brilliant magenta by a willow herb (*Epilobium latifolium*) which flourishes on a diet of river-borne grit. In much the same situation grew two *allardias* (*A. glabra* and *A. tomentosa*). *A. tomentosa* grows six or eight inches high and resembles a miniature marguerite, delicate pink in colour and with silvery foliage scarcely less beautiful than its flowers. *A. glabra* is much smaller and its

117

almost stalkless blooms grow close to the gritty ground. At the sight of such flowers, I used sometimes to experience a feeling almost of despair. How could I ever hope to grow them in England as they grew here? Would they not lose their delicacy and become coarse and lank in the damp British climate?

But the *Allardia* represented only one species in the vast family of Compositae, now in bloom. In stony places, and particularly along the tops of banks, was a white foam of *anaphalis*, and I remembered that after the Kamet Expedition, when its members re-united at a dinner, Raymond Greene, who had brought a number home, presented each of us with a little bouquet—a happy thought.

All over the lower slopes of the valley a little *senecio* had put in an appearance. It reminded me a trifle distastefully of its bigger brother, the ragwort, which is a pest of the British countryside. There is a field of it near my home and my garden receives annually some millions of its seeds, a large proportion of which germinate. There was also an *artemisia* (*A. Roxburghiana*) a member of a family which must have one of the largest distributions in the world, except for the daisy and buttercup families, an *inula* (*I. grandiflora*) which resembled a small sun-flower, and a tall *solidago* (*S. Virgaurea*), a species of the golden rod or Aaron's rod of British gardens, whilst the *erigeron* family was represented by a charming purple daisy (*E. multiradiatus*).

Montmorency had come to an end, but now that there were sheep and goats in the valley it was easy to procure fresh meat. A mile from the base camp an old shepherd had taken up his abode in a stone hut which he had roofed cunningly with strips of birch-bark, and from him I purchased a sheep for five rupees. He was a fine-looking old chap, and his deep-set eyes, seamed at the corners with innumerable tiny wrinkles, had that far-away look acquired by eyes used to searching far horizons. His clothes and footgear would not have fetched sixpence in the Commercial Road, but he had discovered something that untold millions cannot pur-chase—peace and happiness.

Every day he used to bring me sheep's milk in a little brass bowl. He asked for and expected nothing in return, but Wangdi told me that any empty tins I had to give him would be much appreciated, so I presented him with a biscuit tin. He was delighted ; that biscuit tin might have been a golden casket filled with precious jewels.

During the afternoon and evening of July 9th, the weather improved and the following morning was cloudless. On the spur of the moment I decided to camp below the glacier pass which, as already men-tioned, leads over the range of peaks to the north of the valley about two miles to the east of the route described in the last chapter.

A mile or so up the valley the flowers were at their best and I shall never forget the scene where a clear-running stream meandered down to join the muddy glacier torrent. Millions upon millions of the little knot weed, *Polygonum affine*, covered the ground so densely as to form an unbroken carpet of rosy bloom, whilst scarcely less prodigal were the white everlastings, rivalling in their matchless purity the fleecy clouds already gather-ing about the peaks. The hillside was red with the *Potentilla argyrophylla*, blue with *cynoglossum* and purple with *geraniums*, and on the flat stony floor of the main stream bed were acres of puce willow herb.

A little distance farther on we turned up flower-clad slopes which increased in steepness the higher we climbed. Here grew a large purple aster with widely separated petals, which I recognised at once from Holdsworth's description as *Aster diplostephioides*; a noble flower, not growing in colonies but scattered singly over the slopes. As a contrast to these more obvious beauties was a tiny blue forget-me-not-like flower, growing on sheltered gritty slopes where it could not be over-run by larger plants, but the most delightful plant of all, if comparisons are permissible, was a *cremanthodium* (*C. Decaisnei*) which I found in the shelter of a rock at about 14,000 feet, a comparatively low elevation for this height-loving plant. Its little golden flower reminded me of the Alpine *soldanella*, for it is about the same size and droops its head in the same way; a very coy and shy little gem of the high mountain.

After climbing slopes so steep that we were glad of our ice-axe picks on the slippery turf, we gained a ridge sloping at a moderate angle. Some distance up this was perched a huge boulder, forming a cave on the lower side which, to judge from the sheep droppings, was a favourite pull-in for shepherds and their flocks. The men welcomed it, as it reminded them of a Tibetan camping-ground, and wanted to pitch my tent on a solid mass of sheep droppings, being genuinely surprised when I objected. Otherwise, it was a charming spot. Close at hand was a stream, which cascaded down some rock slabs fringed with marigolds, whilst the turf all around was packed tight with innumerable little plants.

Soon after we camped rain fell heavily, but it ceased later, disclosing a lurid sunset. Himalayan sunsets are seldom as colourful as Alpine sunsets, and in atmospheric beauty not to be compared with those of Britain, but this was an exceptional occasion, due no doubt to an excess of water-vapour in the atmosphere, and Gauri Parbat glowed like a forging just withdrawn from a blast furnace, and continued to glow long after the first stars had appeared.

As I lay in my sleeping-bag, I could watch through the door of the tent the upward creeping tide of purple shadow, an iridescent opal at its edge, slowly engulfing the glowing precipices until only the final crest was left to the sun. This faded and the purple deepened ; then, unexpectedly, and it must have been due to the reflection from some high and far-distant clouds, the glow returned, not as brightly as before, but of sufficient strength to lift the great mountain out of the night for a few moments in an unearthly splendour. This was the last of the day and was quickly superseded by the usual pale after-glow that invests high snow-peaks in a light infinitely cold so that they resemble icebergs floating on a dark sea.

I woke in the night with a start to hear a dull roaring sound and above it a succession of sharper crashes. A fall of stones was descending in a neighbouring gully, and looking out of the tent I saw a long line of scintillating sparks as the boulders collided with one another or struck against stationary boulders, an unusual sight which I have seen only once before.

It was a fine morning when Pasang woke me at four o'clock, except that the dawn-light was diffused by high mists. From the camp a grassy boulder-strewn ridge took us easily upwards to a small snow-field sloping to the crest of the pass, which we reached within two hours of leaving the camp. The shepherds who cross this pass to Mana face considerable risks, as the northern slope of the pass consists of a steep and crevassed glacier which forms a tributary glacier of a much larger ice-stream in the valley descending towards that village.

The weather was threatening, and the light early mists had deepened into an opaque pall beneath which

the peaks and ranges to the south stood stark and for-
bidding. More for the sake of exercise than anything
else, we scrambled up a minor rocky eminence immediately to the east of the pass. I had hoped for a view
of the Mana Peak but it and the nearer ranges were
concealed by clouds. Our intention was to climb
something if possible and my attention was immediately
arrested by a striking rock-peak to the east of the pass
which forms an outpost, some 19,000 feet high, of
Nilgiri Parbat. To climb it from the pass would mean
a climb of great difficulty, but the formation of the
mountain suggested that if the ridge between it and
Nilgiri Parbat could be reached, the summit should
prove accessible. To do this, it was necessary to
traverse steep glacier slopes for some distance, then
climb directly upwards. At the same time we must keep
an eye on the weather and be prepared to retreat quickly
in the event of a storm.

In the Alps mountainsides usually turn out to be
less steep than they appear, but the reverse applies in
the Himalayas, and we found ourselves on slopes far
steeper than they had appeared from the pass. Fortunately, the snow was in good condition, but was not more
than a few inches deep and rested on hard ice. A
fall on a slope of this kind must be checked at once, as
it is not possible to drive in the ice-axe deeply enough
to form a good belay for the rope, and I kept a watchful
eye on Pasang. He, however, was going better than
usual, probably because he was unladen, and he accomplished the passage without the semblance of a slip.
Next came a scramble up some rocks to a snow-slope
which brought us to an almost level snow-field immediately beneath the ridge for which we were aiming. At
the sight of the ridge our hopes of reaching it easily were
immediately dashed, for a face some 1,000 feet high

and defended at its base by a *bergschrund* (marginal crevasse) separated us from it. To the left was a belt of overhanging slabs, but to the right of these there was a chance of climbing an exceedingly steep slope to a point on the ridge about a quarter of a mile from the summit. It was no place for a large party, so leaving Pasang and Nurbu on the snow-field, Wangdi and I set out to attempt the summit.

The *bergschrund* was bridged with snow in many places and we crossed it without difficulty. From the snow-field the slope had looked steep and it proved even steeper than it looked. Prior to the recent snow-fall it had been a sheet of ice, but six inches of snow now adhered firmly and had frozen so hard that step-cutting was necessary. We had not progressed far when the sun appeared ; the weather was improving, but we did not altogether welcome this as it meant that sooner or later the snow would soften on the ice. It behoved us to move quickly and we did not pause until we had reached the first of the rock slabs. These were awkward to negotiate, for they were smooth and without belays for the rope. With any other porter I would not have attempted them, but Wangdi had already proved that he could climb safely and steadily on really difficult ground.

As we reached the ridge, a burst of song fell on our ears and looking to the left we saw three or four little brown birds perched on a boulder, all singing lustily and very sweetly. This desolate ridge over 19,000 feet above the sea was a strange place to find song-birds. What were they doing there ? Could it be that, like us, they were impelled to this high and lonely place by the spirit of the hills ?

The ridge stretched almost horizontally to the foot of a rock step fully 100 feet high. There was no turning this either to the right or to the left as far as we could see, and the only chance of climbing it was to tackle it *en face* where there was a crack which widened out higher into a chimney. The rock was excellent, a rough clean granite that reminded me of the Chamonix Aiguilles.

Having seen to it that Wangdi was securely placed and well belayed by the rope to a bollard of rock, I essayed the crack. This was awkward and strenuous rather than technically difficult, but strenuous climbing is tantamount to difficult climbing at high altitudes where even an ordinary arm pull is exhausting ; indeed, of Everest it can be said that if the climber nearing the summit encounters a rock, be it only eight feet high, where an arm pull is necessary he will, failing an alternative route, not succeed in reaching the summit.

From the crack there was an awkward step on to the slab at its side, a balancing movement which I could only accomplish when I had completely recovered my wind. The chimney above had to be climbed by means of back and knee work which involved such a strain that I had to halt and rest after every upward shove of my feet and arms. It was overhanging and roofed above and I had to leave it in favour of the right-hand wall, to do which I had to balance round a corner on small holds. I now found that above me was a slab about fifteen feet high, leading to easier rocks. It needed only a strenuous pull on my arms to take me up this, but I had discovered already that strenuous arm pulls were to be avoided at all costs. The alternative was a route to the right. This was not so strenuous but it was much more difficult, yet tired as I was by the struggle in the chimney, there was no alternative but to follow it. I had taken two steps, and was in the middle of a third, when there was a tug at my waist and a shout from Wangdi announcing that I had run out the whole of our eighty-foot rope. I was within an ace of climbing the slab, but there was nothing for it but to retreat and bring up my companion to the foot of the chimney. I had no belay for the rope and was standing on inch-wide holds, so I shouted down to Wangdi, illustrating my meaning by gesticulating with one hand while holding on with the other, that on no account must he use the rope as a hand-hold and, even more important, that he must not slip as I could not possibly hold him. But Wangdi was always the one to rise to an occasion, and within a minute or two I heard him panting hard at the base of the chimney. There were now thirty feet of spare rope available, just enough to allow me to climb to the top of the step, where Wangdi, now well secured by the rope, presently joined me. It had been a hard piece of rock climbing, the hardest I had ever done at the height.

A little higher, the ridge looked so difficult that, as we were in no mood for further strenuous climbing if it could be avoided, we followed an easier line across the east face of the mountain until we were able to climb directly upwards over steep and broken but not especially difficult rocks to a point above the difficulties. The top of the peak was only a few yards away and soon we were seated on a slab with a detached boulder, the actual summit, resting upon it.

It was 10.30 a.m., five hours since we had left the camp. Wangdi was delighted and full of grins. The first thing *I* did was to take off my boots and rub my feet, which had become wet, cold and numbed during the ascent of the snow-slope. This did not satisfy my energetic companion who, seizing some snow, proceeded to massage them vigorously. If mountaineers have nightmares, the nightmare of the lost boot or

boots must surely take precedence over all other nightmares. On this occasion Wangdi, deciding that my
boots were not in a safe place, suddenly lifted them over
his head and deposited them in a niche behind him. He
did it so quickly that for one awful moment I thought
he was going to drop them.

There was little view owing to mists, but 1,500 feet
beneath us we could see Nurbu and Pasang waiting
patiently. As a reminder of our success Wangdi, who
had already let out stentorian yells, prized some rocks
away which raced down the slabby face and ice-slopes,
leapt the *bergschrund* and finally came to rest only a
few yards from the pair, who jumped up and bolted to
his huge delight.

The weather was windless and the sun warm, but
these very conditions made an immediate descent
imperative ; so after Wangdi's rubbing had restored the
circulation to my feet and my waterlogged socks had
been wrung out and partially dried, I replaced my
boots whilst Wangdi occupied himself in building a
commemoratory cairn, after which we commenced the
descent.

I must confess that I disliked intensely the prospect
of descending the 100-foot step, although, as I knew
from experience, descending difficult rocks in the Himalayas is far easier than ascending them ; so when we
approached the step I looked for an alternative. There
was only one possibility, a diagonal route down the
face to join our ascending track at about two-thirds of
its height, and this I very unwisely decided to take.

In order to reach the snow-slopes about 100 feet of
rock slabs had to be descended. These were not only
steep but singularly holdless. Wangdi went first, firmly
held by me from the ridge. Having run out the full
length of the rope he called on me to follow. I did

so, devoutly hoping that he was well placed. He was not and when, after a very careful descent, I reached him, I found him perched on a tiny ledge supporting himself with one hand whilst taking in the rope with the other. It was a miserable stance, with no vestige of a belay and I implored him to climb very slowly and carefully. He did so, and when at length he reached the foot of the slabs I breathed a sigh of relief. But my relief was short lived, for in another moment he began to cut steps and it was only too plain from the sound of his blows that he was cutting into ice, not snow as I had anticipated. He progressed with painful slowness and appeared to have such difficulty in planting his feet firmly that, standing as I was on small holds and powerless to check a slip, my anxiety was intensified every moment.

Once again the rope ran out and Wangdi called on me to follow. I shouted to him to drive in his ice-axe, and place the rope round it, but this he seemed unable to do. The reason was made plain to me when I descended. The slabs did not end as they appeared to end, but continued covered by a sheet of ice about one inch thick, which in turn was covered by an inch or so of powdery snow. All Wangdi had been able to do was to cut nicks in this ice plating just large enough for the extreme toes of his boots. It was the most evil place I have ever climbed and was fraught with every potentiality for disaster.

I realised now what a mistake I had made to leave the ridge; however, there was nothing for it but to continue and hope that within a few yards we should come to good snow. Driving in the pick of my axe as best I could, and trusting that the toes of my boots would not slip from the minute holds, I descended to Wangdi, who seemed to be standing on nothing in particular. Once again he descended and once again I abjured extreme caution, for I doubt whether he realised what a horribly dangerous place it was we were climbing. And yet he was skill and caution personified : a Knubel or a Lochmatter * could not have descended more confidently. Forty feet more and up came a reassuring shout—he was on the good snow. It was not so hard as formerly, but this was to our advantage, for we were able to face inwards to the slope and kick steps. Moving without pause and both together we presently rejoined our upward track, and half an hour later came up to Pasang and Nurbu, who had throughout watched the proceedings with great interest, but without understanding the difficulties or dangers we had endured.

The snow of the traverse was in good condition and soon we were back on the pass, whence a series of glissades and a downhill run took us in little over half an hour back to the camp, where we had a long rest and a meal.

An hour or two later as we dawdled along the Bhyundar Valley I was able to appreciate once more the joys of climbing in Garhwal. A little while ago we had been straining every muscle on as steep and difficult a peak as I have ever climbed in the Himalayas, and now we were among the flowers ; the perfect mountaineering contrast. It had been a great day's climbing.

* Josef Knubel and the late Franz Lochmatter : two of the finest Swiss guides of their generation.

# CHAPTER XIV

## THE LOWER ALP

So far my flower-hunting had been confined to the upper part of the valley above a height of 11,500 feet. I now decided to camp below the gorge and explore the pastures of the middlemost portion.

The day following the ascent of the rock-peak I spent resting and attending to correspondence. I had been looking forward to a visit from Mr. P. Mason, the Deputy Commissioner of Garhwal, and Mrs. Mason, but a coolie arrived with a note to say that Mrs. Mason was ill at Badrinath and that their visit would have to be cancelled. They sent with the coolie a gift of apples, eggs and onions. The eggs I especially welcomed as since leaving Ranikhet I had been unable to purchase one, the reason being that the Brahmin regards chickens as unclean.

The following morning, July 13th, I descended the valley with Wangdi and Nurbu. We camped on the alp below the gorge, where the flowers, if nothing like so abundant as they were in the upper part of the valley, at least justified an investigation. I found a purple *orchis* and a small arum I had not seen before, whilst the camp was surrounded by the white *Anemone obtusiloba*, and innumerable strawberries, which carpeted the ground so densely it was impossible to take a step without crushing a dozen or more: Nurbu soon collected a hatful, and I had them for lunch crushed up in sheep's milk, but they were lamentably tasteless, not to say indigestible.

129

After lunch I wandered off on my own up the side of a gully, where some monkshood was already in seed. I was not hopeful of finding anything of interest and I was about to turn back when in a moist, mossy place under some rocks above me, watered by a tiny spring, I saw a gleam of pure white. I scrambled up the slope and came face to face with one of the most beautiful little *primulas* (*P. Wigramiana*) I have ever seen. There were a score or more altogether nestling amid cushions of bright green moss. They were white, with a soft butterfly-like bloom on their petals, and they shone out of that shadowed place like stars fallen to earth. I had not seen this *primula* before, not did I see it again.

Thus encouraged, I climbed out of the gully into the forest above it. This consisted partly of deciduous trees and partly of conifers ; there was also a flowering shrub with a syringa-like flower. I ascended, sometimes having to force my way through undergrowth, till I neared the foot of the great cliff which forms one of the jaws of the gorge. Then I stopped. I cannot quite explain *why* I stopped, but immediately I did so, I became aware of a stillness in which not a single leaf quivered. There was one sound : a tree cricket somewhere, droning out a single monotonous note which rose and fell like the hum of a distant sawmill, but suddenly this ended and after that the silence closed in upon me. And with the silence there came to me a curious and wholly inexplicable dread. Dread of what ? I am imaginative but not, I believe, nervous, but when I advanced a step and a twig cracked like a pistol shot beneath my foot, I jumped violently and I could not explain why.

I climbed for a few minutes more until I was not fifty paces from the foot of the great cliff, which loomed above me and above the forest, projecting here and there in black, slimy bulges, whence water dripped with an occasional furtive patter into the forest. Perhaps it was this cliff with its potent and somehow relentless force that impressed itself upon me, that and the silence of the forest. Then I saw that beneath the cliff there was a cave and that all around the cave the damp ground was trampled and crushed as though by some heavy beast. I looked at the dark mouth of this cave, and though I could see nothing, I felt that there was something looking at me—something malevolent. Had I stumbled on a bear's lair? If so, it were better not to investigate further; I was alone, and an ice-axe is a poor substitute for a rifle.

So I retreated, and I do not mind admitting that I cast a glance or two backwards over my shoulder. I had seen nothing and heard nothing, yet some primitive instinct told me that I had been in danger. Was it imagination? If so, why did that great mountaineer, C. F. Meade, write: " The mystery and thrill of travel is always upon one in the Himalayas, but the mystery is awful, and the thrill is sometimes a shudder."

Heavy rain fell in the night, but next morning was bright and clear. The atmosphere had been scoured of water-vapour, and the distances had that brilliant electric-blue tinge, common to mountainous regions after bad weather. The pastures were a vivid green, the forests by contrast dark, the peaks blue and remote against a bluer sky.

We were early astir and after breakfast Nurbu and I descended the valley in search of flowers. Below the alp, a stream hurrying downwards to join the main torrent had been bridged with logs, faggots and stones by the shepherds; beyond it was a slope speckled red with the largest wild strawberries I have ever seen, and beyond this again pine forest. A forest is very beautiful on a fine morning after rain. The sombre shadows cast by the trees emphasise the pools of light spilled by the sun. Here is a mossy place, hoary with dew and lit by a shaft of sunlight, and here a graceful fern frond in sharp and shining relief against the shadow. On such a morning the gloomiest forest seems charged with laughter, the whisper of falling water-drops, the breeze in the treetops, and the cadence of a small stream ; the pipes of Pan sound sweet-noted down the dim sun-flecked aisles.

There were few flowers, and many ferns, but where the path emerged from the forest on to a lower alp, I found a tall *euphorbia* (*E. pilosa*), a yellowish-green undistinguished plant and a purple-flowered, many-headed daisy. The alp had no novelties, but was bright with *potentillas* and *anemones*. I had better luck at the lower end of it, for here I discovered the first *aquilegia* (*A. vulgaris*) I had seen in Garhwal, a blue flower which was growing in one place only, an area of not more than twenty yards square. I never saw it again, and when I returned in the autumn for its seed I found that the sheep had eaten it.

We descended towards the torrent and there, in an alcove formed by two boulders, I found a blue poppy. The altitude was not more than 9,000 feet, which is unusually low for this flower. Then there was a host of rosy *Androsace primuloides* running riot over the boulders, a blue *lathyrus*, a purple motherwort (*Leonurus*) and a white-flowered shrub with singularly long and sharp spines. But the most remarkable plant was a bright pink *Eritrichium strictum* which must have been a freak, as this flower is normally blue. How did this come about ? Was it due to some chemicalisation of the soil, or to some unusual cross pollination ? It is interesting to note that the colour was precisely similar to that of the *Androsace primuloides* which was growing in its thousands a yard or two away.

The monsoon warmth and rain, particularly the heavy rain of the previous night, had roused the torrent to fury. In its presence it was almost impossible to hear oneself speak and as Nurbu and I stood close to it, the raging water ejected a stone weighing several ounces which just missed my head. I have never known such a thing happen before and it was obvious from Nurbu's expression that he placed a magical interpretation on it ; doubtless some disgruntled river-god was having a pot at me.

On the way back to camp we collected a large number of strawberries which compensated in some degree for a joint full of maggots provided by Tewang. After lunch we returned leisurely to the base camp, arriving there in a rainstorm which, however, ceased later, allowing me as usual to enjoy my supper in peace and contentment by the camp fire.

# CHAPTER XV

## THE ABOMINABLE SNOWMAN

SINCE I had first seen that grand mountain named Nilgiri Parbat, 21,264 feet, by Lieutenant R. A. Gardiner of the Survey of India, I had on several occasions turned over in my mind the possibility of an ascent. I had examined the mountain from the west, south and east and from these directions there did not seem the least hope of an attempt proving successful. The sole remaining possibility was a route from the north or north-west. There were two possible lines of approach : one via the Bhyundar Pass and the Banke Glacier and the other via the snow pass, which I had already visited,* and the glacier-filled valley which runs in its uppermost portion roughly parallel with the Bhyundar Valley. I decided on the last-named approach, as it at least involved the exploration of a valley the upper portion of which, as far as I knew, had not been visited by Europeans.

On July 16th I left the base camp, taking with me Wangdi, Pasang and Nurbu with light equipment and provisions for five days. The past week had seen many more flowers come into bloom, prominent among which was the *pedicularis*. This plant goes by the unpleasant popular name of lousewort, from the Latin *pediculus*, a louse, as one of the species, *Pedicularis palustris*, was said to infect sheep with a lousy disease ; but it would be difficult to associate the beautiful *pedicularis* of the

* See Chapter XIII.

134

Bhyundar Valley with any disease, particularly the *Pedicularis siphonantha* with its light purple blooms. There were also many dwarf *geraniums* and the *saussurea*, which grows in an astonishing variety of forms, varying from wide-spreading, flattish leaves with purple corn-flower-like blooms rising almost stalkless in the centre, to curious balloon-shaped plants and little balls of silver-grey wool that grow high up above the snow-line.

Gentians, formerly conspicuous by their absence, with the exception of the ubiquitous *Gentiana aprica*, were also in bloom, and I came across a plant (*G. venusta*) like a small edition of that well-known denizen of the alps, *G. acaulis*. It seems very shy of opening its petals and its little flower is almost stalkless. There was also growing in moist mossy places among the rocks *Primula reptans*, which rivals the *Primula minutissima* in delicacy. With so much beauty and interest attached to the ascent I scarcely noticed that I was walking uphill.

As we passed near some boulders, there was a sudden startled squawking and half a dozen or more young pheasants flew out from a small cave. Wangdi was greatly excited at this, and said that the birds would return to roost. I must confess that my mouth watered so much at the thought of roast pheasant as a change from sheep and goat that then and there I consented to a most nefarious expedition, which was planned to take place after dark.

In order to shorten the morrow's march we camped several hundred feet above our former camping place by the edge of a snow-drift amidst hundreds of *Primula denticulata*, many of which were still in bud. As I had found the same species of *primula* in seed five weeks previously, this struck me as remarkable. As late as October 7th I found flowering plants in ground where avalanche snow had recently melted. It would be interesting to know what process takes place in a plant that is covered for a year or more by avalanche snow, as must often occur in this country. Does it continue to live ? Presumably it does, as even compacted avalanche snow contains an appreciable quantity of air. Small wonder that in England gardeners experience difficulty in growing a high Alpine or Himalayan plant, for these supposedly hardy plants are not really as hardy as plants that grow at much lower elevations, which are exposed to climatic conditions all the year round. It is nothing short of miraculous that a plant which lies dormant, protected by a covering of snow for six months of the year, should deign to grow in our bewildering climate.

It was almost completely dark when Wangdi poked his head in at the door of my tent and with a wicked grin announced himself as ready for the murder of the innocents. Together with Nurbu and Pasang, who were armed with blankets, we descended the boulder-clad hillside. A few yards from the cave Wangdi whispered to me to wait ; then he and the other two conspirators crept forward as softly as cats. The next moment there was a concerted rush and both entrances to the cave were stopped by blankets. There was no answering scurry of startled birds, so Wangdi crawled under one of the blankets and groped about inside. There were no pheasants roosting there, and he retired into the open, saying things in Tibetan which doubtless exercised the nuances of that language, but at the meaning of which I could only guess. For a few moments I was as disappointed as he, then the humour of our attempted murder struck us both simultaneously and we burst into a roar of laughter.

Next morning we were away in excellent weather. Being lightly laden, I was well ahead of the men. On approaching the pass, I was surprised to notice some tracks in the snow, which I first took to be those of a man, though we had seen no traces of shepherds. But when I came up to the tracks I saw the imprint of a huge naked foot, apparently of a biped, and in stride closely resembling my own tracks. What was it? I was very interested, and at once proceeded to take some photographs. I was engaged in this work when the porters joined me. It was at once evident when they saw the tracks that they were frightened. Wangdi was the first to speak.

"Bad Manshi!" he said, and then "Mirka!" And in case I still did not understand, "Kang Admi (Snowman)."

I had already anticipated such a reply and to reassure him and the other two, for I had no wish for my expedition to end prematurely, I said it must be a bear or snow leopard. But Wangdi would have none of this and explained at length how the tracks could not possibly be those of a bear, snow leopard, wolf or any other animal. Had he not seen many such tracks in the past? It was the Snowman, and he looked uneasily about him.

I am not superstitious. The number thirteen even in conjunction with a Friday means nothing to me. I do not hesitate to walk under a ladder unless there is the danger of a paint-pot falling on my head. Crossed knives, spilt salt, sailors drowning when glasses are made to ring, black coats, new moons seen through glass, chimney-sweeps and such-like manifestations leave me unmoved. But here was something queer, and I must admit that Wangdi's argument and fear was not without its effect. The matter must be investigated. So I got out of my rucksack a copy of the "Spectator" and with a pencil proceeded to mark the size and stride of the track, while the men huddled together, a prey to that curious sullenness which in the Tibetan means fear.

About four inches of snow had fallen recently, and it was obvious that the tracks had been made the previous evening after the sun had lost its power and had frozen during the night, for they were perfect impressions distinct in every detail. On the level the footmarks were as much as 13 inches in length and 6 inches in breadth, but uphill they averaged only 8 inches in length, though the breadth was the same. The stride was from 18 inches to 2 feet on the level, but considerably less uphill, and the footmarks were turned outwards at about the same angle as a man's. There were the well-defined imprints of five toes, $1\frac{1}{2}$ inch to $1\frac{3}{4}$ inch long and $\frac{3}{4}$ inch broad, which unlike human toes were arranged symmetrically. Lastly there was at first sight what appeared to be the impression of a heel, with two curious toe-like impressions on either side.

Presently the men plucked up courage and assisted me. They were unanimous that the Snowman walked with his toes behind him and that the impressions at the heel were in reality the front toes. I was soon able to disprove this to my own satisfaction by discovering a place where the beast had jumped down from some rocks, making deep impressions where he had landed, and slithering a little in the snow. Superstition, however, knows no logic, and my explanation produced no effect whatever on Wangdi. At length, having taken all the photographs I wanted on the pass, I asked the men to accompany me and follow up the tracks. They were very averse to this at first, but eventually agreed, as they said, following their own "logic," that the Snowman had come from, not gone, in that direction. From the pass the tracks followed a broad, slightly ascending snow-ridge and, except for one divergence, took an almost straight line. After some 300 yards they turned off the ridge and descended a steep rock-face fully 1,000 feet high seamed with snow gullies. Through my monocular glass I was able to follow them down to a small but considerably crevassed glacier, descending towards the Bhyundar Valley, and down this to the lowermost limit of the new snow. I was much impressed by the difficulties overcome and the intelligence displayed in overcoming them. In order to descend the face, the beast had made a series of intricate traverses and had zig-zagged down a series of ridges and gullies. His track down the glacier was masterly, and from our perch I could see every detail and how cunningly he had avoided concealed snow-covered crevasses. An expert mountaineer could not have made a better route and to have accomplished it without an ice-axe would have been both difficult and dangerous, whilst the unroped descent of a crevassed snow-covered glacier must be accounted as unjustifiable. Obviously the " Snowman " was well qualified for membership of the Himalayan Club.

My examination in this direction completed, we returned to the pass, and I decided to follow the track in the reverse direction. The men, however, said that this was the direction in which the Snowman was going, and if we overtook him, and even so much as set eyes upon him, we should all drop dead in our tracks, or come to an otherwise bad end. They were so scared at the prospect that I felt it was unfair to force them to accompany me, though I believe that Wangdi, at least, would have done so had I asked him.

The tracks, to begin with, traversed along the side of a rough rock-ridge below the minor point we had ascended when we first visited the pass. I followed them for a short distance along the snow to one side of the rocks, then they turned upwards into the mouth of a small cave under some slabs. I was puzzled to account for the fact that, whereas tracks appeared to come out of the cave, there were none going into it. I had already proved to my own satisfaction the absurdity of the porters' contention that the Snowman walked with his toes behind him ; still, I was now alone and cut off from sight of the porters by a mist that had suddenly formed, and I could not altogether repress a ridiculous feeling that perhaps they were right after all ; such is the power of superstition high up in the lonely Himalayas. I am ashamed to admit that I stood at a distance from the cave and threw a lump of rock into it before venturing further. Nothing happened, so I went up to the mouth of the cave and looked inside ; naturally there was nothing there. I then saw that the single track was explained by the beast having climbed down a steep rock and jumped into the snow at the mouth of the cave. I lost the track among the rocks, so climbed up to the little summit we had previously visited. The mist was now dense and I waited fully a quarter of an hour for it to clear. It was a curious experience seated there with no other human being within sight and some queer thoughts passed through my mind. Was there really a Snowman ? If so, would I encounter him ? If I did an ice-axe would be a poor substitute for a rifle, but Wangdi had said that even to see a Snowman was to die. Evidently, he killed you by some miraculous hypnotism ; then presumably gobbled you up. It was a fairy-tale come to life.

Then, at last, the mists blew aside. At first I could see no tracks coming off the rock island on which I was seated and this was not only puzzling but disturbing, as it implied that the beast might be lurking in the near vicinity. Then I saw that the tracks traversed a narrow and almost concealed ridge to another rock point, and beyond this descended a glacier to the east of our ascending route to the pass. Whatever it was, it lived in the Bhyundar Valley ; but why had it left this pleasant valley for these inhospitable altitudes, which involved difficult and dangerous climbing, and an ascent of many thousands of feet ?

Meditating on this strange affair I returned to the porters, who were unfeignedly glad to see me, for they had assumed that I was walking to my death. I must now refer to the subsequent history of this business.

On returning to the base camp some days later, the porters made a statement. It was witnessed by Oliver and runs as follows :

" We, Wangdi Nurbu, Nurbu Bhotia and Pasang Urgen, porters employed by Mr. F. S. Smythe, were accompanying Mr. Smythe on July 17th over a glacier pass north of the Bhyundar Valley when we saw on the pass tracks which we knew to be those of a Mirka or Jungli Admi (wild man). We have often seen bear, snow leopard and other animal tracks, but we swear that these tracks were none of these, but were the tracks of a Mirka.

" We told Mr. Smythe that these were the tracks of a Mirka and we saw him take photographs and make measurements. We have never seen a Mirka because anyone who sees one dies or is killed, but there are pictures of the tracks, which are the same as we have seen, in Tibetan monasteries."

My photographs were developed by Kodak Ltd. of Bombay under conditions that precluded any subsequent accusation of faking, and together with my measurements and observations, were sent to my literary agent, Mr. Leonard P. Moore, who was instrumental in having them examined by Professor Julian Huxley, Secretary of the Zoological Society, Mr. Martin A. C. Hinton, Keeper of Zoology at the Natural History Museum, and Mr. R. I. Pocock. The conclusion reached by these experts was that the tracks were made by a bear. At first, due to a misunderstanding as to the exact locality in which the tracks had been seen, the bear was said to be *Ursus Arctos Pruinosus*, but subsequently it was decided that it was *Ursus Arctos Isabellinus*, which is distributed throughout the western and central Himalayas. The tracks agreed in size and character with that animal and there is no reason to suppose that they could have been made by anything else. This bear sometimes grows as large, or larger, than a grizzly, and there is a well-grown specimen in the Natural History Museum. It also varies in colour from brown to silver-grey.

The fact that the tracks appeared to have been made by a biped, is explained by the bear, like all bears, putting its rear foot at the rear end of the impression left by its front foot. Only the side toes would show, and this explains the Tibetans' belief that the curious indentations, in reality superimposed by the rear foot, are the front toes of a Snowman who walks with his toes behind him. This also explains the size of the spoor, which when melted out by the sun would appear enormous. Mr. Eric Shipton describes some tracks he saw near the peak of Nanda Ghunti in Garhwal as resembling those of a young elephant. So also would the tracks I saw when the sun had melted them away at the edges.

How did the legend originate ? It is known over a considerable portion of Tibet, in Sikkim and parts of Nepal, including the Sola Khombu Valley, the home of the Sherpas on the south side of the Himalayas. The reason for this probably lies in the comparative ease of communication on the Tibetan plateau, as compared with that in the more mountainous regions south of the Himalayan watershed, where it is known only to peoples of Buddhist faith, such as the Sherpas of Nepal and the Lepchas of Sikkim. The Snowman is reputed to be large, fierce, and carnivorous ; the large ones eat yaks and the small ones men. He is sometimes white, and sometimes black or brown. About the female, the most definite account I have heard is that she is only less fierce than the male, but is hampered in her movements by exceptionally large pendulous breasts, which she must perforce sling over her shoulders when walking or running.

Of recent years, considerable force has been lent to the legend by Europeans having seen strange tracks in the snow, sometimes far above the permanent snow-line, apparently of a biped. Such tracks had in all cases been spoiled or partially spoiled by the sun, but if such tracks were made by bears, then it is obvious that bears very seldom wander on to the upper snows, otherwise fresh tracks unmelted by the sun would have been observed by travellers. The movements of animals are incalculable, and there seems no logical explanation as to why a bear should venture far from its haunts of woodland and pasture. There is one point in connection with this which may have an important bearing on the tracks we saw, which I have omitted previously in order to bring it in at this juncture. On the way up the Bhyundar Valley from the base camp, I saw a bear about 200 yards distant on the northern slopes of the valley. It bolted immediately, and so quickly that I did not catch more than a glimpse of it, and disappeared into a small cave under an overhanging crag. When the men, who were behind, came up with me, I suggested that we should try to coax it into the open, in order that I could photograph it, so the men threw stones into the cave while I stood by with my camera. But the bear was not to be scared out so easily, and as I had no rifle it was not advisable to approach too near to the cave. Is it possible that we so scared this bear that the same evening it made up the hillside some 4,000 feet to the pass ? There are two objections to this theory : firstly, that it appeared to be the ordinary small black bear, and too small to make tracks of the size we saw and, secondly, that the tracks ascended the glacier fully a mile to the east of the point where we saw the bear. We may, however, have unwittingly disturbed another and larger bear during our ascent to our camp. At all events, it is logical to assume that an animal would not venture so far from its native haunts without some strong motive to impel it. One last and very interesting point—The Sikh surveyor whom I had met in the Bhyundar Valley was reported by the Postmaster of Joshimath as having seen a huge white bear in the neighbourhood of the Bhyundar Valley.

It seems possible that the Snowman legend originated through certain traders who saw bears when crossing the passes over the Himalayas and carried their stories into Tibet, where they became magnified and distorted by the people of that superstitious country which, though Buddhist in theory, has never emancipated itself from ancient nature and devil worship. Whether or not bears exist on the Tibetan side of the Himalayas I cannot say. It is probable that they do in comparatively low and densely forested valleys such as the Kharta and Kharma Valleys east of Mount Everest, and it may be that they are distributed more widely than is at present known.

After my return to England I wrote an article, which was published by " The Times," in which I narrated my experiences and put forward my conclusions, which were based of course on the identifications of the zoological experts.

I must confess that this article was provocative, not to say dogmatic, but until it was published I had no idea that the Abominable Snowman, as he is popularly known, is as much beloved by the great British public as the Sea-serpent and the Loch Ness Monster. Indeed, in debunking what had become an institution, I roused a hornet's nest about my ears. It was even proposed by one gentleman in a letter to " The Times " that the Royal Geographical Society and the Alpine Club should send a joint expedition to the Himalayas in an attempt to prove or disprove my observations and conclusions. It was obvious that the writer hoped that this expedition, if it took place, would not only disprove them, but would prove the existence of the Abominable Snowman. I can only say in extenuation of my crime that I hope there is an Abominable Snowman. The tracks I saw were undoubtedly made by a bear, but what if other tracks seen by other people were made by Abominable Snowmen ? I hope they were. In this murky age of materialism, human beings have to struggle hard to find the romantic, and what could be more romantic than an Abominable Snowman, together with an Abominable Snow-woman and, not least of all, an Abominable Snow-baby ?

# CHAPTER XVI

## NILGIRI PARBAT

WANGDI and Co. had obviously been severely shaken by
the events narrated in the last chapter, and it was a
subdued little procession that crept down the north side
of the snow pass.   For a while the descent lay over easy
slopes, then the glacier suddenly broke away in a steep
ice-fall, and we had to descend carefully, cutting steps
now and then, so that I marvelled at the hardihood
of the shepherds who traverse this pass, presumably
without ropes and ice-axes, and relying for their safety
on an instinctive rather than a reasoned knowledge of
mountain-craft.   In one or two places, I had to keep
a careful watch on Pasang, for there were crevasses
below waiting, as Professor Tyndall might have said,
for an erratic body.

Having passed the crevasses we came to an unbroken
snow-slope, descending in a steep concave curve to the
main glacier.   There we unroped, the better to glissade.
Wangdi descended skilfully, whilst Nurbu at least
managed to get down without spilling himself, but
Pasang, of course, could not kick more than a few steps
before he slipped.   As usual he let go of his axe, with
which he could easily have stopped himself.   His hat
flew off, his load wound itself round his neck, and down
he came like an attenuated bag of coals, his long limbs
spread out like a star-fish, whilst those below roared
with unmerciful laughter.   It is a hard world for
Pasangs.

Wangdi having good-naturedly retrieved the errant ice-axe and hat we continued on our way. The valley in which we found ourselves contained a long glacier which, like all long glaciers in the Central Himalayas at this time of the year, was largely denuded of snow and consisted for the most part of dirty stone-covered ice. As we turned the corner, where the glacier from the snow pass debouches on to the main glacier, Nilgiri Parbat came into sight at the head of the latter. It had looked magnificent from the south, east and west, and it was no less magnificent from the north-west. Built up on terrific precipices, its summit cut knife-like into the blue. There was no hope of climbing such precipices, yet there was one possibility, the north face. Only the edge of this was visible, but it showed in profile, the best angle of view when gauging the difficulties of a mountain. It was certainly steep ; I should not care to estimate its angle, but it cannot have been less than 40°, on the average. How to get on to it? That problem would have to wait until we could proceed across and over a muddle of ice-falls that formed a half circle at the head of the valley.

I was anxious to push on as far as possible that day, but it was plain that the men had lost all interest in the proceedings. The Snowman had knocked the stuffing out of them, and they lagged limply and sullenly behind as though they fully expected Snowmen to leap out at them from behind every large boulder. There is no dealing with the Bhotia or the Sherpa when he is in this condition ; superstition has much the same physical effect on the native as the fear of high altitudes had on the early climbers of Mont Blanc. My annoyance increased and finally when, after strolling ahead at a snail-like pace, I had to halt and wait for over an hour to allow them to catch up with me, I told Wangdi what I thought about him. But it was no use ; he and the others were tired, prematurely worn out by the terrors of the day : so we camped on the side moraine below, not above, the main ice-fall of the glacier as I had hoped, at a height which cannot have been more than 15,000 feet and may have been less, to judge from the vegetation in the vicinity.

After tea I scrambled up some rocks until I could look over the lower ice-fall of the glacier. What I saw was magnificent, but scarcely encouraging. Above the ice-fall there is an almost level glacier plateau, and above the plateau a semi-circle of precipices and ice-falls. It was a savage and awe-inspiring place and reminded me of that terrible cirque of Kangchenjunga from which we had vainly tried to force a way in 1930. As regards Nilgiri Parbat, I could now see that the upper-most part of the north face was glacier-clad. The slope was steep and intersected in many places by ice-cliffs, but once on it, there seemed a chance that the summit might prove accessible. About 2,500 feet below the summit the mountain is linked by a ridge to a neigh-bouring peak of about 19,000 feet, but any direct approach to this ridge was out of the question owing to cliffs and ice-falls. In one place only was there the remotest hope. This was where a long snow-crested buttress ended against the north-west face of Nilgiri Parbat. If the crest could be gained, it should be pos-sible to traverse a shelf across the face between broken ice to the foot of a steep snow gully ending on the ridge connecting the mountain with an unnamed and un-measured peak on the range extending from it to the north-west. It is a complicated piece of topography and difficult to describe. As for the north face of Nilgiri Parbat, this also is very complicated, so much so that it was impossible to determine whether or not

a route could be made up it.  But was the climb at all
practicable ?  The camp was 15,000 feet or less and
Nilgiri Parbat is 21,264 feet.  We should have to
descend some distance from the initial buttress in order
to traverse the north-west face towards the snow gully.
Assuming such a descent to be 200 or 300 feet it meant a
climb from the camp of about 6,500 feet, a tremendous
climb in one day, even on easy ground, in the Himalayas, and one which in all likelihood would prove too
long should the climbing prove difficult.  So depressing
was the prospect that it seemed best to devote ourselves merely to a reconnaissance and return later with
more food and equipment for a higher camp.

I cannot sleep well when a problem is weighing on my
mind and that night constant and vivid lightning
contributed to my wakefulness.  Once I roused myself
to look out of the tent.  To the west over the Alaknanda
Valley an intense electrical storm was raging.  Towering clouds were piled far up in the sky and these were
illuminated every second by fountains of mauve lightning.  The storm was not far distant and every now and
then the hollow rumble of thunder echoed along the
glacier.  If anything was likely to settle the issue it was
the weather.  But the lightning died away with the
dawn and the day broke calmly and with it the
conviction came to me that we must attempt Nilgiri
Parbat, so at five o'clock I roused the men and we
breakfasted.  I was not sure of their temper after the
previous day's experiences, and I did not tell Wangdi
that I intended to attempt the mountain.  Pasang I
left at the camp to the mercy of the Abominable Snowmen.

At 6 we were off.  A tongue of ice led conveniently
through the ice-fall.  Here and there step-cutting was
necessary and we had to circumvent some wide crevasses,

but there was nothing to cause us more than a moment's pause, and within half an hour of leaving the camp we were on the plateau.

The buttress, which is sharp-crested above, splays out below into precipices, which can be out-flanked by a snow-slope and snow-ridge. Crossing the plateau, we ascended this slope in a diagonal line designed to keep us out of range of a mass of unstable-looking ice pinnacles. The snow was hard frozen and step-cutting was necessary. I always welcome step-cutting at the beginning of a climb, as there is nothing like it to instil vitality and set the sluggish blood circulating. I had no need to look back to see how Wangdi and Nurbu were faring ; in some telepathic way I could *feel* them through the rope. A night's rest, coupled with that power possessed by the Oriental for forgetting unpleasant experiences, had worked wonders. Fire, dash and energy had returned to them.

The slope narrowed into a ridge. Swing—swish. Swing—swish. There is heavenly music in the sound of an ice-axe slicing into hard-frozen snow. The morning was still and cold and the great cirque, out of which we were climbing, silent and immobile. On our left was a steep and narrow gully, polished by falling debris, and bounding it an enormous mass of cold green *séracs*, tinged with a pale opalescent light reflected from some sunlit snow-peaks down the valley.

The ridge petered out into gently sloping snow. Immediately above was a crevasse with a beard of icicles on its lip and above that a steep snow-slope leading up to the sharp crowning ridge of the buttress. The crevasse was choked with snow in one place, and well held on the rope by Wangdi I gingerly crossed the bridge and cut steps up the lip. The slope above was steep and consisted of ice covered with a skin of well frozen snow. Later in the day, when the sun had softened the snow, it would be impossible to descend it without cutting steps in the ice, but there was a rock rib to the right which should serve as an alternative route. Chopping steps and moving all together, we were soon up the slope on to a ridge above. Here the sun welcomed us and we halted for a short rest. It was now no longer necessary for me to keep the men in the dark as to the objective, and I told them that we would go to the summit if possible. Their reply was laconic and typical. " Tikai, Sahib." (" All right, Sir.")

So far the weather had been good, but now mists began to form. Above us we could see the ridge rising in a parabolic curve to a rocky shoulder, then in another curve which disappeared into the mist. A few minutes' rest and we recommenced the ascent. The snow was in good order and to make a step needed only a single vigorous kick. In places the ridge was sharp and needed care, but there was no difficulty and presently, it must have been about 8.30, we stood on the blunt topmost crest of the buttress. As we reached it the mist cleared a little and we could see above us a series of huge ice-walls and square-cut *séracs*. To the left was the shelf I had already seen. It was comfortably wide, which meant that we need not pass dangerously near to the *séracs*, but it was downward sloping and traversing it involved the loss of quite 300 feet of height ; not much, but discouraging when so many thousands of feet remained to be climbed.

It did not take more than a few minutes to reach the end of it and the foot of the snow gully already mentioned, which is about 400 feet high and is bounded on one side by *séracs* and on the other by rock-cliffs. At its base it was defended by a *bergschrund* well choked with snow, so that, although some cutting was necessary

to climb over the lip, we were soon on the slope above.
This was steep, hard and icy. Every step throughout
the whole of its height had to be cut and each step took
several chops with the axe. It was hard work, but exhilarating work too. Wangdi and Nurbu were going
splendidly and had the bit between their teeth. As for
me, I had never felt fitter in my life, and was enjoying
every minute of as fine a snow climb as I had ever
had. The gully was in shadow, but the sharp thin
snow-ridge in which it ended was lit by the white fire
of the sun. Slowly we approached that ridge ; then,
held by Wangdi on the rope, I went ahead, driving in
my ice-axe as I approached the crest, in order to determine whether or not it was corniced. It was not, and
soon we were all moving along the blade-like crest,
which ended after about 100 yards in a little plateau
beneath the final ice face of the mountain. There we
halted for another rest. It was ten o'clock and we had
climbed about 4,000 feet in four hours ; fair going
considering the difficulties.

My mouth was very dry and I longed for a drink. I
moistened it with snow and ate some chocolate though,
as is usual during a hard day in the Himalayas, I had
no desire whatever to eat. Wangdi and Nurbu both
refused food, but I told them that if they did not eat we
should not be able to reach the top, to which Wangdi
replied, " Of course we shall reach the top ! "

As we sat in the snow, the mists parted sufficiently
to enable us to see the face of the mountain. As already
stated, this consists of a steep slope of *névé* some 2,500
feet in height which ended to our left and at about our
level in a line of ice-cliffs overhanging precipices about
3,000 feet high falling to the Banke Glacier. Had its
angle been a degree or two steeper it must have been
rock like the south face of the mountain. As it was, the

downward movement of the *névé* had broken it up into
*séracs* of which the largest formed a wall of ice 100—200
feet high which intersected the face for about three-
quarters of its breadth. I had planned to ascend the
face by its westernmost edge, but this was not practicable owing to broken ice. The sole remaining hope
was to make a route diagonally upwards across it to
the north-east ridge. At first sight this did not seem a
feasible alternative ; for one thing it involved a long
and complicated climb and for another it meant passing
beneath numerous *séracs* and the frowning ramparts
of the great ice-wall. Since the recent snow-fall there
had been two small falls of ice, but the clean-cut nature
of the *séracs* and the ice-wall suggested that avalanches
only broke away very occasionally. The last and most
important point to be considered was the condition
of the snow. In no circumstances could an avalanche
be risked, for with precipices below the end of a party
would be swift and certain. At present it was in good
order, and the danger, if any, would occur later in the
day when the sun had worked on the slope, though at
present mist partially screened the mountain from that
destructive agent.

My examination concluded and my decision made, we
recommenced the ascent. First came a steep snow-
slope which we climbed diagonally to the left. The
snow was hard frozen and vigorous kicking was necessary.
Curiously enough, step-kicking tends to make the feet
colder rather than warmer, possibly because the vibra-
tion deadens the toes. I notice that the same thing
happens to the hands when holding the vibrating wheel
of a badly sprung motor-car. For this reason, and
because the work of kicking in hard snow is tiring, I
varied the work by cutting with the axe.

We had not advanced far when the mist closed in,

this time more densely than before. Nothing saps the energy more quickly than steamy mist at a high altitude. The sun was scarcely visible, yet its heat was suffocating and the absence of a breeze contributed to our inertia. We were experiencing glacier lassitude, often referred to in connection with Himalayan mountaineering but which may be experienced on lower snow-mountains such as Mont Blanc and Monte Rosa. The physical cause is said to be an excess of water-vapour in the atmosphere, but the mental factor enters into it also, for there is nothing more boring or fatiguing than climbing a long snow-slope in a mist. I began to go slower and slower and to breathe more and more heavily ; and my legs were tired, a dead weight of tiredness due no doubt to my having kicked or cut every step since leaving the camp.

At this critical juncture, the mists again parted. We had been climbing for over an hour and traversing to the left at the same time, and I had anticipated seeing the ice-wall well to our right and but little above our level. Far from it. As the sluggish mists slowly and reluctantly released their hold, it loomed out like a vast sea-cliff stretching to right and left as far as we could see and still a long and weary way above us. I had underestimated the scale of the face and it seemed that we were beaten ; time and fatigue had tipped the scale against us. I turned to Wangdi to give the order to retreat, but at sight of the grim-visaged little man standing there imperturbable in his steps, as though his whole life had been spent in climbing arduous snow-slopes, the words on my lips changed themselves into :

" Go ahead, and take a turn at the leading."

I spoke in English, but Wangdi understood. He was at the end of the rope and it was only necessary to reverse the order.

There is nothing Wangdi likes better than leading on a mountain, for he is a leader, with the instincts of leadership, and he went at the slope with a tireless energy which, if not rhythmical, was nevertheless inspiring to watch. It was foolish of me not to have made him lead before, and I at once realised the difference between making steps and walking up steps already made. Quickly my energy returned to me, and with it hope and optimism. Fatigue alone had made the ice-wall seem far away ; actually it was not more than 300 feet above us and we were soon beneath it, close to its eastern-most extremity. To outflank it we had to climb round a steep corner to the left, the approach to which involved the only really dangerous climbing we met with during the whole ascent. Some fifty yards from the corner a piece of the wall had become partly detached, forming a flake of ice about 100 feet high, weighing several hundred tons, which overhung and threatened the route for about thirty yards. Had we traversed the slope some distance below the foot of the wall, we should have been out of the danger zone quickly, as here the angle was less steep than it was immediately beneath the wall, but Wangdi, never a good route-finder, chose a more difficult line at the base of the flake where steps had to be cut. I did not notice what he was doing until it was too late, as I was still recovering from my fatigue at the rear of the rope. Not that it made much difference, for it meant that we were only two or three minutes longer in the danger zone ; yet two or three minutes when the sun is threatening to dis-lodge a piece of ice the size and weight of a fortress wall can seem an unconscionably long time, and I was heartily glad when we were out of range.

The corner was steep and icy and was intersected horizontally by an awkward little crevasse with a vertical upper lip, so I went ahead again and, well belayed by the rope round Nurbu's ice-axe, traversed to the left, then made straight up to the crevasse, cutting steps all the way. I got up at last after some heavy work and was presently joined by my companions. We had turned the ice-wall, the crux of the ascent.

An unbroken but steep snow-slope leading up to the crest of the north-east ridge now remained to be climbed. The snow here was much softer than the snow beneath the ice-wall, as it had been exposed to greater cold, and at every step we went in half-way to the knees, so that even the indomitable Wangdi had to halt and puff for breath every three or four paces. Meanwhile, I kept a sharp look out for wind-slab, but presently came to the conclusion that the slope was unlikely to avalanche, owing principally to the fact that the snow was not of the same consistency throughout.

Nevertheless, it was a relief when the slope steepened into a face of well-compacted *névé* ; step-cutting was arduous work, but it was consoling to know that an avalanche could not possibly occur. Maybe, I was over-anxious as to avalanches ; though I have never been in an avalanche, except for a very minor slide of wet snow during the Kamet Expedition, I have a profound respect for Himalayan snow, which I have always regarded as far more dangerous and less easy to estimate than Alpine snow. Such snow must, of course, observe the same laws as Alpine snow, but the conditions in which it exists are extreme and the changes of temperature, due to the greater height of the sun and colder nights, more variable than in the Alps. It behoves the mountaineer, therefore, always to proceed with the utmost caution, and pessimism is better than optimism when climbing on it.

The slope seemed interminable but at length the angle

eased off and with great relief we stood at last on the crest of the north-east ridge. This was comfortably broad and inclined at a moderate angle, and moving very slowly, for we were now very tired, we tramped along it. Ahead of us the ridge rose to a point. We could see nothing higher; surely this must be the summit? It was not. As we toiled up to it, we saw beyond, a long and weary way beyond, another point.

Disgusted, we slumped down into the snow, breathing heavily, then, a minute later, I glanced cautiously over my shoulder; the summit was not nearly as far away as we had supposed. Distance and fatigue are inseparable at high altitudes. Nothing can appear more remote and inaccessible than the summit of Mount Everest seen by an exhausted climber from a point only 1,000 feet below it, but at 28,000 feet the climber is permanently weary and rest has little effect on him or on his estimation of distance.

We heaved ourselves to our feet and recommenced the ascent; but we had not proceeded more than a few yards when a strong wind suddenly rose. So bitter and penetrating was it that we halted to huddle on every stitch of spare clothing, gloves and Balaclava helmets; thus muffled up we continued slowly to advance along the ridge, which had now attained to the quality and dimensions of a nightmare ridge along which the mountaineer is doomed to climb without ever getting to the end.

During the past hour the clouds had vanished from the immediate vicinity of Nilgiri Parbat, and we became dimly aware of a superb vista extending in all directions. Hustled and blasted by the wind, we toiled on, but the mountain had one more surprise in store. As with leaden legs we breasted the top we had seen, once again it sprang up before us. But this time there was no mistake ; the ridge stretched almost level for perhaps 200 yards, then suddenly narrowed into a blade, which swept upwards in a shining curve to end in a perfect point.

Once more we plumped down in the snow for a rest and once more we heaved ourselves to our feet and continued towards our goal. But there was now a different feeling—that snowy triangle lifting with mathematical exactitude into the blue was assuredly the summit.

We came to the point where the ridge narrowed and steepened. It was impossible to traverse a crest so delicate and thin, so driving in our ice-axes and shuffling along sideways, with toes dug well in at every step, we advanced one by one. Thus we came to the summit. There was room on it for but one of us at a time. I well remember standing in the snow with my arms resting on it while surveying for a few moments a marvellous panorama. My memory is of an isolation and height comparable with far higher summits, for Nilgiri Parbat, like the Matterhorn, stands alone and there is no peak exceeding it in height within three or four miles. The atmosphere that day, probably because of an excess of water-vapour, was blue ; everything was blue, the sky profoundly blue, the hills, the shadows and the distances. In the north, stormclouds were banked up along the edge of Tibet and beneath them I could see the Tibetan plateau, and that was blue and level like an ocean, except for one minute point of white bisecting the horizon. The same ridiculous thought occurred simultaneously to Wangdi and me, but Wangdi was the first to voice it. " Everest." And indeed the peak, which cannot have been less than 200 miles distant, bore a strange resemblance to Everest.*

* Everest is about 400 miles distant from Nilgiri Parbat and would not, of course, be visible.

The wind was blowing hard across the ridge a few feet below the summit, but the summit itself was windless. In this oasis of calm we would willingly have lingered, but there was a long descent before us with the possibility of bad snow. Five minutes we spent on that fragile, unearthly crest, the most beautiful mountaintop I have ever visited, then began the descent.

Now that the need to lever our tired bodies uphill was done with we could appreciate the splendours on either hand : the great precipice which falls to the south and the walls of ice leaning over to the north, seeming almost to overhang the Banke Glacier thousands of feet beneath. The wind was no longer a tormentor and the sun smiled kindly as we strolled along the ridge, and on either side of our splendid path peaks and clouds glowed radiantly in the afternoon sun with an unsubstantial, ethereal beauty. We trod the very parapet of heaven.

And so, at length, the snow-slopes. The upper snow was unaltered, the lower snow softened by the sun, which was now shining on the ice-wall. We hurried past the lurching flake and made all haste to the plateau. Once Nurbu slipped—he was very tired—but Wangdi and I drove in our axes and stopped him before he had slid more than a few feet. On the edge of the plateau we found some rocks with a small trickle of water and I filled my cup again and again, for we were all terribly thirsty.

After a short rest, we traversed the ridge and descended the gully, and here we had a foretaste of what to expect lower down. On the way up we had cut steps, but now we sank almost to our knees into soft wet snow. With the possibility of an avalanche in my mind, I insisted on every precaution, and we descended one at a time keeping as close to the rocks as possible. The snow on the slopes below still retained a crust which would bear for a step or two if trodden very gently ; then it broke, and in we would go, knee-deep and often thigh-deep.  We had not realised before this how tired we were, but the climb of 300 feet to the crest of the buttress was the hardest work of the day.  Wangdi and I took turns at leading, but even Wangdi's amazing strength was on the wane, and he was as glad as I to relinquish the lead after a few minutes' ploughing through the waterlogged snow.  The snow was even softer on the buttress crest, indeed so soft that, as it could hardly become worse, we halted for half an hour on some sun-warmed rocks where Wangdi and Nurbu at last condescended to eat something, while I wrung out and attempted to dry my socks, which as usual had become sopping wet.

The sun was fast declining when we set off again. Wangdi wanted to descend the slope up which we had come from the *bergschrund,* and would not believe me when I told him it was dangerous, so, as an illustration, I rolled a snowball down it.  In a yard or two this had attained to the dimensions of a cart-wheel, the weight of which set a wedge of snow in movement.  The wedge widened and widened and within a second or two a slice of the slope fifty yards wide was sliding down to the *bergschrund* in a formidable avalanche, leaving bare ice in its wake.  Wangdi was suitably impressed, at least I hope he was, and made no demur about descending the rock-ridge to one side of the slope.  This was easy until we came to the *bergschrund,* above which it broke off in a steep little wall.  But the rocks were not as difficult as they looked, and soon Wangdi, whom Nurbu and I let down on the full length of the rope, had found a bridge over the rift.  That was the last difficulty, and the ridge and slopes to the glacier proved so easy that we were able to glissade part of the way.

As we walked across the little plateau above the ice-fall, the shadows were creeping up the cliffs and *séracs* with the stealthy haste of sub-tropical night, but above and around was a rampart of sunlight, whence the great peak we had climbed stood up from a labyrinth of ice to cut a glowing wedge in the darkening blue.

At 7 p.m. we were welcomed by Pasang, who had thoughtfully prepared some tea. We could drink indefinitely, but none of us could eat ; neither could we sleep, we were too tired, and hours later I lay awake going over in my mind the events of the day. We had climbed nearly 7,000 feet up a peak which remains unique in my recollection for its beauty and interest, indeed the finest snow and ice-peak I have ever climbed. Much that is worth while in life had been packed into the space of thirteen hours, but from all that I remember the summit stands pre-eminent and I can picture it as though it were yesterday, simple, beautiful and serene in the sunlight, the perfect summit of the mountaineer's dreams.

# CHAPTER XVII

## RATABAN

AFTER our exertions on Nilgiri Parbat, we arrived tired at the base camp on July 20th : there I slept the clock round, that deep refreshing sleep that comes after the first effects of exceptional exertion have worn off. July 21st was the date that Peter Oliver was to join me, but he had written that he would probably be a day late. However, I decided to descend the valley a short distance to meet him in case he should be up to time.

Various flowers had put in an appearance during the past few days. Near the stream was growing a campion (*Silene tenuis*) and another plant very similar in appearance which turned out to be a *lychnis* (*L. apetala*) with a Chinese-lantern-like flower pendant on a thin stalk, whilst a creeping bellwort (*Codonopsis rotundifolia*) was twining itself about the stalks of large plants.

The *anemones* were past their prime, but a multitude of *geraniums, delphiniums, polemoniums, potentillas* and many smaller flowers filled my garden, as I had come to look upon it, with glowing colours.

It was a perfect morning as Nurbu and I strolled over the meadows. Arriving at the lower end of the gorge we scrambled up to the right through dense undergrowth, then over a series of striated slabs until we were able to see far down the valley. A little ledge formed an ideal belvedere and we spent three delightful hours basking in the sun and lazily watching the slow lights and shadows as the clouds passed.

Rhubarb grew near by and Nurbu munched away whilst I photographed a yellow shrubby *potentilla* (*P. fruticosa*) which grew in cracks and crannies of the neighbouring crags. A botanical miracle of high mountains is the manner in which every vestige of decay is seized upon by the roots of plants. Presumably birds have much to do with the distribution of seed, but the strong upward rising air-currents from the valleys must play a major part in clothing the crags and mountainsides and account for the presence of flowers amid the eternal snows far from alpland and meadow. The study of air-currents and plant distribution in the Himalayas should disclose some interesting facts.

As Peter did not put in an appearance we returned to camp where I spent the remainder of the day attending to my pressed specimens, some of which had been affected by the monsoon damp. After so many delightful weeks, I felt almost depressed at the thought of leaving the Valley of Flowers, for I had discovered a never-ending delight in the growth of the marvellous garden that surrounded me. There are many virtues in wandering about the Himalayas, but to me the ideal life will always be a flowerful country where I can pitch my camp and settle down to observe all that happens about me. To the botanist there is a realm of interest and potential exploration in half a mile of hillside. I had not realised this before, and I remember with regret how often I hastened unseeing through valleys, my eyes fixed on the hilltops when at my feet was lying one half of interest and beauty.

Peter arrived next morning, having accomplished the march from Ranikhet in nine days. He had brought with him two Darjeeling men, in addition to the Dotials who had carried his heavy baggage. These were Tse Tendrup, a Tibetan, and Ang Bao, a Sherpa. Ang

Bao (or " Babu " as his comrades called him) I remembered well, as he had carried my photographic apparatus during the 1936 Mount Everest Expedition. He was the only Sherpa of the party and this was to his disadvantage, for though the Sherpas of the Sola Khombu Valley in Nepal are closely related to the Tibetans and are Buddhists by religion, there is nevertheless a subtle difference. The Sherpas are Tibetans who have emigrated from Tibet into the fertile valleys of northern Nepal close to the southernmost flanks of Everest. They are an exceptionally hardy race and natural mountaineers who have put up a magnificent showing on Everest and other Himalayan expeditions, but it is possible that the Tibetan, wedded to his bleak windswept plains, scorns these emigrants to warmer and pleasanter climes.

It may be that Ang Bao's youth, for he was little more than a boy, and natural willingness and good nature, made him the hewer of wood and drawer of water of the party ; at all events the gulf between him and the Tibetans was manifest, and on more than one occasion we had to interfere to prevent the wholly unscrupulous Wangdi from saddling him with more than a fair share of work.

He was a little fellow with a round boyish face and somewhat sly eyes ; but he was not in the least sly, and it was merely an ingrained diffidence and nervousness that caused him to falter in his gaze and look uneasily about him. He was not a great mountaineer, being naturally timid and clumsy, but he was a trier and a sticker to the $n$th degree. In one way he scored heavily over his companions, for he had acquired, probably at Ranikhet, a brand-new pair of khaki riding breeches. They were fearfully tight at the knees and must have caused him prolonged suffering when marching or climbing, but if they did he never gave a sign, and whatever the menial tasks foisted upon him or the leg-pulls he had to endure, there is no doubt that these breeches and their obvious superiority over all other garments possessed by the party preserved in him a feeling of superiority which stood him in good stead on many trying occasions.

Tse Tendrup I find difficult to describe, for he was one of those men who psychologically and physically are somehow always in the background. In a word he was unobtrusive. You could not imagine him being the focal point of a row or being riotously drunk or being unconventional in the smallest particular. He did his work well, but somehow one never thought about his doing it : I suppose it was because he did it well. He was a fair mountaineer, not rankly bad like Pasang or brilliantly good like Wangdi. Everything that he did was fair ; he gave no trouble ; he commanded no especial praise. Had he been born a European he might have lived in a suburb and travelled up to " Town " by train every day, worked at the same office, lunched at the same restaurant, and spent his fort-night's holiday at the same place, playing golf at the same handicap. It is strange to write of a Tibetan thus, for most people associate Tibet with strange and weird practices, and think of Tibetans as an altogether exciting not to say uncanny race. But I suppose there are ordinary conventional Tibetans just as there are ordinary conventional Englishmen and Tse Tendrup was one of them.

I have hesitated to describe my companion because a hide-bound convention which surrounds mountaineer-ing literature, perhaps more so than the literature of any other subject under the sun, decrees that your companion on a mountain shall remain only a name, a mere cypher which climbs to the summit and back again. On this occasion, however, I am going to violate convention, not to say tradition.

I have accompanied Peter Oliver in the Alps and on Mount Everest. My most vivid memory is of climbing behind him while he cut or kicked steps up the slopes of the North Col in 1936. I remember thinking at the time that here was a man endowed with the physique and spirit of a George Leigh-Mallory. There was the same restless force and fine attunement of the nervous senses to the work in hand, the same exercising of imaginative and artistic qualities, always a surer passport to success in mountaineering and exploration than brute force. I have not the slightest doubt that many have eyed his spare frame, as they have eyed mine, disparagingly, and wondered why something beefier and stronger could not be found for Everest, for the old traditions die hard and to the uninitiated the mountaineer is broad, strong and heavy, with the bunched and knotted muscles of a Sandow, and if he be naturally endowed with a beard of Assyrian luxuriance so much the better. It is hateful to debunk such cherished traditions, but the fact is it is the lean, spare man who climbs best. Lastly, Peter is a genuine lover of the mountains and on such the mountains confer their greatest gifts.

That evening we discussed plans. Our main objective was the Mana Peak, 23,860 feet. This is a near neighbour of Kamet and during the Kamet Expedition it had been the most striking peak of any in view. Now that Nanda Devi had been ascended by the Anglo-American Expedition, the Mana Peak was the highest unscaled peak in the Garhwal Himalayas with the exception of the East and West Ibi Gamin, which form a part of the Kamet massif and are dull-looking, somewhat shapeless mountains. But height alone did not influence our decision ; the Mana Peak is an outstandingly fine mountain, a great pyramid of red granite splendid to look up from all directions and conspicuous even from Ranikhet, some 100 miles distant. It is a difficult peak too, not only because of its steepness but because of the complex nature of the ridges and glaciers surrounding it. In 1931 it was agreed that to climb it from the East Kamet Glacier would involve an expedition with a greater number of camps than were required for Kamet, and that the ascent from this direction would be difficult, perhaps impossible. The remaining approaches are from the west, south and east, and of these that from the west, from the Saraswati Valley to the north of Badrinath and Mana, was evidently steep and intricate, whilst the report of members of the Kamet Expedition, who had explored some distance up the Banke Glacier to the south-east of the mountain, was scarcely encouraging.

Some weeks previously, however, I had received a very interesting letter from Lieut. R. A. Gardiner of the Survey of India, who had been surveying in the Banke Glacier area. He wrote that he had discovered a glacier system between the East Kamet and Banke Glaciers, of which the old map gave no indication, consisting in its uppermost portion of a series of snow-fields forming what was virtually a plateau some six miles in length. Though he had not visited the westernmost snow-fields he had climbed to a height of 20,000 feet on the ridge between the plateau and the East Kamet Glacier and was of the opinion that if three peaks on this ridge, of 21,400 feet, 22,481 feet and 22,892 feet, could be outflanked from the plateau and the east ridge of the mountain reached, the summit should prove accessible. We decided, therefore, to follow his suggestion and first of all attempt the mountain from this direction, to do which it was necessary to cross the Bhyundar Pass, 16,688 feet, at the head of the Bhyundar Valley, and establish a base camp in the Banke Valley at about 14,000 feet. This plan, incidentally, would enable us to diverge *en route* to the snow col I had already visited and attempt the ascent of Rataban, an unwise suggestion on my part because Peter had only recently been at sea-level and Rataban is a difficult mountain, 20,231 feet high, not an ideal training expedition for an unacclimatised mountaineer. Apart from this last scheme the proposed visit to the Banke Plateau had the advantage that, even if we failed to climb the Mana Peak, there were some fine and probably accessible peaks in the vicinity of the plateau.

We estimated that we should require between two and three weeks' food, some of which, such as fresh meat and vegetables and coolie food, could be obtained from the village of Gamsali, which is situated at the junction of the Banke and Dhauli Valleys. With only five porters at our disposal, we had to jettison every unessential, with the exception of cameras and films, which I for one regard as essentials in mountaineering and exploration. It must, however, be added that some whisky which Peter had brought with him was also translated into the same category.

The smallness of our party was dictated by the cost of porterage. Also a small party accompanied by first-rate Sherpa or Bhotia porters is the superior of a large party, even on the greater peaks of the Himalayas, by virtue of its mobility and power to change plans at a moment's notice, thus seizing its opportunities without delay. Shipton is the high priest of the small Himalayan party, and certainly his expedition with H. W.

Tilman in 1934 in the same district was an example of how much may be accomplished.

The flurry of packing and sorting over, the Dotials were sent off down the valley, and the Darjeeling men dispatched with the first relay of loads with instructions to dump them somewhere near the place where I had camped previously below the Bhyundar Pass, leaving Peter and myself to enjoy a lazy afternoon. The men were late in returning, so late that we became anxious for their safety, and went out to meet them. It was a pitchy night, but they arrived at last, having found the glacier very wearisome to negotiate owing to the snow having melted, exposing moraines and ice.

Next morning we left with the remainder of the loads. Despite the first relay, there was enough over to necessitate everyone carrying a heavy burden. I have never taken kindly to load-carrying in the Himalayas and prefer to leave it to men who are used to it and think no more of 60 lbs. than I would of a day's food and equipment in the Alps. In a word, I prefer comfort to discomfort whenever possible. Hugh Ruttledge summed me up during the 1933 Everest Expedition when he called me a " blooming sybarite," only he did not use the word " blooming." No doubt I am, though I do not altogether fancy one dictionary definition of sybarite, " An effeminate voluptuary." In the present instance I was consoled to some extent by some pointed remarks of Peter's on the subject of his own load. It is always comforting to know that others are suffering too.

It was brilliantly sunny when we left the base camp, but within two hours clouds had formed and a drizzling rain set in. The porters had dumped their loads at the foot of the slopes leading to the Bhyundar Pass and not at the old camping site, as they said that there was now

no water there.  As we were very damp outside we
decided to counterbalance this by becoming equally
damp inside, so we sat under a boulder and consumed
an appreciable portion of the necessity already mentioned.  The effect of this upon me was to make me
sing.  Fortunately no avalanche occurred.

Towards sunset the rain stopped and the mists cleared,
revealing the rocky pile of Nilgiri Parbat, glowing in a
green sky at a seemingly impossible height above us.
Then Rataban appeared over the ragged lip of the
near-by ice-fall, but it was on the former peak that the
sun lingered, and long after dusk had fallen and the
stars brightened it continued to shine, at first gold, then
silver, then miraculously gold again, as though the earth
had reversed its rotation for a few minutes.

The following morning was warm and calm and we
made rapid progress to the Bhyundar Pass, finding it
unnecessary to rope for any part of the way.  Just
below the last gentle slope leading to it, we discovered
a pleasant place which needed little preparation in
order to pitch the tents.   There were numerous flowers
in the vicinity, including a yellow *corydalis* (*C. Govaniana*)
with slender feathery foliage, yellow *androsaces* and a
number of golden-brown *sedums*.

In the late afternoon there was a heavy hailstorm
accompanied by thunder.   Thunderstorms are frequent
in the foothills in the Himalayas, but seldom occur
among the high mountains.

The weather did not recover its good humour during
the night and the following morning was misty and
grey.  We waited some time for an improvement, but
as this did not materialise set off to the snow col, taking
with us Wangdi, Pasang, Tewang and Tse Tendrup
and leaving Nurbu and Ang Bao to bring up the remaining loads from the lower camp.  We had not gone

far before Tewang began to show evident signs of
fatigue. Since I arrived in the Bhyundar Valley, he
had had little or no exercise and I thought he was
merely out of training, but when we got to the ice-fall
he suddenly collapsed and we then realised that he
must be in a bad way to judge from the greenish colour
of his face and his racing pulse. There was nothing
for it but to send him back to the camp escorted by
Wangdi and Pasang, while we carried on with Tse
Tendrup.

The ascent was complicated by mist and drizzling
snow, whilst the col, when at length we reached it, was
bleak and bitterly cold with a mixture of hail and snow,
carried along by a strong wind rushing across it. The
three of us crowded into the single tent we had brought
until Wangdi and Pasang arrived with the remaining
tent and equipment, when we were able to warm our
chilled bodies with a hot drink.

It was a miserable afternoon. We lay side by side
in our sleeping-bags in our little Meade tent which
measured approximately six and a half feet in length
and four feet in breadth, whilst the wind and snow
drove furiously at the camp. The porters fared worse
than we, as their tent leaked, wetting their sleeping-
bags. This tent, which was strongly made and of thick
material, had served its turn on Kamet, but as it was
evidently unfit for further use at high altitudes we
decided to scrap it at the first opportunity. Tents, like
wind-proof clothing, need to be replaced every season
in the Himalayas, for the intensely powerful sun at high
altitudes quickly damages canvas, whilst rapidly alternating heat and cold, dampness and dryness, put a
considerable strain on any finely woven material.

At sundown, to our relief, the weather moderated
and we were able to enjoy some pemmican soup cooked

over a "Primus." After my luxurious days and nights in the Bhyundar Valley I cannot say I took kindly to sharing a tent, even with a boon companion, for there are certain penalties and restrictions attached to this : one cannot, for instance, light a candle in the middle of the night and charm away some sleepless hours with a book, whilst kicking or tossing about is regarded unsympathetically ; but thank heavens for one thing, neither of us snored.

The eastern sky was clear at dawn, but heavy clouds were massing over the Alaknanda Valley and the Badrinath Peaks. However, there was no immediate reason why we should not attempt the ascent of Rataban, the summit of which cannot be more than 2,500 feet above the col. With the prospect of some difficult climbing and in all probability iced rocks it was inadvisable to start too early, and we did not leave the camp until eight o'clock, when the weather was excellent.

As already mentioned, the direct ascent of the north ridge from the snow col is impracticable, or at all events desperately difficult, and the one possibility of climbing the mountain from this direction is to force a route to the upper part of the ridge by one or other of a series of rock ribs on the steep north-west face. With this end in view we traversed more or less horizontally from the camp, making for a rib which I had previously decided, when examining the peak, was the most likely line of attack. To gain this we crossed a *bergschrund*, which offered little difficulty, then climbed diagonally over a steep slope of well-frozen snow. The rib to begin with was not particularly difficult and the rock, a granite material, was firm and delightful to climb, but it was slow going on the whole and for the most part we could move only one at a time.

The ridge ended against a rock band, perhaps 200 feet

high and slanting from west to east across the face of
the mountain. The rocks were sheer, even overhanging, and their yellow and red edges bit brutally into
the sky. The one possibility of climbing them was to
the right ; once above the band a minor rib should
lead up to the crest of the north ridge above the impassable section whence the climbing lies over snow to the
summit. It was a difficult and exposed traverse. Moving one at a time and belaying carefully at every rope
length, we edged along a series of minute ledges until
we came to a well-defined chimney. This we attempted
to climb, but it was altogether too strenuous, whilst an
overhang at the top demanded a pull on the arms on
to unknown and doubtful ground, a pull which would
be unjustifiable at any altitude let alone at nearly
20,000 feet. The alternative was to cross the chimney
and continue the traverse past a corner. It was an
awkward movement and meant edging along in the
position of a man crucified. Thence after a steep
climb we came to an ill-defined ridge of snow and
rock that appeared to lead continuously to the crest
of the north ridge. The greatest difficulty had been
overcome and it now remained to be seen whether
there was sufficient time to reach the summit and
return.

As Peter followed round the corner I noticed that he
was climbing slowly and with increasing effort. It was
no surprise to me, therefore, when he announced that
he was feeling very tired and that he did not think he
would be able to continue if the difficulties persisted.
He suggested, however, that I should carry on for
another rope length to determine whether we could
reach the ridge without great difficulty, for once on it
he felt that he might be able to continue to the summit
should it prove merely a snow-plug. I followed his

suggestion, but merely with the idea of prospecting the route for a future occasion, as I knew there was no justification for continuing in such circumstances and, incidentally, we were climbing for pleasure.

After kicking steps up steep snow, and climbing an awkward rock pitch, I saw from the crest of the latter that the rib we were on continued to the north ridge of the mountain and that while there were no insuperable obstacles the difficulties were considerable. Having noted this, I returned to Peter and we rested for a few minutes. It was disappointing to fail when the peak was almost within our grasp, but it was no fault of Peter's ; the fault was mine, and mine alone. I do not suppose any mountaineer has tackled such difficulties at a similar altitude within a fortnight of being at sea-level, and it was foolish of me to suggest the climb, though in my own defence I must state that I had not for a moment anticipated such difficulties as we had encountered. As it was, Peter had put up a magnificent performance in reaching a height of about 19,500 feet after an outstandingly difficult and exacting climb.

Providence walks in many guises. As we slowly descended the sun vanished in a chaos of leaden vapour and within half an hour snow was falling heavily. Had this storm overtaken us near the summit we should have been hard put to it to retreat safely ; as it was the snow filled the interstices of the rocks of the lower rib and rendered the climbing unpleasant, not to say difficult.

When ascending a peak, the mountaineer tends to underestimate the steepness of the climbing, and his mind, particularly when he is on new and intricate ground, is occupied with the technical details of his craft, but during the descent he is better able to appreciate the

steepness and grandeur of a mountainside. The present
instance was no exception, and I do not believe either
of us realised until we descended the formidable nature
of the face we had climbed. Peter said that it was the
hardest and steepest climb he had done in the Himalayas.

The hour or two of warm and sunny weather we had
enjoyed during the ascent had softened the snow on the
slope by which we had ascended to the rib, and as there
was ice below it, to have descended safely would have
meant much step-cutting. We abandoned it, therefore,
in favour of continuing down the rib. This last part of
the descent was disagreeable, for the rocks were not
only running with slush and water, but shaley and
loose into the bargain. Furthermore, we were wet and
cold and the rope had become exasperatingly stiff and
sodden with water. To Peter, who was feeling very
tired, it must have been a very trying descent, but he
gave no hint of this and was a pillar of strength on
more than one awkward slope where everything was
loose and there were no belays for the rope.

As we neared the foot of the rib, we heard distant
shouts from the porters intended to guide us to the
camp through the snowstorm. The rib, which had
seemed interminable, ended at last, and to our great
relief we were able to cross the *bergschrund* without
difficulty. Thenceforward we ploughed through the
soft snow of the glacier and preceded by loud and oft-
reiterated demands for *chha* (tea) eventually reached
the camp, soaked and bedraggled.

It had been a hard not to say anxious climb and we
were thankful to be off the mountain. We agreed as
we poured steaming tea into our chilled bodies that
everything had worked out for the best. Nothing was
to be gained by prolonging our stay, especially as the

snow col formed a natural funnel for every wind that blew, and after a meal we packed up the wet tents and hastened down to the camp near the Bhyundar Pass.

Thus ended my second attempt to climb Rataban. It may be that the mountain is more easily accessible from the south or east, though from what I have seen this appears very questionable, but if it is ever my fortune to attempt it again I should follow the same route ; although very steep and difficult it is, I am convinced, entirely practicable and will afford a magnificent climb to the summit of this grand peak.

# CHAPTER XVIII

## THE BANKE PLATEAU

AFTER our unsuccessful attempt to climb Rataban we proceeded to carry out the next part of our programme, and it was decided to cross the Bhyundar Pass without delay and pitch a base camp in the Banke Valley from which to push up a series of camps on to the plateau whence we hoped to attempt the ascent of the Mana Peak.

When we returned to our camp near the Bhyundar Pass we found that Tewang had not recovered from his indisposition and was now complaining of a pain in his chest. I took his temperature and was aghast to find it only 95·2°. He must be seriously ill if not at death's door. To make certain, I took it again and the laggard mercury rose to normal. This little medical detail satisfactorily settled, the patient was ordered to remain in his sleeping-bag and the onerous task of cooking was handed over to Ang Bao.

All the stores were now at the camp. We had planned to relay them over the Bhyundar Pass into the Banke Valley, but the men were very averse to this as they did not want to return to the pass, and next morning Wangdi said that they would prefer to carry double loads. This meant well over 100 lbs. per man ; it also meant that Peter and I had to carry as much as we could manage and we eventually set off with at least 60 lbs. apiece.

The passage of the Bhyundar Pass is not difficult, but care is necessary when descending the ice-fall on the east side.   Here Wangdi attempted, as usual, to make a better route than we, and proceeded to lead the men across a dangerous ice-slope seamed with crevasses and loaded with loose stones.   We shouted to him to return and follow our route, which he eventually did, and when he came up with us Peter gave him a dressing down, which I fear was entirely without effect as Wangdi is constitutionally unable to differentiate between safety and danger on a mountain.

Below the ice-fall we descended a slope of screes where we came across a beautiful *delphinium* (*D. densiflorum*) growing in close-packed spires of flowers not more than a foot high.   How it lodged in this desolate situation with nothing but stones to root in is a mystery.

From the screes a steep snow-slope led down to the glacier well below the ice-fall where, as was only to be expected, Pasang did his inevitable *pas seul*, or his famous imitation of a sack of coals sliding down a chute into a cellar.   Once on the glacier we had a dull and fatiguing trudge over ice and moraines to its junction with the Banke Glacier.   Here there was a marked change in scenery.   The Bhyundar Valley is moist and fertile, but the Banke Valley is drier, stonier and barer, and its ochre-coloured rock reminds the mountaineer that he is only a few miles south of the main Himalayan watershed and the Tibetan border. Without a doubt it receives much less rain than the Bhyundar Valley, the reason being that the latter runs from south-west to north-east and is linked with the Alaknanda Valley, which forms a natural channel for the monsoon air-current, whereas the Banke Valley runs east-south-east to west-north-west and is linked with the upper part of the Dhauli Valley, into which the monsoon current does not penetrate with the same power that it does into the Alaknanda Valley. I expected, therefore, to find a less luxuriant plant life and one characteristic of a drier climate.

The Banke Glacier, like the majority of the main Himalayan ice-streams, is covered in moraines for the greater part of its length and presents a dreary but not unimpressive spectacle of mountain decay. We followed to begin with a side moraine of the glacier we had descended, a delightful bank forming a home for innumerable *potentillas, androsaces, saxifrages* and *sedums.* I found nothing new until I came to some little rosettes of fleshy leaves, from the centre of which flower shoots were emerging, which I knew must be a house-leek (*Sempervivum mucronatum*). I selected a specimen for my press, and so potent was the power locked up in this little plant that it continued to send out its flower shoot for a full two or three more inches in spite of the weight and pressure applied to it.

It was a tedious crossing of the glacier, over innumerable mounds of moraine, some of them fully 100 feet high, but it was made interesting by the plants which grew even in this barren wilderness of shattered rock, and I came upon many *allardias*, both the large and small varieties, their pink flowers warm and cosy amid silver cotton-wool-like foliage.

By the time we had reached the other side of the glacier our loads seemed even heavier than before and we were thankful to pitch the base camp on a shelf at about 14,000 feet, between two shepherds' bivouacs known as Thur Udiar and Eri Udiar (Cold Cave). There was plenty of fuel in the shape of juniper bushes close at hand, and it was altogether a delightful spot as the ridge immediately above the camp formed a natural rock garden.

Soon after our arrival a shepherd, Alam Singh by name, appeared with the remains of two sheep which he explained had been killed by a rock-fall. As the meat appeared quite fresh we purchased it and afterwards, having discovered that he had an assistant to mind his flocks in his absence, sent him down the valley to Gamsali to purchase vegetables and, if possible, milk.

Tewang, unfortunately, was still unwell, and once again the cooking fell upon Ang Bao, who, unexpectedly, proved capable of turning out excellent chupatties. As a rule I find this particular form of unleavened bread exceedingly indigestible and for that reason had provided myself with biscuits for my stay in the Bhyundar Valley, but it was now necessary to live as far as possible off the country. I think it was General Bruce who once remarked that chupatties made of native flour acted like sand-paper on the inside, though whether he intended this eulogistically or as a warning I did not discover. At all events I have never eaten sand-paper so am not in a position to judge. The General had visited Garhwal in 1907, accompanied by Dr. T. G. Longstaff and the late A. L. Mumm, and his name is legendary along the Himalayas, particularly among the Gurkhas. In such veneration is he regarded that a story is told of an old lady of Mana who asked to be allowed to drink the water he had washed in, as by so doing she would acquire merit and be cured of her various ailments.

Next day was necessarily a rest day, for we had worked hard, and it was only fair to the porters after their great effort. To save time on the morrow, when we hoped to push the first of our camps up towards the Banke Plateau, I spent the afternoon reconnoitring the approach.

Lieut. Gardiner had written that the only practicable route to the plateau lay to the east of Peak 19,212 feet, climbed by Eric Shipton in 1931. The plateau is cunningly concealed, and the only indication that an extensive glacier system exists to the north of the Banke Glacier is afforded by a steep and broken ice-fall which descends to join the glacier. Thus it is easily under-standable why no one had previously suspected the existence of the plateau. Gardiner had given no exact details as to the route to be followed, but from the camp it appeared as though this must lie to one side or the other of a steep and narrow gorge. The crags immediately above the camp were disagreeably loose and shaley, so I climbed the slope to the west of the gorge, halting on the way to admire a large white *anemone* with a golden centre (*A. rupicola*) which covered the hillside in its millions. The slope ended in a ridge clad in juniper against the dark foliage of which galaxies of flowers, *potentillas, androsaces, anemones, polygonums* and *geraniums* made brilliant splashes of colour.

From this point I was forced into the upper part of the narrow and wall-sided gorge and, following a little break across the cliffs, was presently able to make my way almost directly upwards over a series of awkwardly dipping slabs, which were broken at about two-thirds of their height by a small wall.

There were good hand-holds and I was soon up, emerging from the gorge on to a beautiful little alp, ablaze with flowers, of which *geraniums, potentillas* and *polygonums* formed the majority. But the rock gardener must needs turn from such flamboyant beauty to the humble little plants that seek refuge amidst the crags, and on the crest of the cliff I had climbed I found a cushion-plant with a host of white flowers with yellow and red throats (*Androsace Chamaejasme*). For my part,

I would not readily exchange the exotic gardens of a Mogul Emperor for a sight of these little plants that lift their starry heads close to the eternal snows.

It was a beautiful afternoon, for the weather had recovered its good humour, and I spent a delightful hour on the alp, lounging on my back amid the flowers and looking across the Banke Glacier to the ice-crowned precipices of Rataban gleaming in the afternoon sun as though built of liquid but immobile silver.

I did not return by the way I had come, but by another route which crossed the alp above the gorge, and after traversing a narrow ledge, descended pastry-like rocks and steep screes to the camp.

That evening we made ourselves comfortable round a fire of juniper. This shrub has a smell which I shall always associate with travel in the Himalayas, and I have only to sniff the smoke of it to be transported in an instant back to the camp fire. Someone threw some branches into the centre of the fire, and with a roaring crackle a great gust of flame illumined the faces of my companions. The tents stood out sharply and in the background the dim hillsides rose on their long climb towards the stars.

Alam Singh arrived back soon after dark, bringing with him onions, flour and a spinach-like vegetable, but alas no chickens or eggs. More porters' food was required, and it was arranged that Tewang, who was obviously unfit for high altitude work, should descend to Gamsali for it and hire a porter to carry it up, whilst Alam Singh was engaged to transport wood to the lower camps, as it was necessary to husband our petrol and paraffin.

We were off at 7 next morning in doubtful-looking weather. On the slopes below the gorge we halted to collect juniper, after which I ascended the side of the gorge, taking some rope with me, whilst Peter remained below to shepherd the men, whose heavy loads made the ascent very awkward for them. It was not thought necessary to rope them until they reached the point where the route lay straight up the wall of the gorge, but I realised that this was a mistake when I saw Ang Bao struggling to hoist himself and his load up a place which was entirely without difficulty for an unladen man. Peter could not see this from his position, nor could he hear my shouts, owing to the roar of the torrent. With great anxiety I watched the little man striving desperately to balance up on a foothold over a sheer 200-foot drop, and great was my relief when I saw him reach safety. He was evidently a poor rock climber or else overloaded, for the other men made light of the place. Peter roped the men together and I threw them down the end of the 100-foot rope. After this it was plain sailing and at length everyone was on the alp, except Alam Singh, who resolutely refused to have anything to do with the rope, for which he obviously entertained the gravest suspicion, and who eventually succeeded in scaling in his bare feet an entirely different route to the right over some smooth and awkward slabs.

The ascent to the alp had occupied well over two hours, as against the half-hour I had taken when climbing by myself. Such transport difficulties all too often lead to modification of plans in the Himalayas, and so it was in this instance. The preliminary difficulty seemed to have taken the heart out of the men and they climbed very slowly up the easy slopes above the alp. Alam Singh was even slower, and found it necessary to sit down and rest about every fifty yards. It was exasperating when we were anxious to get on and place our first camp as near to the plateau as possible.

Presently, mists gathered, and drizzling rain began to fall.

The flowers were interesting and beautiful. I well remember a rocky place, where water seeped over some slabs, tufted a brilliant green with moss between which, in cracks of the rock, bloomed thousands of yellow *androsaces*. Then, in the screes, were many plants of the same *delphinium* we had seen below the Bhyundar Pass and in turfy places numerous *sedums*, with here and there a woolly *saussurea*. But the most striking flower of all was a *pleurospermum* (*P. Candollii*). An illustration, even a coloured illustration, would probably convey the impression that this flower is interesting rather than beautiful, yet of the many flowers that I saw in Garhwal, there was none that attracted me more. It is one foot or less in height, and at the end of a stout and hollow stem the flower stalks branch outwards in all directions, supporting wide-open white flowers delicately frilled at the edges and with numerous stamens, ending in dark-coloured anthers. Nothing remarkable, you may say, but you must see this plant on a misty day, when it seems to attract the distant sunlight to itself, so that its thin almost transparent petals glow as though illumined from behind. Even if you have little or no interest in flowers, it demands that you pause and pay tribute to its beauty and to the Divinity that raised it among the barren rocks.

We camped at about 15,500 feet, much lower than we had hoped, on a stony desolate place near the steep tongue of a minor glacier. Everyone was wet and miserable, and Peter and I came to the conclusion that we should have to lighten the loads considerably on the morrow and work out in detail a system of relays, else we should not succeed in getting anywhere near the Mana Peak. Rain continued to fall steadily for the remainder of the day, but we had a tent each, which was some comfort. I lay in my sleeping-bag reading Mr. Richard Aldington's cynical book " Death of a Hero." It is an admirable work but I should have preferred Mr. P. G. Wodehouse on this occasion. Ang Bao evidently found the conditions equally depressing, for he did not shine as a cook that evening and the formless lumps of mutton he produced were only fit to strop a kukri. As a result Peter and I had a bad night ; I did not sleep at all but lay awake, as I often used to lie awake on Mount Everest at much greater heights, marvelling at my folly for voluntarily exchanging the comforts of civilisation for the discomforts of the high mountains. Many have marvelled thus, yet they return ; no one has ever satisfactorily explained why.

The weather was still misty next morning but the rain had stopped. Having sent back Alam Singh, who was more of a hindrance than a help, and sorted out the food and equipment we were to take on with us, we set off to the plateau.

Our way lay up a bold moraine on which numerous plants grew, including *Androsace Chamaejasme* and a delightful *saxifrage* (*S. Hirculus*) with yellow petals red at the base and stems covered in rust-coloured hairs.

The moraine ended in a snowy corridor which brought us without difficulty to the foot of a glacier tongue of bare ice, where Peter, who was thirsting for some step-cutting, went ahead and hewed out a staircase. It took an hour to get the men up, after which we found ourselves on a snow-field. Ascending this we halted for some food on a patch of rocks, then continued across another snow-field, which is separated from the main ice-fall of the plateau by a ridge where we saw a cairn, evidently erected by Gardiner. We followed this ridge for a short distance, then traversed horizontally to the plateau, which is here considerably crevassed and broken and which, as already mentioned, is a glacier system with a series of snow-fields at its head. We were able to avoid the crevasses by ascending snow-slopes under an overhanging rock face and presently came to a shelf formed by the lower lip of a wide crevasse, a short distance below the first major snow-field. Here we decided to camp, as the day was well advanced, the weather was once again deteriorating and the men had to return to the first camp by a route which might be difficult to follow in the event of a blizzard. Our tents were pitched entrance to entrance for the sake of convenience, and after we had collected some water from a stream on the neighbouring cliff we retired to our sleeping-bags.

Snow fell lightly for the remainder of the afternoon. I cooked the supper. I cannot remember exactly what I cooked, but I suspect it was a hash of some kind. I am rather good at hashes. There is nothing difficult or niggling about them, no take this and take that and weigh this and weigh that; yet there is a complex grandeur in my hashes which Mrs. Beeton at her best could hardly hope to emulate. My record hash was compounded of eighteen ingredients; I remember it well because I was sick afterwards.

Cooking in a small tent is a filthy business. To begin with, it has to be performed while lying in a sleeping-bag. This affords scope for a professional contortionist, and it often happens that when balancing some tinful of liquid in an awkward and constrained position, one is seized by a violent attack of cramp. But I anticipate; first of all the stove must be lit, and not only lit but kept alight. We had a " Primus " with a burner adapted for use at high altitudes. A " Primus " is far and away the best cooker for Himalayan mountaineer-

ing and is infinitely better than a methylated or solid
methylated cooker, but good though it is, it is subject
to its high altitude tantrums, and if you endeavour to
light it too soon, it fills the tent with noisome fumes
which send you coughing and choking into the open
air.   The tremendous temptation to pump it vigorously
to start with must be resisted, for this is a cardinal
mistake ; the burner lights for a fleeting instant then
goes out and a vast cloud of smoke rises like a volcanic
blast from the apparatus :  strike a match incautiously
and the tent is liable to explode.   A " Primus " must
be humoured, and be worked up gently to do its job.   It
may be cajoled, but never bullied.   It suffers from only
one ailment, a more or less chronic quinsy, and it is
advisable to have an instrument known as a pricker
handy in case, at a critical moment when the hash is
nicely simmering, it chokes and suffocates.   Its diges-
tion is remarkably good, and it can assimilate with
equal ease paraffin, petrol or a mixture of both these
fuels.   Whether it is as accommodating as a Diesel
engine I do not know ;  I have not yet tried one with
whisky, brandy, lubricating oil or treacle.

   After dark the sky cleared suddenly, revealing a
starlit expanse of glacier, and the dim forms of peaks
beyond it.   The night was very cold, the coldest we
had yet had, and a damp chill struck up from the
snow through the floors of our tents.

   At 4 a.m. I set the " Primus " going and we breakfasted.   The sky was unclouded and dawn showed
calmly behind a range of sharp rock-peaks.   The sun
struck the camp at 5.15, and a few minutes later we
left, intending to reconnoitre and if possible climb an
unnamed peak of 21,400 feet on the ridge separating
the plateau from the East Kamet Glacier, the view
from which should enable us to form an opinion as to

whether the two higher peaks of 22,481 feet and 22,892 feet between it and the Mana Peak could be outflanked.

After zig-zagging between crevasses we came to the first of the major snow-fields, whence we saw that the peak was obviously accessible from a col immediately to the east of it and between it and Peak 20,557 feet. We were now able to appreciate for the first time the beauty and extent of the plateau. Westwards it stretched beneath Peak 21,400 feet to the foot of an ice-fall above which there was evidently a further snow-field, and southwards we looked over a snowy rim and the concealed Banke Valley to Rataban, Gauri Parbat, Hathi Parbat and the far blue ridges of Trisul, Dunagiri and Nanda Devi.

Having crossed the snow-field, we followed a ridge of broken rocks where we came upon one of Gardiner's camping sites, and a two-gallon tin of petrol more than half full. This petrol was a godsend as it meant that strict fuel rationing was no longer necessary.

From the surveyors' camp we ascended some rocks and trudged up a snow-slope. Conditions were excellent and we climbed fast, perhaps too fast for I developed a headache and felt slightly sick, though I suspect this was due to the fumes of the " Primus " which filled my tent while I was cooking the breakfast.

Although the surveyors had ascended these slopes several weeks previously their tracks were still distinct, a proof that only a small quantity of snow had fallen in this district during the early months of the summer. At the head of the snow-slope on the ridge overlooking the East Kamet Glacier is a small island of rock which had been visited by Gardiner and had probably served as one of his survey stations, as it commands a superb view. From it we looked down a precipice over 3,000 feet high to the East Kamet Glacier which, with its sinuous curves and level lines of moraines, resembled some vast arterial road. At the head of it stood Kamet in all its superb beauty and majesty. It was the finest view I have ever had of the mountain and I could trace out the route by which we had climbed it in 1931. Five of a party of six Europeans had reached the summit, together with two porters of whom the Sirdar, Lewa, had been so badly frostbitten that he had lost all his toes. That was the only unhappy memory, but it would take more than the loss of toes to dishearten or incapacitate a man of Lewa's calibre and he had accompanied the 1933 Everest Expedition.

I had not anticipated when I climbed Kamet that a few years later I should be attempting the equally fine Mana Peak. From our position the peak was plainly visible beyond three intervening peaks, the 21,400-feet peak which rose immediately above us, and the two peaks of 22,481 feet and 22,892 feet. As we had anticipated, there was no hope whatever of outflanking these to the north for all fell sheer to the East Kamet Glacier thousands of feet below. The wall bounding that glacier to the south extends for a distance of seven or eight miles, and is unassailable from the north. Ours was a unique position on the crest of it, yet in a depression which enabled us to appreciate to the full the grandeur of ice-cliff and precipice down which avalanches roar and smoke, whilst close at hand was the *névé* of Peak 21,400 feet, riven and rent into square-cut turrets the size of cathedrals—altogether a splendid scene of mountain savagery and frigid beauty.

A cold little wind presently decided us to continue with the ascent of Peak 21,400 feet. There was no difficulty whatsoever in the climb, which lay up a slope of snow about 1,200 feet in height. As we had ascended very quickly to the ridge we decided to go slowly, and taking turns at the step-making mounted at the rate of about 1,000 feet an hour. As we climbed the sky clouded over and by the time we reached the summit, which consists of an almost level snow-field an acre or two in extent, a level canopy of cloud truncated all the higher peaks to the south and east. Yet if the view in most directions was disappointing, there was one mountain which showed to great advantage, Nilgiri Parbat. Only the uppermost portion was visible, the great slope on which Wangdi, Nurbu and I had laboured so long, but it seemed to float up in the mist sunlit and serene, as though annexed permanently to the heavenly regions.

Unfortunately we could see little of the plateau or the ridges to the west of our peak. Soon mists began to form about us, and a cold damp wind rustled across the snow. There was no object in prolonging our stay and in five minutes we pelted down slopes that had taken over an hour to climb, then strolled back to the camp.

It was typical monsoon weather : a fine morning, then rapidly forming mists, and a snowstorm in the afternoon, which rendered the remainder of the day in camp thoroughly disagreeable. As previously arranged, three of the men, Wangdi, Pasang and Tse Tendrup, had ascended from the first camp with a second relay of loads, leaving Ang Bao and Nurbu to descend to the base camp for the extra coolie food which was being brought up from Gamsali.

The advent of the porters meant that we needed no longer to cook for ourselves. The chief objection to cooking in the high Himalayas, apart from the work it involves, is the mess and the dirt, and the floor of a tent soon becomes filthy with congealed samples of various foods. The carbon formed by burning petrol and

paraffin is peculiarly obnoxious in this respect. Washing
is impracticable, as water obtained by melting snow over
a cooker is far too precious to be used thus, and the
skin quickly becomes ingrained with dirt whilst finger-
nails go into profound mourning. But my most disagreeable memory in connection with this business of
eating and drinking at high altitudes is of washing up.
This is accomplished by rubbing the pots, pans, plates
and other utensils with snow, a chilly, uncomfortable
and altogether loathsome task. Sherpa and Bhotia
porters, on the other hand, regard cooking from an
entirely different angle. Like children they love to be
given opportunities of making a first-class mess. I
honestly believe that these men are positively unhappy
if accommodated in a clean tent and told not to dirty
it, in which respect they resemble the slum-dweller,
who when transferred to a new tenement promptly
proceeds to use the bath as a convenient receptacle for
coal. Another thing that the Himalayan porter loves
is a fug in his tent, and there is no doubt that cooking
greatly assists in the formation of this. On such an
occasion, the interior of a porter's tent must be experienced to be believed, for the atmosphere generated
is of such density that it seems almost possible to cut
it up into lumps and throw it out of the entrance. This
love of a fug is common among mountain folk and
mountaineers. To my mind, people who pretend to
revel in draughts and cold rooms, who impinge on their
friends at the breakfast table with a horrible heartiness
and in general adopt such manners and costumes as
are most likely to impress on all and sundry their
hardihood and devotion to the open air, ought to be
put away in some special fresh-air asylum where they
may indulge their horrid practices to their hearts'
content.

Perhaps the greatest menace of all is the man, and not infrequently the woman, who insists on filling an already freezing railway carriage with a violent draught, then revels like the sadist he is in the acute discomfort of his fellow-passengers. The Direktion of the Lindenalp Railway settled this vexed question once and for all when they put up the notice :

In the event of a dispute between passengers as to whether the window shall be open or shut, the dispute shall be referred to the conductor, and the window then shut.

I think it was Dr. Howard Somervell who told me that he was once travelling in comfort with the window shut when an old gentleman got in at a station and, after fidgeting and shuffling in that manner peculiar to a fresh-air fiend, said irascibly : " I really must insist on that window being opened." Had he spoken politely, no doubt a compromise would have been effected : as it was the window remained shut. This led to a tirade in which such expressions as " Degenerate young men of the present day " were employed freely. It is a pity that this indignant old gentleman got out at the next station without knowing that he was speaking to one of the toughest and finest mountaineers of the post-war era who had only recently returned from a Mount Everest Expedition. If he has not since died of chronic bronchitis, pneumonia or rheumatic fever, I hope that he will chance upon these lines.

Next morning, August 2nd, we set out to establish another camp. The weather was in poor shape and in a thick mist we groped our way up the first snow-field, steering with the aid of a compass and a detailed and excellent sketch-map supplied by Gardiner. Without the latter, it is probable that we should have kept too far to the south and have got into difficulty on Peak

20,087 feet, which rises from the southernmost edge of the plateau. As it was we were able to make our way through the ice-fall above the first snow-field to another snow-field, which lies to the south of Peak 21,400 feet. Now and again, when the mists thinned, we could see the slopes of this peak to our right, and were careful to keep well away from the base of it, in case of ice avalanches.

We took it in turns to lead and Peter steered a skilful course through the crevasses of the ice-fall, but when my turn came on the snow-field above, I was soon told that I was describing a circle. One reason for bearing off the compass course was the unexpected presence of steep slopes where we had expected none. There was no debris on the glacier to indicate that ice avalanches fall from these, but it seemed advisable to keep well away from them. Up to this point we had made, as was revealed later, an excellent line, but we were now beyond the point we had seen during the previous day's climbing and also, we believed, beyond the farthest point reached by Gardiner. All about us was mist and a waste of snow, and not a landmark was to be seen. Our position was analogous to that of a blind man searching for a black cat on a dark night. Nothing was to be gained by blundering on, and we decided to camp until the weather cleared, so our single tent was pitched and the porters sent back to the second camp.

It was an unusual experience to camp without knowing in the least where we were, and we awaited the lifting of the mists with a feeling akin to that of a child who is all agog for the curtain to rise on the first act of a pantomime. We had not very long to wait. At 4 p.m. the mists began to break up ; a rift of sky showed and against it a sunlit edge of snow. Quickly now the mists melted away, and the almost level snow-field on which we were camped shone out in virgin splendour and beauty.

Immediately to the west of the camp was a snow-ridge easily accessible at one point where it sank down almost to the level of the snow-field, and we set out to investigate what lay beyond it.

The sun was fast sinking as we mounted a slope to a shallow col in the ridge. The view from this col is for ever impressed on my memory. The ridge runs roughly from north to south and is interposed between the snow-field on which our camp was pitched and a snow-field enclosed between Peaks 21,400 feet and 22,481 feet. The last mentioned snow-field is not part of the glacier up which we had come, but forms the head of a glacier descending to join the Banke Glacier.

From the col, a slope about 200 feet in height falls to an extraordinarily steep and broken ice-fall in which the snow-field breaks away at its southernmost edge. Mist still lay below our level and now and then tongues of it licked up the ice-fall between towers of ice to be illumined suddenly and brilliantly by the reddening sun, so that the ice-fall flamed and smoked like a witch's cauldron.

The snow-field above the ice-fall afforded a superb contrast to this savage and uneasy scene, for its level and unbroken expanse stretched calm and serene like a cloth of pure silver. At its westernmost extremity Peak 22,481 feet stood deeply shadowed with a thin wispy cloud, brilliantly sunlit, stealing across it. Here and there other clouds were stationary in a sky of tur-quoise-blue like yachts waiting for a fair wind, and in the south enormous masses and banks of monsoon cumu-lus were ranged along the distant foothills and the peaks of Nanda Devi.

As the sun slipped down behind Peak 22,481 feet

the vast snow-fields about us glowed with an unearthly light. It was a scene that might have been borrowed from an Antarctic plateau and we had much the same feeling of remoteness that the Polar explorer experiences, for no valleys were visible and we gazed over unending wastes of snow and ice, a superlatively majestic vista as restful to the spirit as it was cruel and hostile to the flesh.

We returned to camp moderately satisfied with our reconnaissance. The snow-field we had seen was easily accessible, but as to what lay beyond it, and whether Peak 22,481 feet could be turned to the south, we could only conjecture. Was there another snow-field between it and Peak 22,892 feet? If so, would it be possible to traverse this to the east ridge of the Mana Peak? It was evident that we should have to lengthen our communications considerably and another two camps at least would be necessary. Taking all in all our chances of climbing the Mana Peak from this direction were now very remote.

# CHAPTER XIX

## PEAK 22,481 FEET

THE improvement in the weather was only temporary, and next morning mist again concealed everything. Inactivity was distasteful, and though we should not in any event be able to pitch a fourth camp until the morrow, as the porters would be occupied in relaying stores from the second camp, we decided to make certain of the route to the snow-field. Accordingly, we re-ascended the col and followed the sharp crest of the snow-ridge to the north of it until we came to a place whence it was possible to descend to the snow-field above the ice-fall.

The porters arrived during the day, so that everything was ready to advance the camp on the morrow. Once again the mists cleared and a calm evening was succeeded by a night of intense frost. August 4th dawned brilliantly clear and we were off at 6.30. An inch or so of snow had fallen in the past two or three days, and this had frozen into a light crystalline powder that glittered and sparkled in the sun. It was a morning to delight a photographer, and Peter and I busied ourselves with our cameras during the traverse of the ridge on to the snow-field. Every vestige of haze had disappeared and all of the greater peaks were visible, including Trisul, Nanda Devi and the mountains in the neighbourhood of the Milam Glacier. The finest of all the peaks in the vicinity of the Banke Glacier was Nilgiri Parbat. Mists swathed its lower shoulders, but the upper ice-slope, now so familiar, stood out above them like a tempestuous wave, frozen as it was about the curl over and break. Seldom is the photographer presented with such perfect lighting and beautifully arranged composition and though no photograph can do justice to the grandeur and ethereal beauty of such a scene the photograph I was able to secure does suggest the splendour of this noble mountain.

As we trudged across the snow-field I was reminded of a similar trudge early one morning in the Bernese Oberland over the Ewig Schneefeld, for there is a strong similarity between the " Field of Eternal Snow " and this Himalayan snow-field.

The snow-field sloped gently to the west for three-quarters of the distance, then more steeply to another minor ridge at the foot of Peak 22,481 feet. We gained the ridge without difficulty, and looked expectantly beyond it to the west. We hoped to see another snow-field enabling us to outflank Peak 22,481 feet, but in this we were disappointed. From the ridge, steep snow-slopes fall to the west, and it would be necessary to descend these for some distance before continuing the traverse. Then came a ridge with a steep ice-slope which could not be avoided. Was there an easy route beyond it and was it justifiable to force a route over such difficult terrain ? To do so would mean cutting ourselves off from our base for an indefinite length of time and extending our communications to an unjustifiable length. What would happen in the event of bad weather preventing a retreat for several days ? We were a light party with neither sufficient food nor equipment for prolonged siege tactics. I think we both realised that the game was up and that the Mana Peak was inaccessible from the east.

The sole remaining hope was a higher route past

Peak 22,481 feet. We had taken only two and a half hours to the ridge, so decided to camp in a sheltered hollow, and the same day attempt the ascent of this peak, the view from which should reveal once and for all whether or not there was a hope of approaching the Mana Peak from the east.

It was not an ideal site for a camp, for the slopes of the hollow reflected the sun with terrific heat, so that we felt like flies beneath a burning-glass, but it was better than the wind-swept crest of the ridge. A drink of tea and we were ready to begin the ascent. Meanwhile, the men returned to the third camp with instructions to return with the remaining food and equipment on the morrow, though in case bad weather should isolate us at this camp we had brought up food and fuel for several days.

The easiest route to the top of Peak 22,481 feet is over the south ridge. Unfortunately, with that perverseness characteristic of the monsoon season, mists were already gathering and by the time we had climbed 500 feet of easy slopes we were unable to see whether or not it was possible to continue the route in the direction of the Mana Peak. For 1,000 feet there was no difficulty whatsoever, then the ridge narrowed and rose in an unclimbable rock step. To avoid this we had to ascend an ice-slope to the right. The ice was steep and peculiarly glutinous and many strokes of the axe were required to fashion a step. But if it was hard work for me, it was an equally tedious business for Peter, who for the next hour had to stand in his steps while paying out the rope inch by inch.

Not far from the top of the slope was a shallow scoop that had to be crossed diagonally. In negotiating this my arms became tired and my axe seemed very unready to do its work, but the steps were made at last, and with a feeling of intense relief at having accomplished as strenuous a piece of ice work as I have done in the Himalayas, I secured myself to a rock and, seated in comfort, took in the rope as Peter ascended.

Thenceforwards the ridge consisted of broken rocks and snow. The mists gathered more densely as we climbed and we reached the shoulder in a desultory snow-storm. The final ridge, which runs almost due west from the summit, is broken up into minor pinnacles. For the most part we were able to follow the crest, but in one or two places were forced to forsake it and traverse to one side or the other of the pinnacles. There was no great individual difficulty, but the sum of all the difficulties made a formidable total for a climb at this altitude.

The rock-ridge abutted against the final peak which, though steeper, was less difficult. We climbed slowly, for we were tired, and it was a relief when at length the ridge no longer rose before us but eased off gently into a horizontal snow edge forming the summit.

There was no view, yet we were conscious of standing on a high and isolated peak. We could not see, but we could sense, the precipices that fall for thousands of feet to the East Kamet Glacier. With a chill little wind blowing, there was no inducement to stay, and with common accord we turned and commenced the descent.

The sole difficulty was the ice-slope, where seeping water had damaged the steps. The arduous task of cutting them anew was undertaken by Peter, whom I held from the rocks above while seated in a cold wind, which bombarded me with hail and snow. When my turn came to descend I found that already many steps were unsafe owing to the rapid flow of water, and I must have exasperated my companion by re-cutting them. Descending steep ice is never pleasant when the legs are tired, and the slow balancing movement from one step to the next imposes a greater strain on the knee than in any other form of climbing. The reader can verify this for himself by standing with the toes of one foot on the extreme edge of a high step for a minute or two, then very slowly stepping down with the other foot and gradually transferring the weight. To do this for an hour or two not only provides an excellent illustration but is one of the best training exercises for mountaineering I know.

Back at the camp we imbibed pints of tea and were soon telling one another what a grand climb it had been. Fortunate indeed is man that he can forget so soon the physical stresses of life and remember only the greater blessings of his strenuous endeavours.

Once again the mists cleared in the night and next morning, August 5th, in fair weather we retraced our steps up the lower slopes of Peak 22,481 feet until we were about 500 feet above the camp, then traversed horizontally across a broad ill-defined ridge to a corner, whence we were able to see all that lay beyond.

The Mana Peak is not accessible from the east. We stood on the edge of a semi-circle of precipices, enclosing the head of a deeply cut glacier, on the far side of which rose Peak 22,892 feet, a fang of ice cutting sharply into the morning sky. There was no possibility whatever of further advance, for the precipice fell sheer at our feet to the glacier in vast sheets of ice broken by belts of rock slabs. Even supposing that the col between Peaks 22,481 feet and 22,892 feet could be reached, the traverse of the latter peak would be by itself a long and difficult expedition. We were beaten and must attempt the Mana Peak from some other direction.

Now that there was no further need to concentrate

on one task we were able to take stock of our surroundings. A labyrinth of peaks lay before us, sharply cut, wall-sided peaks with razor-like edges rising from unseen glaciers. Over them our vision passed to the peaks of Badrinath, and the glorious isolated pyramid of Nilkanta. Fleecy cloudlets were slowly sailing along the Alaknanda Valley and in the south a great wall of luminous monsoon mist rested on the foothills. Over 4,000 feet beneath was the Banke Glacier, banded with orderly moraines, sweeping round in parabolic curve between ranks of splendid peaks whose innumerable edges, domes, towers and spires shone serenely in the warm sunlight.

We had failed to climb the Mana Peak from the Banke Plateau, but we had been richly rewarded in other ways and the interesting and beautiful views we had enjoyed during the past few days amply compensated us for any momentary disappointment.

The porters arrived at the camp soon after we returned. It was sad to tell them when they had carried up so many heavy loads that we had failed, but I think they accepted failure as inevitable, for so experienced a mountaineer as Wangdi must have realised already that we were still far from the Mana Peak.

It was necessary to evacuate the camps as quickly as possible, and this meant that everyone must carry a very heavy load. A drink of tea and we set about the task of packing up the tent and stores. This done, we set off to the third camp, at which a single tent was added to the loads. Some lunch, and we continued down to the second camp. None of us were enamoured of this cold desolate site, and Wangdi suggested that we should add still further to our mountainous loads and carry on down to the ridge where the surveyors had camped ; though Peter and I felt as though our necks and shoulder muscles had been branded with red-hot irons.

After several days camping on snow, it was a relief to camp on rocks, for these are always warmer than snow and usually less exposed to strong winds. There were plants on the ridge : a little *draba* (*D. incompta*) and a *saussurea*, with a purple flower in the midst of silvery wool-like foliage. As the men pitched the tents, we spied the unfortunate Nurbu and Ang Bao, toiling up the glacier with additional stores from the base camp, but I suspect that any grief they may have felt for a day of useless work was mitigated by the thought that they would have to go down, not up, on the morrow.

The difference between camping at 20,000 feet and camping at 17,000 feet in the Himalayas is astonishing. An appetite for food, and a capacity for sound, restful sleep, are possible at the lower altitude whereas both are absent at the higher. Medical authorities have put 21,000 feet as the highest altitude at which it is possible to live for a considerable time without serious physical or mental deterioration, but I would place 19,000 feet as the limit in this respect, at all events as regards my own capacities. A great deal of nonsense is talked about the effects of altitude, such as the Italian contention that Addis Ababa is too high from a physical standpoint as their capital in Abyssinia, though undoubtedly the palm must be given to the dear old lady who came fluttering up to Mr. Hugh Ruttledge after his return from Everest, exclaiming : "*I* can understand what you have gone through at those terrible heights. I live at Crowborough." *

Next day we descended to the base camp, and very pleasant it was to get down to the flowers and the balmy

* This reminds me of another dear old lady who said : " So you are going to Everest ; it must be *quite* in the wilds."

air of the Banke Valley. After so many strenuous days, a rest day for the porters, at least, was essential. Both of us had been burned, in spite of copious applications of face cream, for several days on Himalayan snow-fields under almost vertical suns would cause discomfort to an armadillo, and our throats were a trifle sore, due possibly to breathing continuously through the mouth.

Tewang was no better. He was occasionally spitting blood and there was something evidently seriously wrong with him. We decided to send him down without delay to Joshimath, where there is a hospital whence he could be forwarded to Ranikhet and Darjeeling.* As we would have to engage a substitute at the first opportunity we were forced to deprive him of his climbing boots. As already mentioned, he had cherished these with an abounding love, and it went very much against the grain to surrender them. He was allowed, however, to keep his climbing suit, as we had enough spare clothing to equip his successor. The remainder of the Darjeeling men were remarkably callous as to the plight of their companion. They do not understand sickness until afflicted themselves and Wangdi, although he had gone down with double pneumonia on Mount Everest in 1933, despised the invalid for an indisposition that did not allow him to take part in the more strenuous affairs of the expedition and more than once darkly hinted that he was shamming.

So ended our first round with the Mana Peak. We had been afforded an example of the necessity for prolonged reconnoitring in the Himalayas before attempting the ascent of a major peak, and reconnoitring is half the fun and interest of Himalayan mountaineering.

* His trouble turned out to be a mild but chronic bronchitis.

# CHAPTER XX

## THE MANA PEAK:
## THE RECONNAISSANCE

GARDINER had written that he did not think the Mana Peak was accessible from the south ; therefore, all we could hope for was a reconnaissance from the head of the Banke Glacier. We would then follow his route across the Zaskar Range via the Zaskar Pass, 18,992 feet, to the south of the mountain, and descend to Badrinath. For this we needed about one week's food, and the day after we returned to the base camp Wangdi descended to Gamsali for some more sattoo for the porters, and two men to help carry the loads over the pass to Badrinath.

Two days at the base camp gave me time to examine and collect plants in the Banke Valley. As previously mentioned, the climate of this valley is distinctly drier than that of the Bhyundar Valley, as it is less exposed to the monsoon current. Actually I observed few plants which I had not already seen, or was later to see, in the Bhyundar Valley, but it was noticeable that the flora was more advanced than in the latter valley and that flowers which do not normally bloom until late August or early September in the south of Garhwal, bloom here in late July and early August. The valley's proximity to Tibet must have something to do with this, for in that arid country it is remarkable how plants leap into growth during the early part of the monsoon, and it needs but a fortnight of moist warm air to convert an

apparently barren waste into a carpet of flowers. This
haste in plants to perpetuate themselves is doubtless
because of the shortness of the summer season between
the cold winds of spring and autumn. Well to the
south of the Himalayan watershed the summer is longer
and plants need not hasten to complete their cycle of
growth.

I found an excellent instance of this in a lettuce
(*Lactuca Lesserliana*). I was nosing about some rocks
not far from the camp when I noticed a purple flower
on a cliff above me. Not having seen it before, I climbed
up to it over steep and difficult rocks. I need not have
given myself so much trouble, for six weeks later when I
returned to the Bhyundar Valley, I found it growing
in its millions on a slope near the base camp where it
had but recently come into bloom. Another proof of
the greater dryness and possibly windiness of the Banke
Valley as compared with the Bhyundar Valley was
afforded by the large number of cushion plants such as
*saxifrages* and *androsaces*. Except at greater elevations
I did not see such compact foliage in the Bhyundar
Valley. It is impossible that these little cushions
covered all over in almost stalkless starry flowers can
retain their delightful characteristics in the warm moist
climate of Britain; they must inevitably become
lank and attenuated. Yet the gardener can scarcely
grumble; that a plant flourishing at a height greater
than Mont Blanc should grow at all in our climate
pertains to the miraculous.

The weather was now excellent and Peter and I spent
two delightful days at the base camp. Late the second
day, when night had fallen and we were enjoying the
warmth of a fire, Wangdi reappeared together with two
men he had secured at Gamsali. It had not been an
easy task to find porters and these two had only con-

sented to come when he had promised them that they would be engaged for the remainder of the expedition, and be provided with boots and equipment at Badrinath, promises he had no authority whatsoever to make and which as he knew could not be kept. At all events here they were and everything was now ready for our first march up the Banke Glacier on the morrow.

The weather was in cheerful vein when, on the morning of August 8th, we began the ascent of the glacier. A rough shepherd's track followed along the northern bank, sometimes on the crest of the side moraine and sometimes in a corridor, gay with *potentillas* and *allardias*, between the glacier and the hillside. This track continued as far as the shepherds' highest bivouac place, Eri Udiar, but beyond this there is no track and the traveller must fend for himself in a wilderness of stones and moraine.

We made excellent progress, but had to halt many times for the porters, who were continually retarded by the slowness of the two local men. At his best, the Marcha Bhotia is slow compared with the Sherpa or Bhotia (Tibetan). Instead of completing a march in a reasonable time and enjoying a long rest during the afternoon and evening, he prefers to loiter along throughout the day regardless of rain, snow or any other inconvenience. This may suit his book, but it is exasperating to his employers, and I know of no sterner test of patience than to travel with these men.

About Eri Udiar, the Banke Glacier sweeps round almost at a right angle, and the traveller leaves the side of it in favour of a route which cuts across the perimeter of the bend. The ascent was unexpectedly easy, though there was a good deal of up and down going on mounds of moraine which varied from 50 to 100 feet in height. By the time we had turned the corner it was evident that bad weather was brewing, but not even the eloquence of Peter, who has a fluent command of Urdu, could coax the two Gamsali men and they became slower and slower and their halts more frequent. I was ahead, finding the best route through a tangle of moraines, when a shout announced that they had halted once and for all. It was impossible to persuade them to continue. Not for any quantity of clothing, boots or baksheesh would they have ventured farther. They were beyond the grazing grounds ; no one from their village had ever penetrated so far up the glacier ; it was a country of spirits, demons, dragons and psychic phenomena of all kinds. There was nothing to be done ; they returned and their loads were distributed between us and our own long-suffering porters. Wangdi was furious, and if looks could have killed Gamsali would have been two short in its population register. So once more Peter and I trudged along with well-filled rucksacks, and I remember thinking then, and on other occasions too, that the cult of the small expedition can be overdone and that there are occasions when it has its distinct disadvantages.

The mists drooped lower and a blue veil of rain swept down the valley. It was gone within half an hour, leaving the sun to shine brightly through heaped-up masses of cloud. We camped where the surveyors had camped on a medial moraine of the glacier and were cheered a little at finding a load of wood they had left there. But I for one was in a thoroughly bad temper. Perhaps the stones had something to do with this, for nothing is more trying to the temper than a day spent pounding over loose stones. I have never forgotten Bentley Beauman's remarks on this subject in 1931 when for two days we marched up the stony floor of the Arwa Valley. Shakespeare could not have surpassed him in adjectival or epithetical force on the subject of stones.

There was more desultory rain, more doubtful sun and swirling mists, then with magical suddenness the evening cleared, the mists vanished into a frosty atmosphere and, far above, the great boiler-plate precipices the ice-cliffs of Nilgiri Parbat gleamed in the setting sun.

The night was cold and was rendered uncomfortable for me by the puncturing of my air mattress. Air mattresses are very light and provide an excellent insulation between the body and the ground, but once they are punctured, they are very difficult to repair, as not even immersion in water will reveal a small hole. Furthermore, it takes time to become accustomed to them, as if they are blown up too tight they are very uncomfortable, whilst if they are not blown up enough the ground impinges on the hips. Now that I was on the ground, I found it uncommonly hard, and spent a good part of the night fiddling about trying to remove innumerable angular stones from beneath the floor of the tent.

The morning was cloudless and had it not been for our heavy loads we might have enjoyed better the day's march. Beyond the camp, we passed beneath Nilgiri Parbat, the tremendous cliffs of which are crowned by immense walls of ice, which now and again collapse and send avalanches roaring and smoking towards the glacier. Four miles to the north-west of Nilgiri Parbat, and on the same ridge overlooking the Banke Glacier, is an unnamed peak of 21,516 feet, which is characterised by a fluted ice face. Ice flutings are common in the Eastern and Western Himalayas, but are seldom seen in the Central Himalayas. They are formed by a constant downrush of avalanches which carve out parallel channels separated by thin edges of ice : the effect is very striking and adds greatly to the beauty of a mountain. In the present instance, however, the flutings had been weathered into parallel series of ice-pinnacles, in much the same way that earth-pinnacles, of which there are excellent examples in the Alps, are formed by denudation and weathering. The pinnacles were remarkable for their height, which cannot have been less than 100 feet, and must have been more in a great many instances, and for the manner in which they clung to the steep face of the mountain. With the sun shining upon them, they presented a strange scene and reminded us of the ice-pinnacles of the East Rongbuk Glacier, between which the mountaineer passes on his way to Everest. It would be interesting to know why this is the only fluted peak in the district. The pinnacles were on a north-facing slope, and but little exposed to the full power of the sun. Possibly some air-current was responsible, but I could think of no complete explanation for their presence.

It was a relief when after a march of three miles the moraines petered out at the foot of an ice-fall. The latter was not in the least difficult, and soon we were above it on the uppermost ice of the glacier, whence it is nothing but a walk to the Zaskar Pass.

As we had planned to reach the pass on the morrow there was no object in proceeding farther, and we camped on a convenient side moraine. The Mana Peak was in view and exhibited its south ridge almost in profile. If the crest could be gained there was a possibility that the summit would prove accessible, but we disliked the look of an apparently vertical step about 1,000 feet from the summit. There was no hope of gaining the ridge from the Banke Glacier as it ended in a buttress, really a separate point of 20,675 feet, whence impracticable precipices fell sheer to the glacier. It was equally inaccessible from the south-east or east, for there, apart from terrific steepness, hanging glaciers swept every line of approach with their avalanches. As to what lay round the corner to the west of Point 20,675 feet we could only guess, but from Gardiner's letter we knew there were steep ice-falls barring all direct approach to the mountain.

The weather was still improving. No rain or snow fell that day and the evening was cloudless with Nilgiri Parbat glowing like a vast sail down the valley, and casting an opalescent light on the camp long after the sun had left the glacier. Shortly before sunset we strolled across the glacier to the moraine on the far side on which the surveyors had built a large cairn. From this point the Mana Peak appeared totally inaccessible, and we neither of us felt that we stood the remotest chance of success. Yet on this beautiful evening a mundane matter such as climbing a particular mountain could not intrude for long on the mind and we returned to camp through a motionless, frosty atmosphere, which was already forming a film of ice on the pools of the glacier, with the great peak we hoped to climb hard-cut against a deep green sky at a seemingly immeasurable distance above our heads.

In hard frost we set off next morning to the Zaskar Pass. It was all easy going, and we did not need the rope until we came to a few small crevasses. A scramble up a slope of snow and shale and we stood on the pass. Nilkanta rose to greet us beyond the unseen Alaknanda Valley, and to the north of it the snows of the Badrinath Peaks glowed serenely in the calm morning air.

Our first impressions had been confirmed during the walk to the pass that a direct attack on the Mana Peak from the head of the Banke Glacier was out of the question. Between the lower buttress of the south ridge and the ridge on which we now stood was an impassable ice-fall which descended from a recessed plateau enclosed between the south and north-west ridges. I have never seen a more formidable ice-fall. It was a full 3,000 feet high : wall upon wall, tower upon tower the ice rose, riven and rent in all directions as though by an earthquake, whilst tongues of debris stretched far on to the Banke Glacier. One glance was sufficient ; there was no hope there.

But there was one slender chance of success and this was to follow the ridge from the Zaskar Pass over a subsidiary peak of about 21,500 feet to the plateau already mentioned. It would be necessary to descend from the peak to the plateau, and such a descent might well prove impracticable, but once on the plateau there was a possibility of reaching the long north-west ridge of the mountain which connects with Kamet, three miles to the north-north-west, and of traversing it to the summit.

It was a theory, and fact often jostles uncomfortably on the heels of theory. The Zaskar Pass is 18,992 feet ; the Mana Peak 23,860 feet. Allowing for a descent of several hundred feet from Peak 21,500 feet to the plateau, this meant a climb of well over 5,000 feet in a distance of about three horizontal miles. And, incidentally, there was Peak 21,500 feet, a formidable climb in itself. From the Zaskar Pass the ridge, after running more or less horizontally for a short distance, springs up in a sharp and steep snow-ridge which ends against a rock face about 500 feet high, obviously very steep in its uppermost portion. Above this rock face the ridge bends almost at right angles in a snow crest which appeared very narrow, might necessitate much step-cutting, and which eventually ends in the summit of Peak 21,500 feet. Furthermore, we were a small party with provisions and fuel for not more than four days, and it was probable, even supposing that the traverse of Peak 21,500 feet was practicable, that at least two camps, and possibly three, would be needed before an attempt on the summit could be made. On the face of it, all we could hope for was a reconnaissance which would disclose the possibility or impossibility of the route. Should it prove possible, we could descend to Badrinath and return with the necessary sinews of warfare.

Such were our conclusions. It remained only to carry the first part of the programme into effect and reconnoitre the route. Accordingly when the porters arrived we told them to pitch the camp just below the crest of the pass ; then, having provided ourselves with some food, we set out at ten o'clock to climb Peak 21,500 feet.

Although at this stage there seemed no chance whatever of attempting the Mana Peak in the near future we were both of us fired with an optimistic energy ; and it was impossible not to feel optimistic on a morning when there was scarcely a cloud in the sky, and only the lightest of winds rustled across the ridge. We had experienced some dull and misty days on the Banke Plateau, but now the weather was perfect. Perhaps the fact that we had now only a little food and a camera apiece contributed to our lightness of foot and spirits.

After passing along an easy crest of snow and screes we came to the point where the ridge springs up in a series of snow bulges, before tapering into a sharp edge. The first of these bulges was of ice, covered with snow which varied from the merest sprinkling to several inches in depth. Our problem was to find a route which involved the minimum of step-cutting, and though in this we were only partially successful, the step-cutting was speedily accomplished by Peter.

The second bulge was very similar to the first and was followed by snow-slopes, above which the ridge narrowed and rose steeply to the foot of the rocks, where we suspected the crux of the ascent must lie. It occurred to us here that we might be able to outflank this difficult upper portion and possibly Peak 21,500 feet by a traverse to the west and an ascent to the plateau. In this, however, we were mistaken and after a walk across snow-slopes we were brought up short on the edge of impassable ice-cliffs.

Before retracing our tracks we glanced down into a glacier some thousands of feet beneath on to which an ice avalanche had fallen with such force and momentum that the debris had swept along for a distance of nearly half a mile. It was a grim reminder of the fate that had overtaken the Nanga Parbat Expedition, regarding which the Editor of the Alpine Journal wrote : " It lies beyond any man's power to calculate the forces of Nature and their effects on the hanging glaciers and vast snow-fields suspended from those mighty slopes and precipices." It is indeed only possible to climb safely in the Himalayas by keeping not only out of the *obvious* range of ice avalanches but out of seemingly *impossible* range, and parties that attempt such routes as that on Nanga Parbat will always risk destruction. To what extent such a risk is justifiable or unjustifiable must depend always on the climber himself and the store he sets on his life and the lives of his porters balanced against the possible fulfilment of his ambitions.

Having returned to the ridge we recommenced the ascent. Two or three hundred feet higher we came to a point where the ridge was intersected horizontally by a crevasse, the upper lip of which formed an ice-wall about 30 feet high. Before crossing the crevasse we halted to admire the icicles which were suspended from the lip ; gleaming in the sun and with a background of snow-peaks and deep blue sky they made a magnificent spectacle.

The ice-wall was by no means as difficult as it appeared, but even so a number of steps had to be cut before we were able to gain the slope above. We now climbed diagonally upwards and regained the crest of the ridge, which proved so sharp, steep and icy that steps had to be hewn all the way up it. This arduous task was undertaken by Peter, who now seemed at the top of his form. It is a privilege to follow behind a first-rate ice-man and during this part of the ascent I had little to do but step up in the excellent steps made by my companion. When you do not have to make steps yourself there is something very pleasant and lulling in the sound of an ice-axe cutting into snow and ice, and the lazy swish of the dislodged fragments as they skip and spin into the abyss.

At length the snow-ridge levelled out and ended abruptly against the rocks. These proved easier than anticipated, for they were well broken and consisted for the most part of firm material, reddish in colour ; but here and there were loose rocks, including one slab wedged insecurely in a chimney over which we climbed as gingerly as cats on a glass-topped wall. A little way above this was a steep sheep's back of slabs with small holds, which necessitated a long run out of rope for the leader, but apart from this and a short ice-slope with a treacherous covering of snow there was nothing to give us more than momentary pause until we came to a vertical cliff about 50 feet high immediately under the sharp upper ice-ridge leading towards the summit. The rock here was dark and striated and none too firm as compared with that lower down. There was no possibility of climbing directly over the cliff as the crest overhung, so well held by Peter I moved along a little ledge to the right until I came to a corner beyond which a narrow ice gully descended towards the Banke Glacier. This was the crux of the ascent ; if we could climb up and round this corner there seemed every chance of circumventing the obstacle. There were good holds, but a severe arm pull must be avoided at a height of over 20,000 feet. A step or two upwards, then one to the right, and my exploring hand was able to touch a small, sloping, scree-covered ledge. This was covered by a film of ice, which I cleared as well as I could with one hand while supporting myself with the other. Having at last decided that a step was justifiable I balanced up with the delicacy, but scarcely the grace, of a Blondin and a moment later was on the ledge. But this was not the end of it ; the rocks still forced me to the right into the ice-gully, which was here so steep and narrow that it more nearly resembled a chimney. Retrieving my ice-axe from my rucksack in which I had carried it, I cut two or three steps in the ice until I was able to balance across to a hold on the far side. Then, after climbing upwards for a few feet, I cut back across the gully on to a sloping ledge immediately under the crest of the ridge, and above the rock-wall, where I could not resist a triumphant shout of " Done it ! " to Peter.

Soon we were together at the commencement of the ice-ridge. Himalayan ice-ridges are notorious for their sharpness and there are few edges in the Alps to equal these fragile crests that lift into the blue with fairy-like and ethereal beauty. This ridge was no exception.

To the right it fell away in tremendous precipices to the head of the Banke Glacier ; to the left we looked down one of the longest and steepest ice-slopes of my experience. Indeed, I cannot recollect how or where the slope ended ; it dropped and dropped for apparently thousands of feet. Along the crest formed by the intersection of these two slopes we had to make our way ; a crest so thin and knife-like that Peter remarked that it was the sharpest ridge he had ever trodden.

The crest consisted of ice covered with several inches of snow, which varied in depth so that sometimes it was impossible to drive in our ice-axes deeply enough to form a firm belay for the rope. Thus it was necessary to cut good steps. Moving one at a time and taking turns at the work we advanced slowly, keeping just below the crest, which was slightly corniced in places. It was exhilarating work. A Himalayan mountainside often seems to stifle ambition and all those qualities that go to make for success on a mountain, but a ridge is different ; here is a celestial pathway, with nothing to oppress the climber and only the blue sky above.

An hour passed ; the slopes to the north-west were now appreciably less steep and the ridge less acute. Presently we came to a broad snow-slope. Up this we trudged very slowly. To carry heavy loads up to a camp, then indulge in difficult climbing, is a tax on strength, and we were tired. However, what we lost in energy we made up for in rhythm. Nothing is more fatiguing than to climb behind a man who has never learned the art of rhythmical climbing on a snow-slope. Peter is by instinct a snow- and ice-man, and when he led I found myself following docilely in his wake, and with that minimum of effort which is linked inseparably with a rhythmical uphill pace.

So at length we reached the summit of Peak 21,500

feet. It consisted of an almost level ridge and we trudged along to the far end until we could look down to the plateau. We were only about 300 feet above it and a broad and easy snow-ridge, a mere walk, linked it with the summit on which we stood. Beyond the plateau was the north-west ridge of the Mana Peak, a long, gently sloping and apparently easy crest, an obvious route to the summit. The sole remaining problem was how to reach it from the plateau. In one place it sank down, forming a shallow col not more than 1,000 feet above the plateau, and linked with the latter by a slope which from our position seemed inclined at a moderate angle. If this slope, which as far as we could judge was composed of snow, could be climbed and the ridge gained there was every hope of reaching the summit.

The south ridge on the other hand looked far more difficult and the rock step near the top was obviously very steep and likely to prove an insuperable obstacle. And there was no means of reaching the ridge easily, for the one and only route from the plateau lay up a subsidiary ridge, which was not continuous but petered out high up against a steep face. The north-west ridge was the easier of the two routes if the slope leading to it could be climbed.

We returned to camp through the usual afternoon mist, well satisfied with our reconnaissance.

Perhaps it was the hardness of the ground beneath my punctured air mattress, or maybe something I had eaten, but I was unable to sleep well that night. I lay restlessly turning over the events of the day in my mind. The Mana Peak was accessible, or at least there was a reasonable chance of this, and the weather and snow conditions were ideal ; and we were descending to Badrinath on the morrow ; this meant the loss of a week and it was unlikely that the weather would remain good during the height of the monsoon season.

Had we enough provisions and fuel for an immediate attempt on the summit, and was an attempt possible with only one additional camp ? We had no time for more than one camp and in any event it would be difficult to convoy laden porters over Peak 21,500 feet, whilst an ill-provisioned camp in such a remote situation was out of the question. For several hours I lay cogitating the problem and the more I cogitated the more clear did the issue seem ; we must push up a camp to the lower rocks of Peak 21,500 feet and the day after attempt the summit. This point decided, I slept.

# CHAPTER XXI

## THE MANA PEAK: THE ASCENT

WE awoke next morning, August 11th, to perfect weather, and as usual breakfasted in our tents. Meanwhile, the men packed up ready to descend to Badrinath. After breakfast I tore myself reluctantly from my sleeping-bag and crawled out of my tent. The sun was shining from a cloudless sky and not a breath of wind stirred in all that vast arena of glacier, peak and sky. This decided me. I lifted the petrol tin ; there was a full half-gallon of petrol left. Then I approached Peter and with some trepidation put the proposal to him ; that instead of descending we should take a camp as far up the ridge as possible and on the morrow have a crack at the top. I did not expect him to acquiesce, but he did ; the amount of fuel left was the strongest argument. He was not enthusiastic to begin with, for he is a sound and cautious mountaineer, but it was the weather that decided him. We should have to eke out our slender resources with coolie food, but even so there would be plenty left for the men. So it was agreed.

Wangdi was informed of the change of plan. I do not know what he thought, but to judge from his expression I can hazard a shrewd guess. He had been counting the hours till we should arrive at Mana, where there is excellent marwa (native beer) and now this and other pleasures were to be postponed. Undoubtedly the Sahibs were mad and especially Ismay * Sahib. Gloom

* The nearest the Tibetan can get to my name.

settled on his hard face, but it presently vanished. It was a *fait accompli* and must be accepted as such ; he would see us through with the job.  So the tents and stores were unpacked, resorted and repacked, and an hour later we set off up the ridge.

Climbing even moderately easy snow and ice with laden porters is a very different matter to climbing without them, and it was necessary to enlarge considerably the steps we had already made.  Then, of course, there was Pasang, who might slip at any moment, whilst of Tse Tendrup and Ang Bao it cannot be said that they were pillars of strength to the party.  However, Wangdi and Nurbu were well able to take care of their less competent companions and Nurbu, in particular, had acquired a knowledge of rope craft which was astonishing, considering that less than two months previously he was a raw novice unversed in the finer points of mountaineering.

Two hours later we reached the uppermost limit of the snow-ridge and cast around for a place to pitch the tent.  There was only one—immediately beneath the crest on the precipice falling to the Banke Glacier.  At first sight it seemed an impossible situation, but nothing is impossible to the Tibetan or Sherpa when it comes to pitching a tent and in a few minutes the men had descended a wall of snow and ice fifteen feet high and were busy excavating a platform at the base of it where it rested on some rocks.  An hour later the tent had been pitched, the sleeping-bags arranged inside, and a pan filled with water from a drip nearby.  This done, some tea was prepared for the men after which they set off down to the Zaskar Pass, having previously had instructions to return on the morrow and await our arrival.

Perched on the rocks we watched their descent.  It

was a ragged little procession.   Pasang and Tse Tendrup
in particular seemed to regard their feet as the least
important part of the anatomy, and contrasted oddly
with Wangdi and Nurbu, who moved with the confidence
of experienced mountaineers, plunging in their ice-axes
at every step and belaying the rope in readiness to check
a slip.

Having seen them disappear in safety we surveyed our
surroundings.   It was certainly the most sensational
camping site of my experience.   Like certain houses of
ill design and antique origin it was possible to step
straight out of the bedroom and down the stairs, only
in this instance there was a 1,500 feet precipice in lieu of
stairs.   Immediately behind the tent the ridge crest
concealed the view to the west, but to the east we looked
across a precipice crowned by an ice-wall from which
were suspended huge icicles gleaming in the sun like
sheaves of Titanic spears.   Beyond this was the edge of
the plateau with a frozen cataract of ice descending from
it towards the Banke Glacier which stretched south-
eastwards in two great curves before disappearing
behind a distant shoulder under the shining snows of
Nilgiri Parbat.  Immediately beneath was an ice-
sheeted gully scored and seamed by stones which, dislodged by the fierce sun from masses of decaying crags,
never ceased their whirring and humming, with now
and then the resounding crash of a bigger block, until
the evening frost had set its seal on the mountainside.

The weather was good and not even heavy mists
charged with desultory hail squalls could dim the
optimism we now felt about the outcome of the morrow's
climbing.   We spent the afternoon lounging about the
warm rocks and in my case collecting flowers, for even
at this inhospitable altitude, far above the permanent

snowline and the nearest alps and meadows, plants had obtained a lodgment on the crags. I found the same little woolly *saussurea* I had already seen on the edge of the Banke Plateau (*S. bracteata*),* and a beautiful little yellow-flowered *saxifrage* growing from woolly, densely tufted foliage which clung close to cracks and crannies of the rocks (*S. Jacquemontiana*).

During the afternoon I lost my pipe and spent a considerable time searching for it. No doubt it fell from my pocket and descended the gully to the glacier, from which it will emerge a century or so hence above Gamsali to gladden, I hope, one of the inhabitants of that village. This was a tragedy and Peter commiserated suitably with me on my loss ; at the same time I suspect that as a non-smoker he was secretly relieved because it was a particularly foul pipe and the tent we shared was very small.

Our eyrie lost the sun early and the increasing cold forced us to seek the shelter of our sleeping-bags. From this vantage point we looked out through the entrance of the tent on the glories of a monsoon sunset. At this season, when there is an abundance of water vapour in the atmosphere, sunrise and sunset are far more colourful than in the dry periods before and after the monsoon. The clouds bear witness to this and the towering masses of cumulus that are built up during the afternoon glow with a fiery splendour at sundown. That evening the colourings were especially fine. Shortly before sunset we witnessed the phenomenon known as the Brocken Spectre, the conditions for which are a low sun and a wall of mist. There was a point not far from the camp still bathed in sunlight and standing on it I saw my shadow surrounded by a halo of prismatic colourings cast on the mists that lingered in the gully to the

* Unfortunately I lost my specimens of this plant.

east of the camp.  I attempted to photograph it, but
though I was using panchromatic film the attempt was
unsuccessful.

Soon after this the mists rapidly cleared from the
vicinity of the Mana Peak, and lying in our sleeping-
bags we gazed out of the tent on to the group of snow-
peaks south of the Zaskar Pass and far beyond them to
a vast range of cloud, sunlit above and shadowed below,
spanning the distant foothills.  Quickly white changed
to amber and amber to gold as peaks and clouds reflected
the enormous conflagration of the setting sun.  Then,
even more quickly, the shadows welled upwards, a
delicate opalescent blue at their edges where they met
the sunlight, and within a few minutes the peaks had
gone out and only the cloud mountains were left to
carry the day to its peaceful ending.  A little later when
I looked out of the tent entrance the world had been
drained of all sunlight and was pallid and deathly
cold.

We supped off pemmican soup thickened with the
porters' sattoo.  Soup is perhaps scarcely descriptive
for Peter, ever a lover of the latter commodity, which
to me tastes like pulverised blotting-paper, added so
much that the resultant mess was practically solid and to
assimilate it needed all the gastronomical fortitude of
which I was capable.

My last memory before attempting to sleep is of the
stars.  Those who have only seen stars through the
dense atmosphere of low levels cannot conceive their
grandeur when viewed through the thin keen atmosphere
of the High Himalayas.  The firmament is crowded
with innumerable archipelagoes of brilliant fire shining
undimmed from horizon to horizon, except when the
Milky Way interposes a spectral luminescent veil, apparently so near that a hand outstretched could tear it down

from heaven.   Beneath these serene eyes the mountaineer must needs forget his little woes.

> Sit, Jessica.   Look how the floor of heaven
> Is thick inlaid with patines of bright gold.
> There's not the smallest orb which thou behold'st
> But in his motion like an angel sings,
> Still choiring to the young-eyed cherubims ;
> Such harmony is in immortal souls ;
> But whilst this muddy vesture of decay
> Doth grossly close it in, we cannot hear it.

Neither of us slept much.   I doubt whether I slept at
all, but my memory is vague on the point.   It is easy
at high altitudes for a man to wake up in the morning
convinced that he has not slept at all.   But the bogey
of sleeplessness is not as formidable as it is at sea-level ;
the deprivation of oxygen results in the mountaineer
lying in a semi-comatose condition and the hours pass
quickly, not drag by on leaden feet as they do at sea-
level.   I remember clearly the silence ; there was not
a breath of wind or the rumble of an avalanche the
whole night through.   I remember too in more wakeful
and alert periods turning over again and again in my
mind the fortunes of the morrow, for this was likely,
as we both realised, to be the greatest mountain day
in our lives.

At 3 a.m. I got the Primus going after some ineffectual
attempts which filled the tent with fumes.   It was
bitter cold at that hour and everything that could
freeze had frozen, including our boots, but a hot porridge
of sattoo and a cup of chocolate put life into us.

At five o'clock the light was sufficiently strong to
permit of our starting.   Stiffly we mounted to the ridge
and began the ascent of the rocks.   The stars were
paling rapidly in the fast-strengthening light, and the
weather was perfect ; not a cloud.

As we climbed, at first up the chimney and broken

rocks, then over the slabby section where my hands, which I had to remove from my gloves to grasp the small holds, became very numb, our muscles soon lost their stiffness and we began to enjoy the ascent.

We made good progress to the foot of the wall immediately beneath the ridge but here we were checked. The trickles from the snow melted by yesterday's sun had frozen in ugly sheets of ice on the holds and on the scree shelf above, and the ice-axe pick had to be requisitioned to clear the rocks, an awkward business when only one hand was free, the other being occupied as a support.

The landing on to the frozen scree-covered shelf was particularly delicate, but at length we were over the obstacle and on the snow-ridge above. Here, thanks to the steps cut two days previously, we made rapid progress and at 6.30 were on the summit of Peak 21,500 feet.

A downhill walk of about 300 feet brought us to the plateau, which was still in shadow and very cold. Crossing this and ascending gently we made for the north-west ridge ; but the nearer we approached the slope leading to it, the more formidable did it appear, and it soon became evident that we had been misled as to the angle.

Splitting the base of it was a *bergschrund,* half choked with snow. Peter crossed, held on the rope round my indriven ice-axe, and cut a step or two over the shallow lip of the crevasse to the slope above. Once on this I hoped to see him advance quickly, kicking or slicing out steps in frozen snow, but instead he cleared away what was evidently a surface layer of loose, powdery snow and swung his axe ; it met the slope with a dull thud—ice. And ice of the toughest quality to judge from the time it took to fashion a step. Two or three steps, and he called on me to join him. I did so. There was no mistaking the fact that the slope was an ice-sheet from base to crest, covered not with a layer of firm well-consolidated snow, as we had hoped, but in snow of the consistency of flour or castor sugar. To climb the slope would involve the additional labour of clearing this surface snow away in order to cut a step. And the slope was about 1,000 feet high; it meant a day's work at least, in all likelihood two days' work, even supposing we had the strength to do it at a height of nearly 22,000 feet. There was nothing for it but to descend.

Having returned to the plateau, we discussed the situation. The game was up, but was it quite up? There was one possibility, a very remote possibility— the south ridge. We had already agreed that it could in all probability be reached from the plateau along a subsidiary ridge ascending to a point about 1,500 feet from the summit of the mountain, but we had also agreed that the ridge was more difficult than the north-west ridge and that the rock step some 800–1,000 feet from the summit appeared very formidable. Still, it was the only alternative open to us and we decided to attempt it, though I do not believe either of us had any hope of ultimate success.

To reach the foot of the subsidiary ridge we had to cross the plateau and descend some 300–400 feet, which descent increased twofold the work of the day.

There was no difficulty in approaching the foot of the subsidiary ridge but to reach the crest we had to clamber up a steep little gully with an awkward rock step. The ridge consisted of a thin edge of icy snow sweeping up like the blade of a scimitar before petering out in the west face of the south ridge about 400 feet from the crest.

Sometimes step-kicking was permissible, but for the most part it was safer and less fatiguing to slice steps out of the ridge crest. Peter did most of the work and we progressed steadily along this sensational edge with feet turned outwards like a pair of Charlie Chaplins.

The angle of the ridge increased the higher we ascended so that by the time we got to the point where the ridge ended in the face it cannot have been less than 50 degrees. Much depended on the condition of the face ; if there had been the least possibility of the snow sliding we should have had no option but to retreat ; but the slope was in good order, a hard slope of compacted snow and ice ; mostly ice. It was also very cold, being as yet untouched by the sun, and we gazed longingly at some sun-warmed rocks on the ridge crest far above us.

From the point of view of sheer hard work this last 400 feet was one of the toughest jobs I have ever engaged in and there is no doubt that Peter, who rose splendidly to the occasion to do a lion's share of step-cutting, although he had already worked hard on the ridge below, must attribute his failure to reach the summit to the energy he expended at this stage of the climb.

Here and there were rock slabs which afforded welcome resting places but seldom security for the rope. At length the angle eased off a little and a minor rib of rocks and snow led up to the crest of the south ridge which we gained with a vast sense of relief at ten o'clock.

Here the sun met us for the first time and we plumped down on a rock to revel in its warm rays. Peter's feet had become numbed with cold during the ascent and the first thing he did was to take off his frozen boots and restore the circulation with a vigorous massage. If I remember aright we tried to eat some chocolate but with little success ; after breathing hard through the mouth in the cold dry air there was little saliva in our mouths and our throat muscles would not function efficiently. This disability is common at high altitudes and is, I believe, partly responsible for loss of appetite when climbing. For this reason liquid food is far to be preferred to solid food.

From our position the south ridge stretched roughly horizontal for some distance, though considerably broken up into minor points, crests and rock towers ; then it sprang upwards in a steep rock ridge alternating with occasional snow edges to the sharp-pointed summit. We were looking at it *en face* so could not estimate the difficulty of the rock step which we knew was likely to be the crux of the climb.

Had we been climbing in the Alps we might have appreciated the grandeur and complexity of the edge along which we scrambled, but at nearly 23,000 feet these qualities are seldom appreciated by mountaineers who have already expended much energy in overcoming initial difficulties.

For the next hour we made little or no height and in several instances lost it when descending some rock tower or snow point. In places the ridge was a snow crest, sometimes corniced on its eastern side, and we traversed cautiously one at a time across the steep western slope ; in other places we moved both together over broken rocks.

This horizontal section ended in two or three little rock towers more formidable than any yet encountered and we had to descend some fifty feet to the west and traverse across the face to avoid them. Fortunately the slope we traversed was composed of hard snow, not ice, and we were presently able to regain the ridge without difficulty at the point where it swept steeply upwards to the summit, which now seemed close to us but was in reality a full 1,000 feet higher.

Now at last we were at grips with the final problem, and what a splendid problem it was. I shall always regret that we were too tired to enjoy those red granite slabs that lifted up and up in a great sweep towards the finely tapered summit edging proudly into the blue. Here was something to warm the heart and blood : clean, firm granite and a perfect day with not a breath of wind to chill us ; what more could we have desired in different circumstances ? But now a weight of tiredness opposed us and out of the tail of my eye I could see that my companion was climbing with increasing effort and that every upward step was a painful weariness to him.

We came to a sloping platform on the crest and there Peter seated himself wearily and told me that if he continued he would become unsafe as he was now very tired. He was not exhausted but might become so with further effort. It was a terrible disappointment to us both. Seated side by side we discussed the situation. There was no doubt that he was suffering primarily from the effects of altitude. As long as he rested he felt fit and strong, but directly he exerted himself uphill intense fatigue supervened. To climb downhill is, as I knew from my experiences on Everest, easy, even to a man who cannot muster the energy for another upward step. I asked myself, firstly, was it justifiable to leave him resting at that point and, secondly, was I justified in making a solitary attempt on the summit ? Had the weather been anything but perfect there would have been no choice in the matter— we should have had to descend. But the weather *was* perfect ; although it was nearly noon the sun was shining with unabated fierceness and the rocks even at this great elevation were warm to the touch. So I asked him if he minded my carrying on alone. Though he gave no positive indication of his feelings I do not believe he liked the idea ; it was not the prospect of being left alone but my safety that worried him, and afterwards he told me how anxious he had been, which is typical of him—the most unselfish man I have ever climbed with. So it was agreed and, leaving him seated on the platform, I recommenced the ascent.

A few feet above the platform the ridge narrowed into an awkward bank of snow overlying a length of slabs tilted downwards to the east and projecting as a thin flake over the precipice to the west. Along the uppermost edge of the slabs the snow had melted, leaving a high bank of snow on the one hand and on the other a drop so sheer there was nothing a falling object could touch for some hundreds of feet. The strange little path thus exposed, which was never more than two feet wide, continued unbroken for twenty or thirty yards and reminded me of the ledge on the Grépon euphemistically known as the " Route aux Bicyclettes."

At the end of the ledge was a low wall and beyond this broken rocks and snow leading to the foot of our *bête noire*, the step in the ridge. I should estimate this as 150 feet high, and at first sight it appeared a formidable obstacle. It was built up of horizontally stratified rocks and overhung in places, but the fact that the strata were well defined and dipped if anything slightly inwards encouraged the hope that perhaps a way could be made up it from ledge to ledge. A direct approach from the ridge crest was out of the question, but immediately to the right of the step was a shallow, ill-defined little gully, and it occurred to me that if this were climbed a horizontal traverse could be made across the face of the cliff to a point whence the upper portion was practicable.

To my relief the snow of the gully was in excellent order and though so steep that I halted to rest at every step with my chest against it, the fact that I could drive in my ice-axe to its head gave me a feeling of security. After about 100 feet of this arduous work I was able to step to the left on to a ledge a few inches in width which traversed the cliff more or less horizontally. Edging sideways along this under some impassable overhangs I reached a point where a series of rock leaves projected from the face. Although fragile in appearance they were perfectly firm and climbing slowly up them with some halts for breath I presently found myself at the top of the step. The worst had been accomplished—or so I thought—and I shouted joyfully to Peter, who was now busying himself with his camera.

Above the step the going was easy until I came to a slab about 25 feet high. There was no avoiding this and it had to be climbed. There were few holds, but a tongue of snow well frozen to the rock afforded an excellent purchase for the ice-axe and by utilising the friction of my knees I was soon at the top.

After this the climbing was more laborious than difficult and with nothing to occupy my full attention I realised how weary I was and that every step involved a conscious effort of will-power. As I have discovered on many occasions, easy climbing can seem more fatiguing than difficult climbing, though, of course, this only applies up to a certain point in tiredness beyond which difficulties become insuperable owing to sheer muscular weakness.

Going very slowly, with halts to rest every few steps, I approached the most remarkable obstacle I have encountered on a mountain. By some extraordinary geological chance a boulder the size of a cottage had wedged itself athwart the ridge. There was no climbing over the top of it for it overhung, nor could I see a way of clambering over a vertical wall of rock to one side, really a tongue of the boulder. Had I been climbing in the Alps I might have scaled this wall, but it meant an upward pull on the arms alone and for this I had insufficient strength ; gymnastics are not possible over 23,000 feet. There was no hope of turning the obstacle to the left, for here the precipice fell with appalling steepness, but there was one way—and it is this that makes the obstacle unique in my recollection of Himalayan climbing—there was a way *under* it.

The boulder was hollowed beneath and this hollow persisted from one side to the other. The cave thus formed was perhaps five feet high at its entrance but it was more than half choked with ice, leaving just room for a man prepared to crawl.*     Stooping down I looked through a little funnel of glistening black ice and perceived a gleam of light at the far end. It was a last hope and I crawled inside.

Describing these events now makes them seem straightforward enough, but at the time they possessed a queer dreamlike quality which is consonant with my former experience of severely difficult climbing at high altitudes. I believe the absurdity of the situation must have struck me because I remember halting my crawl to laugh aloud, but my laugh deteriorated into a gasp ; laughter is hard work at high altitudes.

I had hoped that the hole would end conveniently on the ridge above the boulder but this was too much to expect. It ended to one side—the side overlooking the western precipice.

Crawling forwards, I looked out through the ice-encumbered exit. Once again Fortune smiled. The

* When free of ice at the far end and with snow-free rocks at the exit this passage would be comparatively easy.

precipice beneath was sheer but there was a ledge half hidden by snow and ice running forwards beneath the boulder towards the ridge. The difficulty was to get out of the hole on to this ledge. Having got my head and shoulders out, I twisted to the right until I could grasp satisfactory hand-holds, then half pushed with my knees and half pulled with my arms. For a moment my full weight came on my arms, then I was in safety on the ledge. It sounds a sensational manœuvre; at the time, however, it seemed obvious and straightforward. But it was very exhausting and when, a minute later after a short pause, I regained the ridge I had to rest before I could summon up the energy to continue.

As to the ridge immediately above the boulder I have the vaguest recollection; I think it was easy snow and rock, but I do remember that the snow was softer and more powdery than lower down. I remember too looking up and seeing the summit apparently an immeasurable distance away, just as the summit of Everest had appeared from over 28,000 feet in 1933.

Then to my dismay I came on yet another obstacle— a step in the ridge some fifty feet high. Had I been stronger I might have climbed this, for the rocks, though steep, were broken, but I had no further strength for strenuous rock-climbing and was now fast drawing on my last reserves of energy.

The alternative was a snow-filled gully to the left. This lay on the south-west face of the mountain and was exceedingly steep. At its base it narrowed into what was virtually a chimney, but above it broadened out into a snow-slope which I told myself must surely lead to the summit. It was the sole alternative; the one breach in the topmost defences of the mountain.

Traversing horizontally to the left I entered the gully.

Thank heavens it was filled with snow, not ice, but deep soft powdery snow into which I sank almost to the knees. Fortunately there was well compacted snow beneath and I was able to drive in my ice-axe to the head, which gave me a feeling of security, especially when the surface layer poured off in loose streams and hissed down the gully and out over the precipice.

Once or twice I was able to use rocks, including a little outcrop where the gully broadened. It was funereal going ; at every step I had to halt and rest before I could muster sufficient energy for the next step.

As the gully broadened the angle of the slope lessened. I now saw the ridge to my right ; it was unbroken snow, but I did not venture too close to the crest for fear of cornices. It ended at a point of snow, but I scarcely dared believe that this was the summit. I trudged towards it. There was no cornice and a few minutes later, at about 1.30 p.m., I sank down in the soft snow, the Mana Peak beneath me, after the hardest solitary climb of my life.

For a minute or two I was too fatigued to do anything but sit breathing heavily, blissfully conscious that whatever else befell me I had no longer to lever myself uphill. Then as my speeding heart and lungs quieted I became gradually conscious of my position and the view.

Since I left Peter I had been concerned with climbing and my whole physical and nervous energy had been concentrated to that one end, but now that the deadening work of hoisting the weight of my tired body uphill was at an end my mental faculties were released from physical bondage. The one concession of high altitudes is that as soon as the climber rests for any length of time he is enabled to forget his physical weariness. To me that day it was as though I had been led blindfold up the mountain and that the bandage had been removed on the summit. It was this more than any sense of " conquest " or achievement that made my few minutes on the summit unforgettable, so that if I live to be old and feeble I can still mount the golden stairs of memory to inspiration and contentment.

The summit of the Mana Peak is the highest and southernmost point of an undulating snow-ridge about 200 yards long which extends northwards in the direction of the group of peaks known as the Ibi Gamin. Kamet is immediately to the west of this group, and the first object I saw when I had recovered from my fatigue was its huge reddish pyramid, to which clung a vast banner of cloud floating slowly westwards yet ever forming against the mountain as it did so.

It would be easy to reel out a string of names of ranges, peaks, glaciers and valleys, but to occupy the mind with trifling topographical details on the summit of a great Himalayan peak is a petty anticlimax to weeks of reconnaissance, strenuous work, and a final glorious scramble. On a mountain-top time's sands are grains of pure gold ; must we then obscure their brightness with a leaden mess of trifling detail ? After Kamet I remember clearly but one detail in all that enormous landscape, the plateau of Tibet. I saw it to the east of the Ibi Gamin, a yellow strand laid beyond the Himalayan snows, shadowed here and there with glowing clouds poised in a profound blue ocean like a fleet of white-sailed frigates. For the rest there were clouds and mountains ; clouds alight above, blue caverned below over the deeper blue of valleys, citadels of impermeable vapour spanning the distant foothills, and mountains innumerable—snow-mountains, rock-mountains, mountains serene and mountains uneasy with fanged, ragged crests, beautiful mountains and terrible mountains, from the ranges of Nepal to the snows of Badrinath and the far blue ridges of Kulu and Lahoul.

Would that Peter had been there to share this with me.

But of all my memories, distinct or vague, one memory stands pre-eminent : the silence. I have remarked before this silence of the high mountains. How many who read this have experienced silence ? I do not mean the silence of the British countryside or even of the northern hills and moorlands, for though we may strain our ears and hear nothing there is always life not far distant. I mean the silence of dead places where not even a plant grows or a bird dwells. That day there was no wind, not the lightest breathing of the atmosphere, and I knew a silence such as I have never known before. I felt that to shout or talk would be profane and terrible, that this silence would shatter in dreadful ruin about me, for it was not the silence of man or earth but the silence of space and eternity. I strained my ears and heard—nothing. Yet, even as I strained, I was conscious of something greater than silence, a Power, the presence of an absolute and immutable Force, so that I seemed on the very boundary of things knowable and things unknowable. And because I have felt this more than once before on the high mountains I know that death is not to be feared, for this Force is a part of Heaven and a part of us ; how else should we be aware of it ? From it we have been evolved ; into it we quietly and peacefully return.

The minutes passed. Presently I mustered up the effort needed to take some photographs ; then I began the descent.

The ascent had been hard work ; the descent was absurdly easy by comparison. My strength returned with each downward step and once again I realised, as

I had realised on Everest, that altitude alone is responsible for exhaustion on high Himalayan peaks.  To judge from the speed at which I descended the difficulties of the Mana Peak are also primarily dependent on the altitude, but it was a steep descent nevertheless and the reverse passage of the hole under the boulder, while being considerably easier, especially as I discovered more holds, was awkward, and so was the slab below it and the big step in the ridge.

An hour later I rejoined Peter, who had regained his strength so well that he had scrambled about to take photographs and had ascended the ridge for a short distance.  No time was to be lost if we were to get back to camp before dark and we descended without delay.

All went well till we turned off the ridge on to the ice-slope, but here we had to recut many steps which had been damaged by the sun and lost much valuable time in regaining the lower snow-ridge.  Such work coming after a great climb is particularly irksome and it is on such occasions that risks are taken and accidents occur, but Peter rose nobly to the task and deepened the steps with unfaltering precision.

At last we were on the plateau.  The afternoon mists had risen and we passed along the crest of Peak 21,500 feet in a desultory hailstorm.  Before turning off it we shouted to the porters, who should be awaiting our arrival at the camp, in the hope that they would hear us and prepare some tea and were relieved to hear a faint response.

At 6.15 the camp loomed out of the mist and a few minutes later hot tea was moistening our parched throats.  How good it was ; no nectar is more revivifying at the end of a hard day on the mountains.

A few minutes' rest, while the men packed up, and we set off once more, down the ridge to the Zaskar Pass.

At last the snow and ice were behind us ; no longer was it necessary to place each foot with exact care ; through the dusky mist we moved shadow-like along the easy scree ridge. Already the strenuous events of the day were in the remote past, no longer linked to us by any thread of difficulty or danger. Trudging along, very weary now, through the swift-gathering darkness we came at 7.15 to the camp.

So ended the longest, grandest and hardest mountain climb of our lives.

# CHAPTER XXII

## NILKANTA

On August 13th, the day following the ascent of the Mana Peak, we reached Badrinath after a fatiguing march from the Zaskar Pass, and there remained for the next two days comfortably ensconced in the little rest-house.

Kedarnath and Badrinath are the two goals of the pilgrims who throng annually to the Himalayas to worship the five deities of Hinduism, Siva, Vishnu, Devi, Genesa and the Sun, Kedarnath being dedicated to Siva, the Destroyer, and Badrinath to Vishnu. The Rawal, or High Priest, of Badrinath is a Brahman from Southern India, and the temple of which he is the keeper, a little building with a gilded roof, contains the image of Vishnu carved in black stone. From the temple a flight of steps, polished smooth by the feet of innumerable pilgrims, leads down to the Alaknanda River in which the devout dip themselves, holding on to ring bolts to prevent the swift torrent from sweeping them away. There is also a hot spring believed to be very efficacious, especially every twelfth year when the planet Jupiter is in the sign of Aquarius.

Architecturally Badrinath is a mean little place, being composed for the most part of single-storied houses which display a wealth of corrugated iron roofing, and its situation in a barren boulder-strewn valley almost completely destitute of trees adds still further to its ugliness. Its greatest interest lies in its proximity to the source of the Alaknanda River, the " true source " of the Ganges, which issues from the Bhagat Kharak and Satopanth Glaciers a few miles distant, though a nearer and remarkable waterfall is acknowledged to be the stream mentioned in the Skanda Purana, " where the Ganges falls from the foot of Vishnu like the slender thread of a lotus flower."

The pilgrimage is not undertaken merely for abstract religious reasons but in many cases as deliberate self-immolation and penance for sins, and this accounts for the presence of many ascetics, Yogis, Bairagis and Sanyas. The Yogis come from all classes of the community, from the noblest Rajput families to the lowest castes, and having renounced everything material, except the barest necessities of life, strive towards Nirvana through mortifying the flesh. To what extent a man is justified in severing all social ties and battening on the charity of his neighbours in pursuit of selfish, yet in one sense selfless, ends, is only one of the innumerable social and religious problems of India. At least he sets an example in simplicity of living, the secret of earthly happiness.

Only one great mountain is visible from Badrinath, Nilkanta. This peak is associated in Hindu mysticism and mythology with Siva, for Nilkanta or Nilakantha, the Blue-necked, is an allusion to the god whose matted locks are represented by the torn glaciers and eternal snows. It is easy to understand why Nilkanta should be held in superstitious awe and reverence by the pilgrims, for there is no more majestic and awe-inspiring peak of its height in the world. It rises 21,600 feet above the sea and its summit is only five miles from Badrinath, 10,159 feet. Like the Matterhorn it stands alone and has no rival within eight miles, and is beautifully proportioned, being pyramidal in form with a graceful ice-clad summit whence sweep down three great ridges, of which the south-east terminates in the Alaknanda Valley at an elevation of only 7,000 feet.

My first view of the mountain was as dramatic as it was beautiful. The Kamet Expedition, after exploring the Arwa Valley, descended to Badrinath *en route* to Ranikhet. We knew that Nilkanta is visible from Badrinath but were frustrated by monsoon mists from seeing it during the day. But as we dined the mists cleared, revealing it full in the light of the rising moon. Of many moonlit views I have seen the snows of this glorious peak framed between the dark walls of a gorge was the most beautiful.

Peter had also seen the mountain and it was agreed before I left England that we should attempt the ascent. Such views of the mountain as we had already seen had convinced us that the only possible line of approach was via the south-east ridge. Though the longest of the three ridges it seemed likely that it was accessible from the Khiraun Valley which bifurcates with the Alaknanda Valley four miles below Badrinath and which, as far as we knew, had not been entered previously by a European. If the crest of the ridge could be gained at a point within reasonable distance of the summit there appeared to be a possibility of climbing the mountain.

Our first concern at Badrinath was to engage some more porters. So far we had managed with our five Darjeeling men, but they and we had carried very heavy loads, and for peaks such as Nilkanta, which are within easy reach of villages, the ultra-small party loses its point and inadequate porterage merely complicates an expedition. So word was sent to Mana and soon a number of Marcha Bhotias arrived from that village. Several had " chits " from former expeditions and one produced a recommendation given him by Mr. C. F.

Meade in 1913. We engaged four of them, picturesque fellows with wild locks and dressed in a weird and wonderful assortment of costumes.

Two days passed restfully and pleasantly during which time we received generous gifts of fruit, vegetables and sweetmeats from Pandit Neryan Dutt, who befriended the Kamet Expedition in 1931, whilst I must record here the courtesy of the postmaster who, although suffering from malaria, put himself out to further our arrangements.

By the evening of August 15th our "banderbast" was complete and we left next morning after seeing over Pandit Neryan Dutt's garden, which contrives to exist and flourish miraculously in this stony valley and includes fruit trees, although snow lies for several months of the year and winter temperatures must fall well below zero.

Unfortunately the weather was bad. Since we arrived at Badrinath rain had fallen almost continuously and the monsoon was now very heavy. There is no doubt that we should have remained in the north of Garhwal near the Tibetan frontier, where the monsoon air-current is sheered away by the dry winds of the Tibetan plateau, but we were encouraged to attempt Nilkanta by the success of the Anglo-American Expedition which succeeded in climbing Nanda Devi during the height of the monsoon season.

The bungalow at Pandukeshwar is four miles south of the Khiraun Valley but it was necessary to spend a night there in order to pick up some more food and equipment as well as leave certain items which were not needed for Nilkanta. This done, we set off on the following morning, August 17th, for the mountain.

Retracing our way up the Alaknanda Valley we crossed the Alaknanda River by a primitive little bridge, built however on the correct cantilever principle, and entered the Khiraun Valley. The impression we had gathered from the map was of a steep-sided valley narrowing into a gorge, for Nilkanta rises 10,000 feet out of the valley in about two horizontal miles, a steep angle even in a country of tremendous mountainsides. Such, however, is by no means the case and on entering the valley we found ourselves amid fields and woodlands watered by clear-running streams.

For a little distance we followed a rough shepherd's track but presently lost it and had to force our way through a wilderness of pink-flowered balsam (*Impatiens Roylei*) growing fully eight feet tall. Had it not been for the labour we might have appreciated the beauty of these flowers which covered acres of the valley floor in a sheet of bloom ; as it was, we were heartily glad to regain the path, dripping with sweat after the unusual exercise.

Crossing the valley torrent, which by its size suggested a considerable glacier system, we climbed a steep track to a hamlet set amid cultivated fields on a sloping shelf of the valley-side. Europeans were evidently something of a curiosity here and I nearly scared a small girl out of her wits when I attempted to take her photograph.

We camped half a mile beyond this village at a height of about 9,000 feet, a pleasant peaceful spot within sound of several streams.

Rain fell in the night and the morning of August 18th was dull and misty. After wading through dripping vegetation, which included thistles fully seven or eight feet high, we traversed forest-clad hillsides, then climbed steeply up the northern side of the valley. The local men were so slow that we began to wonder whether we should ever get on to our mountain. Every boulder, ledge and terrace was a potential halting-place for a prolonged puffing at their pipe, which had to be passed from hand to hand, and even Wangdi soon abandoned all hope of persuading them to move until the ritual was ceremoniously and inflexibly fulfilled ; this was their method of travel and the immemorial customs of the country were not to be violated by impatient Europeans.

To judge from its vegetation, the Khiraun Valley receives an abundant rainfall and enjoys a warm climate due to the proximity of the deep Alaknanda Valley, which is a natural funnel for the monsoon current, and I noticed oaks growing at between 11,000 feet and 12,000 feet, an unusual height for this tree. There were also many plants, including an annual blue gentian (*G. tenella*) which a week later covered the upper slopes with innumerable blooms, and the curious woolly spires of a *saussurea*.

At length, and quite unexpectedly, we arrived at a most beautiful alp, hundreds of acres of perfect turf grazed over by flocks of sheep and goats. There was a stone shepherd's shelter and the shepherd came forward to greet us, a soldierly looking fellow who told us that he had served for ten years with the Garhwal Rifles and that we were the first Europeans he had ever seen in the valley.

We camped on the alp and it would be difficult to imagine a more delightful spot for, as Peter remarked, good turf is rare in Garhwal and here were hundreds of acres of fertile meadows where we had anticipated finding steep and barren hillsides. Indeed it was difficult to imagine that we were on the slopes of one of the steepest and most formidable peaks in the Central Himalayas, especially as we had seen nothing of it as yet owing to mist.

Next morning we awoke to hear the patter of rain on our tents. Mist shrouded the hillsides but the shepherd accompanied us some distance to direct us to a higher alp. After scaling about 1,500 feet of grassy hillside we traversed horizontally and eventually came to a little shelf with plenty of dwarf rhododendron at hand for fuel, whilst juniper was not more than half an hour away. As we were unable to see more than a few yards owing to mist and were quite unable to estimate our position in relation to the south-east ridge, of which we had seen nothing, we decided to camp, having estimated our height as being close on 15,000 feet.

So dense was the mist that when Peter ventured away from the camp on a tour of inspection he lost his bearings and only found his way back with difficulty ; such dense and persistent mist is rare in the Himalayas and for all we could see of our surroundings we might have been camped on an English fell-side.

The mist cleared from our vicinity at nightfall, revealing the Khiraun Valley, and eastwards, far beyond the Alaknanda Valley, the dim forms of Gauri Parbat and Hathi Parbat, the massive bulk of Dunagiri and the thin keen peak of Nanda Devi. For a minute we gazed at these great mountains, then, instinctively, our eyes passed upwards. Immediately above the camp was a hillside, its wet herbage white and frosty in the moonlight, ending in a dark shoulder ; above and beyond the shoulder a slender ribbon of snow tailed upwards into the stars—Nilkanta.

The following morning was fine but did not appear likely to remain so for long, and at 6.30 we set out on a reconnaissance which would, we hoped, determine whether or not we could reach the crest of the south-east ridge, and if so whether the ridge afforded a practicable route to the summit.

The hillside was unexpectedly easy and after mounting over grass and boulders we approached a small glacier descending into the Khiraun Valley. As this was apparently uncrevassed and the snow was old and well-compacted, we proceeded to cross it, but had not gone far when we came to an unpleasant bottle-mouthed hole of unknown depth which had remained invisible until we were within a yard or two of it. After this we did what we should have done before, roped together, and without further incident crossed the remainder of the glacier to a broken rock face leading up to the crest of the ridge. The rocks were not in the least difficult and presently we stood on the ridge.

Considering the general angle from which Nilkanta rises from the Khiraun Valley we were not surprised to find that the ridge was very steep ; at the same time it was broken up in its lowermost portion into a complicated mass of rock pinnacles : could these pinnacles be outflanked and, if so, was the ridge above them less broken and complicated ? Only through practical trial could we determine this and we decided to push forward with our reconnaissance as far as was possible in the day.

Immediately above us the ridge broadened out to form a commodious camping site ; then, after continuing almost horizontally for another hundred yards, sprang upwards towards the first of the rock pinnacles. Seen *en face* the rocks appeared very difficult ; actually they were well broken up and we proceeded unroped. It was an enjoyable scramble for, although mists had again gathered and there seemed every prospect of a snowstorm, the weather was windless and warm.

Climbing rapidly, we followed the ill-defined ridge crest for a short distance, then traversed to the right above the depths of a gully, stepped round a corner, and scrambled up a series of slabs and ledges interspersed with screes, steering as well as we could in the mist for a point on the ridge crest above the initial group of pinnacles.

After several hundred feet of this work a fault in the cliff tempted us still further to the right along a ledge, but this proved a mistake as the ledge petered out in an impassable precipice, so retracing our steps we climbed directly upwards and presently gained the ridge crest above the more formidable of the lowermost pinnacles.

The rock here was mostly firm and plentifully supplied with holds and we progressed rapidly over a minor pinnacle, descended from it into a gap, and climbed up to the right of the ridge over broken ground towards the next pinnacle. And here we encountered the first serious difficulty.

The pinnacle we were aiming for was thin and sharp and the gap beyond it deep. We decided that it must be outflanked if possible. To the west was a narrow gully leading down to broken rocks but it was an unpleasant place, loose and with a mixture of grit and snow resting on slabs. The alternative was a traverse on the east face. The rock here was firmer but the climbing, technically speaking, was more exposed and difficult, and we had to descend greasy rocks down and round a nearly vertical corner overhanging a terrifically steep gully cleaving the east face of the mountain.

After this came a long stretch of easy rocks and once more progress was rapid ; indeed the climbing on the whole had been much easier than anticipated, though the route-finding throughout had been tricky and we were lucky to have discovered at a first attempt a comparatively easy breach in the lower defences of the mountain.

But Nilkanta had a surprise in store, and we had not advanced far when there rose before us a thin and elegant pinnacle with sheer sides falling into unknown depths and so formidable in appearance that it seemed our reconnaissance had come to a premature end.

At such moments it is a sound plan to stop and eat, for rest and food have an optimistic effect on a mountaineer, but in this instance the more we stared at this hard-faced sentinel of the ridge the less we liked it.

One thing was in our favour, the rock. The best that Chamonix can muster is no better than the clean-cut granite of this part of the ridge.

For the first rope length all went well and the climbing while steep was more strenuous than difficult. Then we came to a little corner immediately under an overhanging slice of rock. It was only twenty-five feet from the crest, but there was no climbing the overhang. To the left ran a ledge which appeared to tail out in the precipice ; but to the right there seemed just a chance that we might work across the face of the pinnacle and regain the ridge beyond it.

Well held by Peter—the belays for the rope were splendid throughout this part of the climb—I edged along an outward sloping gangway and after a delicate traverse to the right and an awkward movement round a corner, made principally on the hands, and a further traverse, reached a little recess under an overhang beyond the pinnacle. The only hope of regaining the ridge was to climb a curiously grooved slab to the left. The holds were sloping the wrong way, but by getting my feet on the slab and lying back with my hands grasping an edge—in technical parlance a " lay-back "—I was able to work my way up, a very exhausting manœuvre at nearly 19,000 feet which I could not have done without the climbing and acclimatisation to altitude of the past few weeks.

Twenty-five feet more of steep climbing, this time on good holds, and I reached the crest of the ridge above the pinnacle which proved to be more of a step on the ridge than an isolated point.

Peter joined me, and in so doing douched with cold water any little vanity I might have felt at overcoming a difficult obstacle by loitering negligently up the rocks. However, on such occasions it is possible to repair injured pride by reflecting that there is a right and a wrong end to a climbing rope.

The ridge now continued almost horizontally for a short distance, then rose abruptly in another step formed by a wall several hundred feet high, of which the lowermost 200 feet consisted of a belt of very steep slabs.

Here in all probability was the crux of the climb. We could not tell what lay above, but hoped that once up this step, if it were practicable, we should find ourselves on the upper snow- and ice-slopes of the mountain.

There was no time for a further reconnaissance for the afternoon was well advanced, and after examining carefully this next problem we began the descent convinced that we must contrive to pitch a camp as near as possible to the foot of the step, though, as we had already agreed, it was beyond the scope of our small party to convoy laden porters up the difficult place we had just climbed : it would mean fixing ropes and indulging in " siege tactics " for which we were ill-equipped and incidentally had no intention of undertaking.

In the hope of finding an easier alternative route past the pinnacle we explored downwards to the west and there, as luck would have it, discovered that the ledge I had rejected on the way up was a fraud and continued on out of sight round a corner to end in easy rocks. We had put ourselves to a great deal of unnecessary trouble by selecting the other and much more difficult route.   Nevertheless, it was a sensational little causeway.   We had to crawl along a narrow sloping shelf over as sheer a drop as any seeker of the sensational could wish to experience, then lower ourselves on to some footholds and in spreadeagle fashion edge round a corner.

The lower traverse and the slimy corner were also avoided by the gully we had looked down, but this, though technically easier, was an unpleasant alternative as the rocks were loose and covered with a treacherous mixture of snow and grit.

For the rest, the descent was uneventful until we came to the complicated hillside above the camp, where the mist was so dense that we could see only a few yards. Every now and then we paused to shout in the hope of attracting the porters' attention.   Our shouts were heard and answered, but even so it was difficult to find the camp, and when at length we reached it, the light was rapidly failing.

The weather was in a sullen mood and it was no surprise when heavy rain set in soon after our arrival. But we could hardly grumble ;   whatever Nilkanta had in store for us, we had enjoyed a splendid day's mountaineering and we celebrated the occasion with a feast of " Maggi " soup, mutton, potatoes, onions, delicious wild rhubarb gathered near the camp and " Ovaltine," after which a certain bottle husbanded by Peter at Pandukeshwar circulated steadily between the tents.

It is seldom that bad weather fits in with a plan on a mountain, but heavy rain next day not only offered no temptation to push up a camp but enabled one of the local men to descend to Pandukeshwar for another pair of boots for Peter who had lost many nails from his present pair.   Still, if I had to choose where to spend an " off day," I would not select a small and leaky tent battered ceaselessly by torrential rain.

Fortunately, Peter had plenty of reading matter and he loaned me " Dr. Johnson." As I lay in my sleeping-bag listening to the dreary sound of the rain on the canvas and occasionally making vain attempts to check a steady drip on to my sleeping-bag, I tried to picture the worthy Doctor. Under similar circumstances would he have written something such as this?

SIR,

I address you from within the miserable confines of a tent, a leaky, plaguy structure into which a proportion of moisture finds its way with a scurrilous persistency. This inclemency of the elements is as irksome as it is irritating and taxes considerably the moral fortitude while imposing discomfort on the human frame. In a word, Sir, it is shrewish weather and foully damp.

The rain continued until the afternoon of the 22nd, and the temperature fell sharply, so that when the mists cleared the peaks showed heavily plastered with freshly fallen snow.

The following morning was bright and as further inactivity was thoroughly distasteful we decided to push up the camp to the site we had already noted, taking with us the five Darjeeling men and three Mana men, Kharak Singh, Mangal Singh and Nater Singh.

The Mana men jibbed at crossing the little glacier, except for Nater Singh, whom we had already marked out as exceptionally keen and willing, and it was some time before Peter's fluent Urdu could persuade them to continue.

Several inches of snow had fallen and this and stones had to be cleared away before level platforms could be made for the tents. Meanwhile the weather quickly deteriorated ; snow fell heavily and the atmosphere both in gloom and dampness did its best to emulate an English November day.

The camp having been pitched the Mana men were sent down, after which we settled into our damp sleeping-bags to continue a dreary and apparently useless vigil.

Fortunately the snow did not accumulate deeply on the rocks and under the influence of the sun next morning melted so quickly that we decided to push forward our next camp.

It was essential to load the men lightly for steep rock-climbing and we cut down equipment to the minimum. Thus we made rapid progress, climbing for the sake of speed and convenience in two parties widely separated, so that the second was in no danger from stones dislodged by the first.

But the dice were still loaded against us, and a heavy snowstorm broke before we reached the awkward slimy corner of the first difficult pinnacle, quickly covering the rocks with slush. There was nothing for it but to camp, as it was out of the question to allow the men to return unaccompanied in such conditions from anywhere beyond this point.

There was no semblance of a ledge on the steep and broken mountainside, but after an hour's work a little platform was built up just large enough for our single tent. This done the porters returned to the lower camp, leaving us on our damp and uncomfortable little eyrie.

My memories of this camp are exclusively of dampness and discomfort. The reader of travel books expects and demands that the traveller should endure hardship and discomfort ; but these make a weary catalogue, and I will content myself by remarking that the tent leaked freely, that our sleeping-bags were wet, and that the only means by which we could dry our under-clothing was to sleep in it. Is it not a strange thing for men to endure such discomforts for the sake of climbing

a mountain ? I have often asked this of myself but
have never been able to find an answer. Let there be
no mistake ; the true explorer or mountaineer derives
no feeling of superiority over his fellow-men from his
achievements ; his "conquests" are within himself
and over himself alone.

A space of six and a half feet by four feet, when
occupied by two men and an assortment of foods, food
utensils and cooking apparatus, tends to become a
trifle cramped and is not conducive to restful sleep. In
such circumstances it is a major folly to broach a tin of
condensed milk and expect what is left to remain within
the tin, and when next morning came the sight of the
tent floor afforded convincing testimony as to the vola-
tile qualities of this substance. It was no hardship,
therefore, to wriggle out of our steam-filled sleeping-
bags and after a melancholy breakfast set off on what
we realized could only be a forlorn-hope attempt on
the summit.

The sun was shining brightly when we started and the
view from our lofty perch ranged from Kamet and the
Mana Peak to Dunagiri and Nanda Devi, but we had
no illusions left as to the unsettled state of the weather
or the rapidity with which a fine morning deteriorates
during the monsoon season.

The condition of the mountain was now far worse
than it had been before and we had a foretaste of what
to expect when, instead of climbing round the steep
corner of the initial pinnacle, we elected to descend the
narrow gully, where snow several inches deep and frozen
stones and grit made a disagreeable and dangerous
combination. We moved with the greatest care and
were unanimous in condemning the place when at
length we reached the safety of the gap beyond the
pinnacle.

After this the climbing was easier despite the freshly fallen snow on the rocks and we made good progress over the thin pinnacle to the foot of the step in the ridge.

Already the weather was breaking. Within an hour the brilliant morning had been snuffed out by fast-gathering mists and the great crags above us loomed cold and hostile through the thickening vapour. Our attempt was doomed to failure ; the condition of the mountain alone warranted that assumption ; still, we determined at all events to climb the step and reconnoitre as far as possible towards the summit.

If the rocks of the thin pinnacle were firm and delightful to climb, the rocks at the foot of the step were the exact reverse, for here we found a flaky pastry-like substance. Moving one at a time and very carefully we edged across a series of rickety ledges, then clambered upwards to a sloping scree-covered shelf which traversed the band horizontally. The belt of rotten rock ended here and above the shelf were firm slabs broken here and there into projecting crags and seamed with incipient gullies.

Our first attempt to climb the slabs failed. Then we attempted to follow a shallow scoop-like gully. This quickly steepened into unclimbable rocks, but there seemed just a chance of forcing a route out of the gully over the slabs to the left.

It was a bad place. Peter had no belay worth speaking of and was standing on small holds as I slowly worked my way out across the slabs. The climbing reminded me of the harder routes on Lliwedd in North Wales ; there were the same small slabby holds and unrelenting exposure except that on Nilkanta the climber who " comes off " falls, not hundreds, but thousands of feet, not that the result in either case is likely to be different.

There was one particularly awkward place where a long step on tiny toe-holds had to be made. I hesitated a long time before making it for the reason that to return would be even more difficult; however, I decided to "burn my boats" in the hope that the climbing would become easier beyond. The climbing did not become easier; indeed, after running out about sixty feet of rope, I found further advance impossible. I remember very well clinging to the tiny rugosities of the rock and wishing devoutly that instead of nailed boots I had on felt-soled shoes. Then, at this critical juncture, when I knew that retreat was inevitable, a terrific hailstorm burst on us.

One moment the rocks were warm and moderately dry, the next they were cold and streaming with slush and water. So violent was the storm that soon our situation became dangerous owing to the torrents of hail that poured down the slabs.

I have a vivid recollection of my retreat, but it must have been equally painful for Peter, insecurely placed as he was and powerless to check a fall.

Soon my fingers lost sensation on the slush-covered holds, but there was no opportunity to warm them, nor was it possible to wear gloves when handling such small holds. The stride was the worst as I had to rely on wet finger-holds which I was totally incapable of feeling, but it was done at last and I rejoined Peter thankfully, after one of the nastiest bits of rock climbing of my experience.

The hailstorm ended a few minutes later. There was one last possibility of climbing the step, by a line to the right of our last line. The rocks here were steeper, but they were more broken, and this time we were successful in forcing a route after a difficult and exposed climb.

The upper portion of the step consisted of broken slabs and snow on which we were able to move both together for the most part. Making rapid progress, though we were both feeling tired after our strenuous efforts, we scrambled to the crest of a conspicuous point which forms the uppermost limit of the step. Here we rested and lunched.

There was no question of proceeding further. We were fully 2,000 feet below the summit of the mountain, the weather was against us, the day well advanced, and the mountain in impossible condition : at this height, which cannot have been more than 19,500 feet, fully a foot of new snow was lying, and higher the conditions were manifestly worse.

From our position a snow-ridge rose parabolically to a point on the ridge beyond which another snow-ridge swept up to the foot of another and, as far as we could judge, very formidable step.   If this last could be climbed the summit should be accessible via snow- and ice-slopes.

There is no doubt that we had under-estimated the length and difficulty of the south-east ridge.   To climb Nilkanta another camp or possibly two camps will be necessary, one at our highest point and another above or below the final step.   To carry up camps over rocks such as we had encountered will be no easy task, and a week of perfect weather may be required for the job.

But whatever the trials and difficulties of the route the prize will be well worth while, and the climber who eventually treads the crest of this peak will be conscious of having climbed one of the most beautiful peaks of its elevation in the Himalayas.

Much splendid mountaineering awaits the climber who, sick and tired of high altitudes and the spirit of nationalism and competition which surrounds the highest summits of the world with an atmosphere more stifling than the oxygenless air, turns his attention to peaks such as Nilkanta. At moderate elevations he is able not only to test himself to the uttermost of his strength and skill but to appreciate the beauties of Nature and enjoy the same thrills that the pioneers of Alpine mountaineering enjoyed. It will be a happy day for Himalayan mountaineering when the " conquest " of high altitudes is achieved.

We returned to camp drenched by hail, rain, sleet and snow. There was nothing further to be done and the following morning we signalled to the porters at the lower camp to ascend and carry down the camp, which they did so expeditiously that we were able to descend the same day to the lower alp. Next day we descended to Pandukeshwar and on August 28th arrived at Joshimath.

# CHAPTER XXIII

## DUNAGIRI

AFTER Nanda Devi, the undisputed goddess of the Central Himalayas, one of the finest peaks in the group of mountains between the Milam and Dhauli Valleys is Dunagiri, 23,184 feet, which is situated to the northwest of the Nanda Devi basin. For many years past it has attracted the attention of mountaineers, and there is no grander sight in Garhwal than its ice-clad summit soaring in a tremendous sweep out of the Dhauli Valley which, at the confluence of the Dhauli and Rishi Rivers, is only 6,170 feet above the sea.

Dr. T. G. Longstaff who in 1907 crossed the Bagini Pass to the east of Dunagiri, was of the opinion that the mountain was accessible from the south. Acting on this opinion Messrs. Oliver and D. Campbell attempted to reach the south-west ridge from the west but found all approach barred by precipices and hanging glaciers. It was left to E. E. Shipton to find a route to the ridge from the east in 1936, and to reach the shoulder of the mountain at a height of about 22,000 feet accompanied by one Sherpa porter. From this shoulder knife-like ice-edges lead toward the final peak which is distant nearly one mile.

Peter was naturally anxious to attempt once again this splendid mountain and it was the lodestone which drew us south after our failure to climb Nilkanta. We had hoped also to attempt the ascent of the unclimbed East Peak of Nanda Devi, but as there was no time for this we resolved to devote the whole of our energies to Dunagiri.

The mountain is more difficult of approach than Nilkanta, and the climber must work his way up the great Rishi Valley before entering the Rhamani Valley which leads up to the south-east face. We estimated that three weeks' coolie food, weighing about 350 lbs., would be required, and to carry this eight local porters were engaged, including Nater Singh, who had proved his worth on Nilkanta. As it was necessary to retain two men for work on the mountain, Nater Singh and a youth named Dharam Singh were selected and provided with boots and other equipment. Dharam Singh, who to judge from his appearance had more Tibetan than Indian blood in him, had served with the Nanda Devi Expedition, and had become possessed of an ice-axe of which he was inordinately proud. In build and manner he suggested an experienced mountaineer, but in point of fact he was not, and though invariably cheerful and willing, proved the least competent of our new recruits.

After some uncomfortable days and nights on Nilkanta, Joshimath seemed a haven of rest and repose and the two days that we spent there were devoted almost exclusively to eating and sleeping. It was an effort to tear ourselves away from the dak bungalow, but on August 31st we set off up the Dhauli Valley.

We had hoped that the weather would improve, as it must do if we were to stand the smallest chance of success, and there certainly did appear some prospect of this when we left Joshimath.

At the village of Tapoban we had a stroke of luck in being able to purchase seven eggs. Some eggs had been bought at Joshimath, but as half of them were bad we were taking no chances. Accordingly, a bowl of water was requisitioned and the eggs tested : if they sank all was well, but if they swam the reverse was the case. These proceedings were watched by the inhabitants of the village with the greatest curiosity and astonishment, including the vendor, who obviously looked upon them as impugning his good faith and the faith of his hens. Happily all sank. In addition to the eggs we acquired an aged rooster and thus set up for one meal at least proceeded cheerfully on our way.

Once again the weather was profligate, and rain set in later, so that we arrived at the village of Lata damp and cheerless. There was no camping ground and we pitched our tents on a path near the village. But we reckoned without the cows coming home from the upper pastures and a mêlée ensued in which the opposing forces were the cows, whose inflexible determination was to proceed as they always had proceeded along the path, and ourselves, who strove to make them realize the wisdom of by-passing a crowded thoroughfare.

The inhabitants of Lata are cheerful, friendly people and soon called on us with gifts of vegetables. Among them was an old shikari who had accompanied Dr. Longstaff in 1907 and Peter when he climbed Trisul in 1934, a charming old gentleman armed with an antique rifle which projected through the medium of caps and gunpowder, an assortment of ironmongery and stones. He was particularly anxious that we should assist him in stalking a bear which had recently killed one of the cows of the village, but as we had left our rifle at Joshimath we were unable to accept this invitation; no doubt he would be able to deal with it effectively if he could get within close enough range for a blast of nails and pebbles. There was also an impression abroad that I was a doctor and I was called on to treat cases of conjunctivitis and blood-poisoning. On this, as on other occasions, I was amazed at the implicit and touching faith in the Sahib.   It was no use telling my patients that they must go to the hospital at Joshimath to be treated by the Indian doctor there ;  no, the Sahib was worth a thousand Babu doctors, however well qualified.

During the night we were plagued by mosquitoes which, if not malarial at this altitude, were so venomous that I woke next morning scarcely able to see out of my eyes.

From Lata to the alp known as Lata Kharak a steep track scales 5,000 feet of hillside, at first through dense sub-alpine vegetation, then between pines, birches and rhododendrons.   The morning was showery, but the weather improved later and we spent the remainder of the day pottering about the camp collecting seeds or gazing on the stupendous panorama of mist-swathed ridges, deep blue valleys and the remote snows of Hathi Parbat shining through windows in slow-moving columns of thundercloud.

Rain fell in the night but the morning was fine. Our route lay along the north-west side of the Lata Ridge to a grass pass south-west of Tolma Peak.   We now entered the Rishi Valley and at once had a foretaste of the next three days' travelling in a goat track which wound sinuously in and out of gullies.

Before we had gone far the weather broke in a sharp hailstorm which cleared as we breasted a ridge and saw at our feet the bright green alp of Durashi.   Down we went over slopes blue with gentians and frosted silver with edelweiss, just in time to pitch the tents before hail and rain again deluged the valley.   Wet mists surrounded us for the remainder of the day, but when night fell the stars shone out and through the clear air we saw the twinkling light of a shepherd's fire on the slopes of the Kuari Pass many miles away.

We left early next morning and walked up slopes of grass and boulders to the ridge we must cross to the alp, Dibrugheta. Immediately ahead, towering from the jaws of the Rishi Valley, was Nanda Devi with light mists stationed on its dark precipices. Small wonder that until Shipton and Tilman penetrated the tremendous gorges of the valley to the inmost sanctuary of the goddess, this district was reputed locally to be the abode of demons and dragons, for there can be no more awe-compelling scenery in the world than the vista of gorges framing this glorious mountain.

The weather was perfect and we were able to enjoy to the full the beauties of Dibrugheta which Dr. Long-staff described as a " horizontal oasis in a vertical desert." Our tents were pitched on a sward of flowers with forests above and below, and in the background the sunlit slabs known as " The Curtain " ; a peaceful, beautiful place where we rested through the sunny afternoon in lazy contentment.

Unhappily the fine weather did not last ; rain fell during the night and we set off next morning in mist and drizzle. In the dripping forest above the alp we disturbed a black bear, who quickly made off. A red currant grows here but, like the Himalayan strawberry, it is almost tasteless. After climbing some 1,500 feet we emerged from the forest on to a shoulder where I found monkshood in seed, then traversed steep hillsides covered here and there in juniper and *berberis* (*B. aristata*). There were also numerous flowers, including *lloydias*, *potentillas*, *anemones*, *gentians*, *saxifrages* and *androsaces*. I noted the seed of *nomocharis* and was able to collect some when we returned. There is no doubt that the Rishi Valley and the Nanda Devi basin would well repay botanical exploration.

The Nanda Devi Expedition had made a well-defined

track which we followed without difficulty. Yet even so progress was slow, for the track was seldom level and to travel one mile takes two or three hours in this valley with its innumerable gullies and buttresses.

Two goats had been purchased ; one had been slaughtered at Durashi, and the survivor now accompanied us. It was a cause of much tribulation to the man leading it, but all my sympathies were with it. Twice it escaped and was recaptured with difficulty after an exciting scramble across the hillside.

Shortly after midday we came to two draughty caves where the Nanda Devi Expedition had camped, but we were determined to make a longer march, and Peter eventually persuaded the local men to continue despite a good deal of grumbling.

Just beyond this place a steep stream rushes down a series of slabby scoops and falls. From sheer laziness we tried to cross too high instead of at a safe and easy place a little lower. The agile Wangdi got over, but the next man failed although assisted by an ice-axe. Then I tried. There was a small hold in the middle of a smooth, water-worn slab, and I managed to get one foot on it, but when I tried to raise myself my foot slipped and down I went. Fortunately the stream narrowed into a scoop and in this I wedged above a drop of fully fifty feet with water cascading over me. I managed to force my way up against the torrent until one of the men grasped my hand and dragged me to safety, soaked to the skin, with one elbow skinned and feeling something worse than a blithering idiot.

The remainder of the march was miserable, but I obtained a grain of vicarious comfort in the torrential rain which was now falling ; it was impossible for me to become any wetter.

We found a camping place near a trickle of water and levelled tent platforms on the steep hillside. Everything was damp and the tents being muddy leaked like sieves. Our luck with the weather could scarcely be worse, and conditions for the porters were wretched in the extreme as they had no spare underclothing to change into ; their cheerfulness under such conditions is inspiring.

A supper of dhal (lentils) and rice curry made the world seem a better place and it became positively rosy after a jorum of whisky. The night that followed is memorable to me above many nights. With us we had a two-pound tin of black treacle. This had been drilled through the top with the usual holes to allow of the treacle coming out and the air going in. The tin was placed in my tent, but deliberately turned itself upside down and oozed all night over the floor, my sleeping-bag, mattress and sweaters. The last-mentioned article does not combine harmoniously with black treacle and I shall never forget the anguish on Nurbu's face when he looked in next morning.

It was a dull, sullen morning and snow was falling down to the 17,000-foot level. For a few minutes there was a suspicion of sunlight then, inexorably, the mists shut down and rain began to fall.

The going was easy on the whole and we reached the entrance of the Rhamani Valley earlier than expected. The mist made the way up this difficult to find, but we ascended a gully and traversed hopefully along hillsides considerably less steep than those of the Rishi Valley. Presently, after crossing two streams, we came to a grass slope where there was a large overhanging boulder, the ground beneath which showed evident signs of former occupation. This was Shipton's camping place and it was remarkable that we should come across it after groping our way up the valley and over complicated hillsides in a thick mist.

Here we camped. There was juniper handy and soon Ang Bao had contrived to light a fire in the shelter of the boulder and brew tea. We next dismissed the local men, with the exception of Nater Singh and Dharam Singh, and settled down to make ourselves as comfortable as possible.

Any optimism we might have had as to climbing Dunagiri had long since evaporated. It was now September 6th and since August 13th when we arrived at Badrinath there had been only one completely fine day. There is no doubt that had the Nanda Devi party experienced similar weather they could not have succeeded, for snow had fallen every day, and the mountain had been continuously plastered. Yet there is no reason to suppose that we experienced especially bad monsoon weather, and mountaineers visiting Garhwal during the monsoon season should keep as far north as possible until the monsoon ends, as it usually does, in September.

Rain fell most of the night and as usual we dressed next morning in damp clothing. Once again it was a day of continuous mist and rain, and as we had little idea as to where we were we steered by Peter's compass, making more or less directly up the valley to begin with, then in the approximate direction of Dunagiri. In good weather it would have been a delightful walk as we passed many slopes and lawns bright with flowers, some of which were now in seed, including *allardias*, yellow *potentillas* and *primulas* of the *nivalis* section.

Then we made uphill by the side of a moraine. We could see little or nothing and presently when sleet and snow fell heavily we decided to camp, for there was no object in continuing on what might well prove to be a wrong route to Dunagiri. Three men were retained and the other four sent back to the base camp. As for the remainder of the day, my diary records simply, " Rain, sleet, snow. Tent leaking."

Six inches of snow fell in the night, but next morning when we looked out of our tents the weather was clear, and we saw the long summit ridge of Dunagiri, white and brilliant in the sun, peeping over a nearer ridge.

To reach the col at the foot of the south-west ridge we had to cross two intermediate glaciers and ridges. Just beneath the crest of the first ridge we had an inkling as to the snow to expect on the mountain when a little snow-slope peeled off in a miniature slab avalanche. Tse Tendrup, who was holding me on the rope from the ridge crest, apparently thought I was in great danger (there was none as the slope was not fifty feet high and ended in screes) and planting both heels in the snow pulled for all he was worth. A volley of half-strangled curses was his sole reward for an action which, on the face of it, was entirely praiseworthy.

The second ridge involved us in a steep descent of some 300 feet, but at length we stood on the glacier immediately beneath the slopes running up to the col. Mists had again formed, but the day was warm and the snow soft and unpleasant to tread. As far as we could see the best route to the col was to one side of a wide and steep bulge of ice. At the foot of the slope was a partially choked *bergschrund* which we crossed without difficulty. We had progressed less than 200 feet and I who was leading was cautiously prodding the snow with my ice-axe when there was a dull thump. We came to a sudden halt ; then, through the mist and above us, we heard the unmistakable rushing sound of an avalanche. There was a slight hesitation, then we turned and fled, making for the shelter of the ice bulge.

It was a nasty moment, for we could see nothing in the mist, only hear that ominous grating rush of sliding snow. As we ran, balls of snow scampered past us, nothing more.

The main body of the avalanche stopped just above our farthest point. It was a small one, an affair of an inch or two of surface snow, scarcely enough to have carried us down with it, much less buried us, but it gave us a fright and with common accord we turned our backs on the slope and after some little trouble found a camping place on the glacier, well protected from avalanches by wide crevasses. The porters were then sent back to the lower camp with instructions to return on the morrow with food, fuel and equipment for the camp we had planned to pitch on the col.

It was a desolate situation. All about us was snow and ice, great crevasses, frowning *séracs* and the mist-wreathed precipices of Dunagiri. Our height was about 19,000 feet, and as this is equal to approximately half atmospheric pressure at sea-level, we found it impossible to cook potatoes and after boiling them for over an hour gave them up as a bad job and ate them hard.

There was a sharp frost during the night, and next morning we climbed quickly up hard snow to the col. A biting wind was blowing across the crest, but even this could not detract from the grandeur of the view. I know of few situations where the climber is more conscious of his height. He stands on the edge of a labyrinth of snow and ice, looking down into fertile valleys and away over ranges of low hills towards the distant plains. No human brain can take in the immense panorama, and it was almost a relief to turn to objects more easily calculable : the glorious twin spires of Nanda Devi and the terrible precipices of

Changabang, a peak that falls from crest to glacier in a wall that might have been sliced in a single cut of a knife. No journey is more sublime than this visual journey from the remote depths of sub-tropical valleys to the terrific summits that girt about the " sanctuary " of Nanda Devi.

From the col the south-west ridge of Dunagiri springs up in a series of sharp snow-edges to a rock band about two-fifths of the way to the summit ridge. Above this band the ridge is flattened to the east and forms an edge rather than a ridge between the south-east and west faces of the mountain. Thus the climb above the rock band is more of a face climb than a ridge climb until the south-west shoulder of the peak is reached, whence a series of sharp edges lead towards the final snow-cap of the mountain.

Shipton found ice above the col, but when we set off to prospect the route we found soft snow on the initial ridge and the climbing was wearisome rather than difficult.

Perhaps an hour later we reached a little plateau at the foot of the rock band, an obvious site for a camp, though it was doubtful whether the summit was accessible in one day's climbing from this point, taking into account the length of the final ridge.

The rock band was still plastered by recently fallen snow which had melted here and there to form an ugly ice glaze. Our first attempt to climb it round a corner to the left was unsuccessful, and we found ourselves in an uncomfortable position on snow-covered rocks with, in my case, boot soles caked with ice and numbed fingers. After this we did what we should have done before, tackled the problem frontally ; and after a difficult and exacting piece of work succeeded in climbing it,

Thenceforward the ascent was comparatively easy until the ridge petered out in the face of the mountain. Judging from photographs, this face is some fifty degrees in angle in its lowermost portion and steepens several more degrees before connecting with the south-west shoulder. In good conditions it should be possible to climb it over rocks, but these were now buried beneath snow or glazed with ice and we were forced to the east on to a snow-slope.

Whether further advance was justifiable depended on the condition of this slope. At the point where the ridge merged into it the snow was suspiciously wind-rippled, and held by Peter I went a full rope-length ahead to test it. Wind ripples inevitably suggest that deadliest form of avalanche trap, wind slab. The climber is proceeding on hard and apparently safe snow when the surface layer cracks and sweeps down, carrying him with it. A slope of two or three hundred feet may well prove fatal as the snow, which has been compacted by the wind, splits up into hard blocks.

The two essential conditions for wind slab are a slope which permits of the snow accumulating on the lee of a ridge or buttress and a humidity of the atmosphere not less than about 80 per cent. These conditions persist on the North Col of Mount Everest during the monsoon season, and combine to render the east side a death-trap. On this slope of Dunagiri, however, though the required degree of humidity was certainly present in the atmosphere, the slope was exposed to the wind, which instead of indirectly depositing snow on a lee, had directly compacted it by pressure. Yet, when all is said and done, and the mountaineer has taken into account the implications of weather, snow, temperature and position of the slope, the casting vote between safety and danger must as often as not be based on intuition, a *feeling*, as Mr. Win-throp Young would have it, for the mountains. Just as the old sailor can " smell " bad weather or danger in his environment, so can the mountaineer sense danger on a mountain. This intuition is the product of ex-perience and a love for the mountains ; it springs from something far deeper than superficial logic or rule of thumb ; no text-books can analyse it, nor words describe it ; it is the still small voice of Nature, and woe betide him who turns a deaf ear.

The slope was safe, but it was steep ; not until we approached the shoulder did we tread rock, then there was an awkward little wall and an icy gully. Meanwhile the weather had steadily deteriorated and the signal for our arrival on the shoulder was a sudden snowstorm, accompanied by a strong and bitterly cold wind. We paused just long enough to see the first of a series of sharp snow-edges leading towards the summit. There was no question of advancing further as, apart from the bad weather, we were both tired after a climb of well over 3,000 feet on snow which reminded me of mid-winter snow on a high Alpine peak.

The porters meanwhile had carried up the camp to the col, and by the time we had descended through mist and snow the tents had been pitched.

September 9th dawned clear after a cold night and soon after the sun had risen we packed up preparatory to carrying the camp up the ridge. In such unsettled weather and difficult conditions there was no possibility of taking it beyond the little plateau at the foot of the rock band. From this point retreat is possible in bad weather, but a camp above the band might be isolated for a considerable period, quite apart from the difficulty of pitching it on the steep and exposed slopes beneath the shoulder.

Our steps of yesterday had been filled up with snow and had to be made anew, and with laden porters the ascent took nearly twice the time previously taken by Peter and myself.

Except that there was a nearly level platform for the tents the site had nothing to recommend it, for it was fully exposed to the wind. Our advent was the signal for the worst Himalayan weather I have known, except for the storms on Mount Everest in 1933. My diary is terse on the point.

" *September 9th.* Pushed camp to plateau below rock step. Blizzard at 11 a.m., lasted 22 hours. Terribly cold. Zip fastener broke and powdery snow invaded tent (Peter and I were sharing his tent). The coldest night I've ever spent bar high camps on Everest.

" *10th.* Wretched day. Blizzards. Descended to col for more provisions. Snow 1–2 feet deep on ridge and avalanches peeling off the slopes ; steps had to be re-made. We were working with two porters, Tse Tendrup and Ang Bao, the remainder having returned to the lower camp for more provisions and equipment.

" *11th.* Clear early. Gale later, then blizzard. Lightning at night. Hopeless conditions.

" *12th.* Clear morning but snowstorm in afternoon. High wind blowing clouds of snow off mountain. Sun cleared some of the snow from rocks above the camp."

In such conditions there was little hope of reaching the summit and we were not in the position to play a waiting game. We determined, however, to push an attack through as far as possible, in which we were encouraged to some small degree by the quantities of snow stripped from the mountain by the wind. If we could regain the shoulder there was a chance we might find the summit ridge in fair condition.

The night of the 12th was starlit and calm and at

4 a.m. on the 13th we roused ourselves and began the wretched business of cooking a meal. The cold was intense ; our boots were iron-like, and as usual the condensed milk had spilt overnight, and frozen in a horrid mess to the floor of the tent.

We were off at 6. The rope, which had become wet, had frozen and was as intractable as a steel hawser. The cold was still intense, and my toes soon became so numb that nothing I could do would restore circulation. The one thing in our favour was the weather, which was clear and calm.

If the difficulties had been considerable before they were now far worse, and it was all we could do to force the ice- and snow-plastered rocks immediately above the camp.

We led in turn. The upper snow-slope had been safely swept by the wind, but our former steps had disappeared and had to be made anew. The shoulder is about 1,500 feet from the plateau, but it took three and a half hours to reach. As we climbed, the fine morning quickly deteriorated ; mists were forming as we trod the first of a series of snow-crests leading towards the summit, and a rising wind carried powdery snow into our faces.

The ridge rises and falls in a series of scallop-like edges. Of the precipices on either hand, that to the south-east is a mere 4,000 feet, but that to the west is appalling in its steepness and magnitude. At first sight it seems to fall direct into the Dhauli Valley, 15,000 feet lower ; actually, however, the *sheer* drop into a side glen of the valley cannot be less than 8,000–10,000 feet and constitutes one of the highest mountain walls of the Central Himalayas.

We had hoped against hope that we would find the ridge in good condition, but in this we were disappointed.

The fierce blizzards of the past few days, instead of sweeping it bare had accumulated loose snow upon it, building it up in the process to a razor-like edge.

The first crest was merely fatiguing, as at every step we sank deeply into the soft, floury snow, but on the second we encountered cornices which increased in size the farther we advanced. And they were cornices of the most treacherous type. The ridge crest was continuous in appearance and it was the *undercut* that varied in width. Thus in one place the undercut would be practically nil, and in another place a few yards away, eight or ten feet, without any perceptible difference in the run of the ridge crest to indicate this variation in the overhang.

The solution to such a problem is, of course, to traverse a ridge at a safe distance from any possible cornices, but in the present instance the steepness of the south-east slope, coupled with the loose deep snow, made such an alternative disagreeable, not to say dangerous.

The wind increased steadily as we advanced, and the ridge reeked and smoked with blown snow, so that it became more and more difficult to estimate our position in relation to the cornice. These conditions contributed more than any negligence on our part to a narrow escape from disaster.

We were taking it in turns to stamp out a track through the loose snow, and Peter was in the lead. He was some thirty feet ahead of me and half concealed every few moments by clouds of wind-driven snow, when without a sound the ridge crest peeled off beneath him. As the loosely packed snow collapsed the wind caught it and whirled it upwards, so that it seemed almost to explode. For a moment he disappeared from view, then I saw him ; he had been at the edge of the break, and though he had fallen with the cornice he had landed on the true crest of the ridge a few feet lower.

It all happened in a second.  He stopped, while the collapsed cornice went smoking down the ice-slopes, then scrambled back to the ridge and safety.

A question I have often asked myself since is would I have been able to stop him had he followed the cornice down the ice face ?  I could only have done so by throwing myself down the other side of the ridge. Once in the Alps I had to do this, but that was to check the fall of a companion, and I had a second or two in which to decide upon a course of action.  Here I had less time and at high altitudes the brain works slowly. I can only *hope* that I would have done the right thing.

We were shaken by the experience, and when Peter regained the ridge, almost exhausted by the effort, the one thing I could think of to say, and it flashed illogically, absurdly and brutally into my mind, was, " You have been warned ! "

After this little misadventure we traversed the southeast slope some distance from the ridge, but we had not gone far when it was brought home to us that we were beaten.  I was now taking a turn ahead and so steep was the slope that I was edging along sideways.  Worse than this was the loose snow ; at every step we sank in to the knees ; and beneath the snow was ice, so that it was impossible to secure ourselves by driving in our axes, and we felt that the snow might cascade off at any moment and take us with it.  Our attempt had been pushed to the limit of justifiability.  There was nothing for it but to retreat.

We had traversed about one-third of the ridge, and beyond our highest point there appears to be no insuperable obstacle.  Given good conditions Dunagiri is a safe climb, but it will never be an easy one, especially if much ice is present.

The descent was a miserable experience. I did not realise until we retired how cold I was. Never have I felt so cold ; my feet were without feeling, and my fingers so numb and stiff that I could scarcely grasp my ice-axe. To halt on the ridge was impossible, but a short distance below the shoulder we found a partially sheltered place under a rock where I removed my boots. My feet were white and entirely without feeling, so Peter set to work to rub them. For half an hour he worked away and I can never be sufficiently grateful to him ; there is no doubt that he saved me from serious frost-bite.

As we sat on an uncomfortably sloping rock we were able to take stock of ourselves and of what we had endured on the wind-blasted ridge. We were caked with ice, and our faces looked out from the midst of a solid mass of ice matting our beards, moustaches and Balaclava helmets.

We turned back at 10.15 and regained the camp at 1.15, after a descent complicated by yet another snowstorm. There Tse Tendrup and Ang Bao set to work on my feet. Their skill was surprising ; an experienced masseuse could not have done it better ; no doubt Tibetans are used to dealing with frost-bite, and experience in treating it is hereditary with them. It was an agonising process when the circulation began to return, and so prolonged was the rubbing that raw patches appeared.

There was no question of a further attempt on Dunagiri, and we packed up the camp and descended through weather that was working up for another blizzard. On the col we collected the remainder of our gear and hastened down to the glacier, meeting Nurbu and Pasang on the way, who relieved us of some of our loads.

Wangdi had pitched a camp on the glacier, and

there my feet had another rubbing which restored the circulation, except to my big toes which had already suffered on Everest, and which continued to remind me of Dunagiri for some months to come.

Altogether we were thankful to be off the mountain safely, for what with avalanches, blizzards and collapsing cornices, we felt that we had had more than our fair share of excitements. I remember coming across a copy of " Punch " which had arrived by a previous mail. In it was a questionnaire entitled, " Are You Alive ? " I read it very carefully and decided that we were, but only just.

Snow fell heavily at the lower camp, and the weather increased in spitefulness during our return through the Rishi Valley, reaching a climax the day we marched from Dibrugheta to Durashi, when rain fell in such torrents that the stream between the two alps had to be forded one man at a time tied to a rope.

But this day, September 16th, was the last day of the monsoon. As I lay shivering in a soaked sleeping-bag I saw the stars shining steadily, and next morning the alp lay white and frosty beneath a cloudless sky. The fine weather lasted, and all day as we marched to Lata Kharak the sun blazed with a new-found vigour. The monsoon had ended as though turned off by a tap.

In brilliant sunshine we ran down to Lata to receive a warm welcome from the friendly populace of that little village, and the following day strolled back to Joshimath.

We had been beaten, soundly thrashed, by Dunagiri, but it was an experience we could hardly regret. Within the space of three weeks we had tasted all that mountaineering has to offer in the Himalayas. Swiftly perish the memories of failure and success ; imperishable are the memories of good adventuring.

# CHAPTER XXIV

## AUTUMN IN
## THE VALLEY OF FLOWERS

ON September 21st Peter and I parted at Joshimath, Peter to return to Ranikhet and I to return to the Bhyundar Valley to complete my botanical work. So ended the happiest mountaineering partnership of my experience.

It was a perfect morning as I strolled along the Alaknanda Valley. The air was charged with a new sweetness and strength. The humid, waterlogged vapours of the past two months had been replaced by an atmosphere of crystal clarity ; the sun was no longer a fierce despotic tyrant, but warm and genial.

The last of the pilgrims were descending from Badrinath, and they too seemed imbued with the vigour of the atmosphere and greeted me cheerfully. In a week or two Badrinath would be evacuated for the winter, when snow accumulates to a great depth and renders the Alaknanda Valley inaccessible.

The cycle of life and growth had entered a new phase. Here and there were fields of millet ripening to a deep magenta, and the hillsides were tinted with brown and gold. The predominant note was the intense stillness. The streams after their turbulence had regained tranquillity ; the weather, freed from its recent passions, had lapsed into a profound peacefulness ; the air was entirely without movement, and a great hush had fallen on hill and valley.

Once again I crossed the crazy little suspension bridge over the Alaknanda River and climbed through the forests to the same camping place at the edge of the Bhyundar River.

Nothing had changed since I entered the valley three months earlier. The remains of the half-burnt tree-trunk were still lying there ; the evening was the same with the distant peak alight between the walls of the gorge. Then, miracle of miracles, and I must ask the reader to accept this as true, the same little bird sang the same little hymn from the tree above my tent. In this changelessness lies Nature's greatest message to men. Beside it our hurly-burly of rush and bustle can be viewed in its true proportions ; our little snobberies, our puffed up self-importance, become as naught when viewed against this supreme indifference of Nature. Yet the message is not purely negative ; it should not inspire hopelessness or passivity. In Nature we see a force building up from limitless materials to some unimagined end ; we are part of a growth infinitely serene ; why then should we not partake of serenity ?

At the upper village next morning I met the old shepherd who had supplied me with milk. He and the other shepherds had driven down their flocks and were about to descend to the Alaknanda Valley for the winter. The grain had been reaped, and lay in golden piles on rushwork mats or in the flagged court-yards of the houses.

Above the village I saw no one, until I came to the pastures below the gorge where some goats were still grazing. Beyond these alps the valley was deserted, and it seemed strange that it should have been aban-doned thus early ; probably there are seasons when snow falls deeply early in October and the shepherds dare not risk their flocks later than the third week in September.

On the last occasion I had crossed the bridge below the gorge the torrent had raged furiously, but with the ending of the monsoon it had shrunk to peaceable dimensions, for winter cold was now gripping the high snows.

It was good to pass through the gorge into the upper meadows. Peter and I had left them under scowling skies, but now the sky was the colour of the gentians that were blooming in their millions at the base camp, except where a few light plumes and tufts of glowing cloud clung to the peaks or floated lazily between them. When I had left, green was the predominant shade, now it was brown and gold; the floor of the valley was enriched with soft colourings, varying from the deep red of the *potentilla* leaves to the yellow of the withering grasses and the faintest tinge of russet in the birch forest. Here and there drifts of white everlastings matched the snows on high, and down by the stream blue *cynoglossum* and deep red *potentillas*, growing from turf only recently evacuated by avalanche debris, were in bloom, hastening to complete their cycle before winter should come.

The predominant note was peace; not the faintest breeze ruffled the herbage and the silence was the silence of a vast ocean utterly calm, though always the sound of the streams came to the ear as a soft almost imperceptible cadence.

The evenings were cooler now and frost rimed the herbage at nights, so that I was glad of a fire. Otherwise there was little difference. The same evening mist swept up through the gorge, hurried along the valley and melted away as quickly as it formed, and the same stars looked down when the snows of Rataban had flamed and paled in the swift tide of night.

The morning after our arrival I set the men to work to dig up *nomocharis* bulbs. It was no easy task, as the *nomocharis* seems to prefer the company of bracken roots and grows a full six inches deep ; ordinary forks and spades were useless, and ice-axes had to be employed.

Meanwhile I collected seeds. Unfortunately the sheep had done considerable damage and numerous plants that I had carefully marked had been nibbled down to the roots. Thus I had great difficulty in finding such plants as the *Cypripedium himalaicum* and even the *Polemonium caeruleum*, which had flourished in the vicinity of the camp.

Thanks to a friend of Peter's, Lieut. Robertson, I now had a rifle with which to stalk the Abominable Snowman. Alas, at Joshimath I had received a telegram from London which read " Tracks made by bear " so all that remained to be done was to search for the bruin. It was sad to have my romance rudely shattered, for I had long nourished the secret hope that there really was an Abominable Snowman and that he lived in the Valley of Flowers. I had wondered, too, what my legal position would be were I to shoot him, and had pictured an intricate argument in the Law Courts hinging in all probability on whether the Snowman was the man-eating variety or merely a devourer of yaks. If the former I could at least plead justifiable homicide, but if the latter my position would be intricate and difficult and I might have to face a charge of snow-manslaughter at the very least.

So far from being grateful to the scientists who had elucidated my measurements and photographs, I cursed them roundly as destroyers of my romantic illusions. I endeavoured to explain to Wangdi that the tracks had been identified as those of a bear by the scientific pandits in London, but he dismissed their conclusions contemptuously and said something in Tibetan which I was unable to understand, but which I am certain was derogatory to zoological science. He even evidenced a scepticism as to the power of the rifle and explained that even if I did not drop dead before I had time to fire it the bullet would pass straight through the Abominable Snowman without incommoding him in the least. It says well for his bravery that he did not hesitate to accompany me on my stalk.

It was a perfect morning when we left the base camp, with hoar-frost on the ground and the sun rising in a cloudless sky from behind Rataban. My plan was to climb the hillside to the east of the base camp, then to traverse more or less horizontally across the end of the glacier into which the tracks had descended.

Our best route lay up a steep and broken ridge, and we were scrambling up this and had arrived at the foot of a little rock step perhaps fifteen feet high, when of a sudden there was a rushing sound from above. Thinking for a moment that a stone was coming, we ducked in close to the rocks and next moment a musk deer jumped over our heads and was gone in a flash. I had a momentary glimpse of it as it bolted down the ridge with incredible surefootedness and speed, before disappearing from sight over a brow.

A few yards higher we found its cave, which was full of droppings and highly charged with musk. Except for this incident the ascent was uneventful, and we came at length to a boulder-strewn shoulder where we were surprised to find a cairn, which had probably been built by the Sikh during his survey of the Bhyundar Valley. A little higher the ridge ended against a sheer rock face, two or three thousand feet high. Here we halted, for the ridge was an excellent viewpoint and commanded a view of the glacier and mountainside to which the tracks had descended.

Needless to say there was no animal life to be seen, not so much as a barhal, though we had seen their tracks during the ascent, so we divided our time between scanning the hillside through my monocular glass and collecting seeds from various small plants which included *androsaces*, everlastings, dwarf *potentillas* and gentians.

Light mists had formed in the valley and between them the stream showed, a straggling silver line, but the sky was unclouded, a deep royal blue into which the snow-laden peaks rose unfuzzed by a single breath of wind. Gauri Parbat in particular loomed spectacularly magnificent, whilst the snow-peak we had climbed lifted a gleaming crest on dark-banded precipices dusted with winter snow.

There seemed little object in pelting across hillsides after a bear or even an Abominable Snowman when we could lie at our ease on the warm sun-soaked turf, and it was a full two hours later before we bestirred ourselves from our lethargy to continue with the hunt.

Having descended from the ridge we crossed the tongue of the glacier and traversed steep hillsides, buttresses and gullies until we came to another grassy ridge, which rose to a craggy top. It was a perfect luncheon place, whilst many plants in seed more than compensated me for any regret I may have felt at not sighting our quarry. So for the next sunny hour or two we rested there or filled envelopes with seeds, and what better way is there of spending an autumn afternoon on a hillside? Which would you prefer: a flower in your garden or a mouldering head on your wall?

Before returning to the base camp we descended to

the buttress beneath which was the cave into which I had seen a bear retreat. The bear had left or was not at home, but on the buttress I discovered a gentian I had not seen before, light purple in colour and with a light green throat which I decided was worth any number of bears.

We arrived back at the base camp without having fired a shot, and for this I am glad. Long may the peacefulness of the Valley of Flowers remain undisturbed.

The days passed all too quickly and with their passing the autumn hues brightened until the valley glowed golden in the sunlight. Twice showers fell in the late afternoon and once thunder rumbled among the ranges but the weather otherwise remained perfect. I wish that I could convey some picture of this perfection. The sun shone daily from unclouded skies of indescribable purity, all Nature slept and dreamed and the very spirit of Peace pervaded the still atmosphere. As I had felt on the Mana Peak so did I feel now, that to shout would be profane, that this peacefulness in which we lived was a precious experience.

A clever friend once told me : " The trouble with you is that you feel more than you think." If this is so, thank God for my disability. For solitude in the Valley of Flowers taught me the insignificance and incapacity for happiness of thought as compared with a meditation that knows no intellectual limitations but is content to accept with childlike faith and delight the infinite beauties and grandeurs of the universe. So limited is the scope of thought when brought to bear on the splendours of the Universe that we must first of all rid ourselves of its ensnaring tangles before we can turn our eyes to heaven and read the message of the hilltops and the stars. What a man gains in cleverness he may lose in spiritual perception ; he is indeed great who can conquer his own cleverness.

The day came when the Dotials arrived to carry my loads to Ranikhet. This was September 29th, my last day in the Valley of Flowers, and that evening I sat late by the camp fire. The night was supremely still and the smoke of the burning juniper stood straight up into the stars. The porters had long since ceased talking and were fast asleep and no sound came to me but little hissing whispers from the fire and the eternal note of the stream. All about me was the great peacefulness of the hills, a peacefulness so perfect that something within me seemed to strain upwards as though to catch the notes of an immortal harmony. There seemed in this peace and quietude some Presence, some all-pervading beauty separated from me only by my own " muddy vesture of decay." The stars, and the hills beneath the stars, the flowers at my feet were part of a supreme Purpose which I myself must struggle to fulfil. Poor little man, from ignoble depths to starry heights, from hill-top to valley in a reckless run ; poor, slogging little man, how hard and wearisome the climb, how besetting the winds and difficulties. Surely the hills were made that we should appreciate our strength and frailties ? The stars that we should sense our destiny ? Yet through all this tangled skein of earthly life must run the golden thread of beauty. Beauty is everywhere ; we need not go to the hills to find it. Peacefulness is everywhere, if we make it so ; we need not go to the hills to seek it. Yet because we are human and endowed with physical qualities, and because we cannot divorce ourselves from these qualites we must needs utilise them as best we can and seek through them beauty that we may return refreshed in mind and spirit. So we go to seek beauty on a hill, the beauty of a larger freedom, the beauty that lifts us to a high window of our fleshy prison whence we may see a little further over the dry and dusty plains to the blue ranges and eternal snows. So we climb the hills, pitting our strength against difficulty, enduring hardship, discomfort and danger that through a subjugation of body we may perceive beauty and discover a contentment of spirit beyond all earthly imaginings. And through beauty and contentment we gain peace.

It is the ugliness man creates that leads to discontentment and war ; the ugliness of greed, and the ugliness that greed begets ; a vast ocean of ugliness in which he perishes miserably. It is because men are beginning to realise this that they long to escape from an environment of mechanical noises, of noisome fumes and hideous arrangements of bricks and steel into the beauty and quietude of the countryside, to carry themselves naturally on their legs, not artifically on wheels, to travel at God's pace, to listen to the song of Nature, the birds, the streams and the breeze in the cornfield, to look upon beautiful things, flowers, meadowlands and hill-tops, to live for a time simply and rhythmically in airs untainted by factory smoke, to discover the virtues of simplicity and goodwill.

Beauty, health, good comradeship, peace, all these had been mine in the Valley of Flowers. For a while I had lived simply and happily and I like to think, indeed I know, that those about me had been happy too.

Such memories are imperishable for they rely on their perpetuity not on physical action, but on a contemplation that reaches into the very soul of beauty. For I had seen many beautiful things and not least of these was the loyalty and devotion of my companions, those hard bitten men who were ready to dare all and risk all if by so doing they could further my plans and ambitions. Such loyalty as this is rarer than gold.

So I spent some of my last hours in the Valley of Flowers, seated by the camp fire, until the flames died down and the stars brightened beyond the hill-tops ; and all about me was the serenity of God.

# APPENDICES

## BOTANICAL NOTES

My flower collecting was confined to altitudes over the 7,000-foot level. Above this level flowers should prove hardy in the British climate, though there are some species which have found their way up from lower elevations to live precariously between 7,000 and 8,000 feet which may not be hardy. There are also many flowers below the 7,000-foot level which should prove hardy as the frost-line is considerably lower. The subtropical vegetation in the Central Himalayas is a study in itself, and though I came across many flowers, I did not collect them for fear of complicating my object, which was to collect seeds and specimens which should prove hardy in the open British garden. The majority of my specimens were collected over 10,000 feet and there are a great many flowers not collected which grow between the 7,000 foot and 10,000-foot levels, whilst there are of course scores of plants awaiting the collector above the 10,000-foot level ; I did little more than scratch the surface of a rich mine of plants.

The following list of plants collected would be incomplete without plants that Mr. R. L. Holdsworth found in 1931 but which I did not find, or if I did find rotted in my presses when they had to be kept without attention at Joshimath for some weeks during the monsoon season.

There are also plants which grow in the foothills, such as *Paeony Emodii* and *Lilium Giganteum* which do not find their place in a list concerned solely with the High Himalayas.

Being very ignorant of botany it seemed to me best to concentrate on one particular district, and the Bhyundar Valley proved ideal for this purpose as there is a marked range of climate and rainfall within a few miles with corresponding variety in flora.

The specimens were identified at the Royal Botanic Garden, Edinburgh, and I am greatly indebted to Dr. J. Macqueen Cowan, the Assistant Keeper and his staff for the trouble they took in identifying my indifferently pressed collection.

The plants have been arranged in the order adopted by Sir Richard Strachey and Mr. J. E. Winterbottom, who made a scientific survey of Garhwal and Kumaon between the years 1846 and 1849, and whose herbarium of dried plants from these districts and the adjacent portions of Tibet has been described as " one of the most complete and valuable that has ever been distributed from India."

I am also indebted to Dr. Cowan for permission to quote from a communication he made to *The Times* :

" The richness of the flora of the Western Himalaya,* at least of some of the upper valleys, is now beyond dispute. Mr. F. S. Smythe by his recent expedition has established this fact, for he has brought back from there some 250 plants, many of them representatives of the most popular garden genera. This is not only a matter of general interest, but also an important addition to our knowledge of plant geography.

" For more than a century the long line of the Himalaya, from Kashmir to Bhutan, has been known as one of the World's richest treasuries of flowers. Slowly from

---

* I have referred in my book to the ranges of Garhwal and Kumaon as constituting a part of the Central Himalayas.

time to time the hidden valleys revealed their wealth, until it seemed that the storehouse must be empty. Plant collectors then turned to different fields.

" It is true that there is scarcely a plant of high altitudes in the Eastern Himalaya that does not adorn our gardens. Only by a close comparison of lists of Sikkim plants with garden catalogues can one appreciate how much our gardens owe to the flora of that region.

" From the Western Himalaya, Kashmir, Garhwal and Kumaon, fewer plants have come, and we have been accustomed to look eastwards, away from this drier region, for luxuriance of plant life.

" Mr. Smythe has drawn our attention again to the west ; it is not without justification that he names the Bhyundar Valley ' The Valley of Flowers.' It is as rich as, and probably richer than, any valley in Sikkim. This valley, and the country around it and beyond it, is in a region which has not had much attention from botanists and plant collectors.

" While on the one hand some of the plants are not confined to the west but occur throughout the whole Himalaya, on the other hand there are many which occur only within a limited range and do not extend far eastwards, penetrating only a little way into Nepal. Mr. Smythe's collection is the more interesting because it contains mainly plants with a restricted distribution and very few of those which extend to Sikkim."

Being a gardener and not a botanist I looked at the flora through a gardener's eyes. The principal points that struck me were firstly the power that many plants possess to adapt themselves to varying conditions and altitudes. I have already mentioned in the text that I found a balsam growing eight feet high at 7,000 feet and as many inches high at 14,000 feet. Such flowers should be able to adapt themselves to the British climate. It is, I maintain, wrong to define a plant as hardy from a garden standpoint because it flourishes at great altitudes, for it must be remembered that such plants exist under more equable conditions than flowers indigenous to Britain ; they are covered with snow for the greater part of the year and exposed to genial warmth during the summer months. For this reason they are difficult to grow in a country such as ours which varies in its climate between a muggy Christmas and sharp frosts in May. I see, however, no reason to suppose that flowers from elevations of 7,000 to 13,000 feet should not flourish in Britain, and I dare venture the prophecy that they will more readily adapt themselves to the vicissitudes of the British climate than the flowers of Sikkim which have added so greatly to the beauty of British gardens, for the reason that the spring, summer and autumn climate of Garhwal is far less extreme in temperature and rainfall than the climate of Sikkim. I have already compared the midsummer climate of the Bhyundar Valley with the midsummer climate of Britain and the similarity is significant to gardeners.

Secondly, as a gardener I was intensely interested in the cycle of growth in the Bhyundar Valley, and it seems to me that many valuable lessons are to be learnt from it ; I wish now that I had made it an intensive study. I refer to the manner in which flowers grow in association one with another. In the halcyon days to come when gardeners will renounce the formal herbaceous border in favour of the natural garden the study of association and rhythm in plant life will receive the attention it deserves. Anyone can cultivate an herbaceous border, but to grow a natural garden is an art and a science. I have hesitated to refer to what I mean as a wild garden, for this suggests something completely untamed and composed largely of weeds. The natural garden is necessarily composed to a great extent of flowers and grasses and has no formal limitations.  To achieve such a desirable end we must study flowers in far greater detail than we need do when we plant an herbaceous border, for we must not only copy and emulate Nature but adapt her to our particular needs.  Thus, in the Bhyundar Valley I saw ground that was so closely packed with fritillaries that it seemed impossible that other plants could grow, yet when the fritillaries had died down they were succeeded by other plants such as *potentillas* which grew equally densely.  And this cycle persisted throughout the summer, one plant being replaced by another with perfect precision.  It seemed to me also that the time factor was not the only factor but that soil and association must enter into it.  Why is it, for instance, that the purple *orchis* which grows in the Bhyundar Valley loves the near presence of thistles ?  Is it possible that there is some interacting effect of nourishment, or some rhythmical effect not as yet properly understood ? A vast subject awaits the natural gardener in this direction, and there is no doubt to my mind that it is one of intense interest, for it brings us in touch, as no ordinary gardening can, with the marvellous rhythm of Nature.

The soil is another complex factor.  Dr. Cowan very kindly had a sample of soil surrounding the roots of *Nomocharis oxypetala* analysed and the analyst's report was that : " It is slightly acid ($p$H = 6·26) and moderately fertile as far as the amounts of available plant food are concerned.  It has a large amount of organic matter, the loss on ignition being 33·8 per cent."

From this and my own observations I suggest that the flowers of Garhwal are likely to flourish in a light soil with plenty of organic matter present, i.e. leaf-mould and peat-mould which is sharply drained and, almost needless to say, exposed to full sunlight.

I cannot close these brief notes without thanking Dr. Cowan for the immense help he afforded me. I was about to leave England with no other idea but to do a little desultory seed collecting when I met him. Shortly afterwards I found my luggage augmented with about a hundredweight of presses, drying papers and seed envelopes, and it seemed that my ambition of travelling light had received a serious setback. I can only write now that the trouble was very well worth while and that I now realise what I have missed in the past. Merely to travel in a district such as the Himalayas without some additional interest, whether it be surveying, geology, anthropology or botany, is to miss one of the vital interests of a region that abounds in beauty and interest.

# PLANTS FROM THE BHYUNDAR VALLEY AND NEIGHBOURHOOD COLLECTED IN 1937

RANUNCULACEAE

   *Clematis montana* Buch.-Ham. (Virgin's Bower)
      *grata* Wall.
   *Anemone rupicola* Camb. (Wind-flower)
      *obtusiloba* D. Don
      *rivularis* Buch.-Ham.
      *polyanthes* D. Don
   *Thalictrum elegans* Wall. (Meadow Rue ; Tufted Columbine)
      *cultratum* Wall.
      *Chelidonii* DC.
      *pauciflorum* Royle
   *Callianthemum cachemirianum* Camb.
   *Ranunculus hyperboreus* Rottb. (Crowfoot ; Buttercup)
      *hirtellus* Royle
   *Caltha palustris* Linn. (Marsh Marigold)
      *scaposa* Hook. f. et Thoms.
   *Trollius acaulis* Lindl. (Globe Flower)
   *Paraquilegia grandiflora* Drumm. et Hutch.
   *Aquilegia pubiflora* Wall. (Columbine)
   *Delphinium denudatum* Wall. (Larkspur)
      *densiflorum* Duthie
      *Brunonianum* Royle
   *Aconitum heterophyllum* Wall. (Wolf's-bane ; Monkshood)
   *Actaea spicata* Linn. (Toad-root, Baneberry ; Herb Christopher)

BERBERIDEAE

   *Berberis aristata* DC. (Barberry ; Jaundice Berry)

PAPAVERACEAE

*Meconopsis aculeata* Royle (Blue Poppy)

FUMARIACEAE

*Corydalis cachemiriana* Royle (Fumatory)
    *cornuta* Royle
    *Govaniana* Wall.
    *Moorcroftiana* Wall.
    *meifolia* Wall.

CRUCIFERAE

*Arabis auriculata* Lam. (Wall Cress ; Rock Cress)
    *amplexicaulis* Edgew.
*Draba lasiophylla* Royle (Whitlow Grass)
*Erysimum repandum* Linn. (Alpine Wallflower ; Hedge Mustard)
*Capsella Bursa-pastoris* Medic.

VIOLACEAE

*Viola biflora* Linn. (Violet)

CARYOPHYLLEAE

*Gypsophila cerastioides* D. Don (Chalk Plant)
*Silene Cucubalus* Wibel. (Campion ; Catchfly)
    *Moorcroftiana* Wall.
*Lychnis apetala* Linn. (Campion ; German Catchfly ; Rose Campion)
*Cerastium glomeratum* Thuill. (Snow in Summer ; Snow Plant)
*Arenaria kashmirica* Edgew. (Sandwort)
    *musciformis* Wall.
    *glanduligera* Edgew.

HYPERICINEAE

*Hypericum elodeoides* Chois. (Aaron's Beard ; St. John's Wort)

GERANIACEAE

*Geranium pratense* Linn. (Crane's-bill)
    *collinum* M. Bieb.
    *Wallichianum* Sweet
    *Grevilleanum* Wall.

*Impatiens Roylei* Walp. (Balsam)
   *sulcata* Wall.
   *Thomsoni* Hook. f. et Thoms.
   *scabrida* DC.

SAPINDACEAE

*Acer caesium* Wall. (Maple)

LEGUMINOSAE

*Piptanthus nepalensis* D. Don (Nepal Laburnum)
*Thermopsis barbata* Royle
*Parochetus communis* Buch.-Ham. (Blue-flowered Shamrock)
*Trigonella corniculata* Linn. (Fenugreek)
*Guldenstaedtia himalaica* Baker
*Astragalus chlorostachys* Lindl. (Milk Vetch)
   *himalayanus* Klotzsch
   *Candolleanus* Royle
*Pueraria peduncularis* Grah.

ROSACEAE

*Spiraea Aruncus* Linn (Meadow Sweet)
   *bella* Sims
   *canescens* D. Don
*Geum elatum* Wall. (Avens)
*Potentilla Sibbaldi* Hall. f. (Cinquefoil)
   *fruticosa* Linn.
      ,, var. Inglisii Hook. f.
   *ambigua* Camb.
   *eriocarpa* Wall.
   *polyphylla* Wall.
   *Leschenaultiana* Ser.
   *peduncularis* D. Don
   *leuconota* D. Don
   *microphylla* D. Don
   *argyrophylla* Wall.
      ,, var. *atrosanguinea* Hook. f.
      ,, var *leucochroa* Hook. f.
*Agrimonia Eupatoria* Linn.

*Rosa macrophylla* Lindl. (Rose)
    *sericea* Lindl.
*Sorbus foliolosa* Spach
*Cotoneaster rotundifolia* Wall. (Quince-leaved Medlar ; Rose Box)

SAXIFRAGACEAE

*Astilbe rivularis* Buch.-Ham. (False Goat's-beard)
*Saxifraga cernua* Linn. (Rockfoil ; London Pride)
    *Hirculus* Linn.
    *diversifolia* Wall.
    *Jacquemontiana* Dcne.
    *fimbriata* Wall.
    *Flagellaris* Willd.
*Parnassia nubicola* Wall. (Grass of Parnassus)
*Bergenia Stracheyi* Engl.
*Ribes glaciale* Wall. (Red Currant)

CRASSULACEAE

*Sedum Rhodiola* DC. (Stonecrop)
    *heterodontium* Hook. f. et Thoms.
    *crenulatum* Hook. f. et Thoms.
    *tibeticum* Hook. f. et Thoms.
       ,, var. *Stracheyi* (Hook f. et Thoms.)
    *quadrifidum* Pall.
    *asiaticum* DC.
    *trifidum* Wall.
*Sempervivum mucronatum* Edgew. (House-leek)

ONAGRACEAE

*Epilobium latifolium* Linn. (Willow Herb)
    *origanifolium* Lamk.

UMBELLIFERAE

*Bupleurum longicaule* Wall. (Hare's-ear)
*Anthriscus nemorosa* Spreng. (Chervil)
*Cortia Lindleyi* DC.
*Pleurospermum Candollii* Benth.

CAPRIFOLIACEAE

*Viburnum erubescens* Wall. (Guelder Rose ; Snowball Tree)
*Lonicera obovata* Royle (Honeysuckle)

RUBIACEAE

*Galium acutum* Edgew.
*Asperula odorata* Linn. (Woodruff ; Squinancy-wort)

VALERIANEAE

*Nardostachys Jatamansi* DC.
*Valeriana dioica* Linn. (Cretan Spikenard)

DIPSACEAE

*Morina longifolia* Wall. (Whorl-flower)

COMPOSITAE

*Solidago Virgaurea* Linn. (Golden Rod)
*Aster diplostephioides* Benth. (Starwort ; Michaelmas Daisy)
*Erigeron alpinus* Linn. (Fleabane)
    *multiradiatus* Benth.
*Microglossa albescens* Clarke (Shrubby Starwort)
*Leontopodium himalayanum* DC. (Edelweiss)
        *Jacotianum* Beauv.
        *monocephalum* Edgew.
*Anaphalis nubigena* DC. (Pearly Everlasting or Immortelle)
        *cuneifolia* Hook. f.
        *contorta* Hook. f.
*Carpesium cernuum* Linn.
*Siegesbeckia orientalis* Linn.
*Allardia glabra* Dcne.
        *tomentosa* Dcne.
*Tanacetum nubigenum* Wall. (Tansy ; Alecost)
*Artemisia Roxburghiana* Besser (Old Man ; Old Woman ; Lad's Love)
*Cremanthodium Decaisnei* Clarke
        *arnicoides* Good

*Senecio chrysanthemoides* DC. (Jacobaea ; Cineraria ; Rag-
    wort)
    *diversifolius* Wall.
    *Ligularia* Hook. f.
    *quinquelobus* Hook. f. et Thoms.
*Saussurea obvallata* Wall. (Saw-wort)
    *piptanthera* Edgew.
    *hypoleuca* Spreng.
    *sorocephala* Hook. f. et Thoms.
*Gerbera Kunzeana* Braun. et Asch. (Barberton or Transvaal
    Daisy)
*Lactuca dissecta* D. Don (Lettuce)
    *macrorrhiza* Hook. f.
    *Lessertiana* Clarke

## CAMPANULACEAE

*Codonopsis rotundifolia* Benth. (Bellwort)
*Cyananthus lobatus* Wall.
    *microphyllus* Edgew.
*Campanula latifolia* Linn. (Bellflower)
    *cashmiriana* Royle
    *aristata* Wall.
    *modesta* Hook. f. et Thoms.

## ERICACEAE

*Gaultheria trichophylla* Royle (Canada Tea ; Creeping Winter-
    green)
*Cassiope fastigiata* D. Don.
*Rhododendron campanulatum* D. Don
    *lepidotum* Wall.
    *anthopogon* D. Don

## PRIMULACEAE

*Primula denticulata* Sm.
    *Heydei* Watt.
    *involucrata* Wall.
    *elliptica* Royle
    *macrophylla* D. Don
    *Wigramiana* W. W. Sm.

*Androsace primuloides* Duby (Rock Jasmine)
    *Chamaejasme* Host. var. uniflora Hook. f.
    *Poissonii* R. Knuth

OLEACEAE

*Jasminum humile* Linn. (Jasmine)
*Syringa Emodi* Wall.

GENTIANACEAE

*Gentiana tenella* Fries (Gentian)
    *argentea* Royle
    *cachemirica* Dcne.
    *venusta* Wall.
    *tubiflora* Wall.
*Pleurogyne carinthiaca* Griseb.
*Swertia purpurascens* Wall. (Marsh Felwort)
    *pulchella* Buch.-Ham.

POLEMONIACEAE

*Polemonium caeruleum* Linn. (Jacob's Ladder ; Greek Valerian)

BORAGINEAE

*Cynoglossum glochidiatum* Wall.
*Hackelia glochidiata* Brand
*Eritrichium strictum* Dcne. (Fairy Borage ; Fairy Forget-me-not)
*Myosotis sylvatica* Hoffm. (Forget-me-not)
*Macrotomia perennis* Boiss.

SCROPHULARINEAE

*Verbascum Thapsus* Linn. (Mullein ; Aaron's Rod)
*Mazus surculosus* D. Don
*Picrorhiza Kurrooa* Benth.
*Veronica deltigera* Wall. (Speedwell)
    *himalensis* D. Don
    *capitata* Benth.
*Euphrasia officinalis* Linn.

*Pedicularis siphonantha* D. Don
   *bicornuta* Klotzsch
   *pectinata* Wall.
   *porrecta* Wall.
   *Roylei* Maxim.

ACANTHACEAE

*Strobilanthes Wallichii* Nees (Cone-head)

LABIATAE

*Elsholtzia eriostachy* Benth.
*Origanum vulgare* Linn. (Sweet Marjoram)
*Thymus Serpyllum* Linn. (Thyme)
*Calamintha Clinopodium* Benth. (Calamint ; Basil Thyme)
*Nepeta eriostachys* Benth. (Catmint)
*Scutellaria prostrata* Jacquem. (Helmet Flower ; Skull Cap)
*Brunella vulgaris* Linn.
*Stachys sericea* Wall. (Woundwort ; Chinese Artichoke)
*Lamium album* Linn. (White Dead Nettle)
*Phlomis bracteosa* Royle (Jerusalem Sage)

POLYGONACEAE

*Polygonum delicatulum* Meissn. (Knot Weed)
   *filicaule* Wall.
   *viviparum* Linn.
   *affine* D. Don
   *vacciniifolium* Wall.
   *polystachyum* Wall.
   *rumicifolium* Royle
*Oxyria digyna* Hill

EUPHORBIACEAE

*Euphorbia pilosa* Linn. (Spurge)

CUPULIFERAE

*Betula utilus* D. Don (Birch Tree)

SALICINEAE

*Salix elegans* Wall. (Willow ; Osier)
   *flabellaris* Anderss.

CONIFERAE

*Juniperus Wallichiana* Hook. f. et Thoms. (Juniper)
*Abies Pindro* Spach (Silver Fir)

ORCHIDEAE

*Orchis latifolia* Linn.
      *Chusua* D. Don
*Platanthera acuminata* Lindl.
*Cypripedium himalaicum* Rolfe (Lady's Slipper)

SCITAMINEAE

*Roscoea alpina* Royle

HAEMODORACEAE

*Aletris nepalensis* Hook. f.
*Ophiopogon intermedius* D. Don (Snake's-beard)

IRIDEAE

*Iris kumaonensis* Wall. (Flag)

LILIACEAE

*Polygonatum Hookeri* Baker (Solomon's Seal)
      *verticillatum* All.
*Smilacina pallida* Royle (False Spikenard)
*Allium humile* Kunth (Onion)
*Nomocharis oxypetala* Balf. f.
      *nana* E. H. Wils.
*Fritillaria Roylei* Hook. (Fritillary)
*Lloydia serotina* Reichb. var. unifolia Franch. (Mountain
  Spiderwort)
      *tibetica* Baker
*Gagea lutea* Schultz f. (Yellow Star of Bethlehem)
*Clintonia alpina* Kunth
*Trillium Govanianum* Wall. (American Wood Lily)

JUNCACEAE

*Juncus membranaceus* Royle
      *coninnus* D. Don

AROIDEAE

*Arisaema Wallichianum* Hook. f. (Arum)
　　　　*Jacquemontii* Blume

CYPERACEAE

*Kolbesia laxa* Boeck.
*Carex obscura* Nees. (Blue-grass ; Sedge)
　　*fuscata* Boott
　　*nivalis* Boott
　　　　,,　　,,　var. *cinnamomea* Kükenth.
　*inanis* Kunth

GRAMINEAE

*Phleum alpinum* Linn.

FILICES

*Adiantum venustum* D. Don (Maidenhair Fern)
*Cryptogramme crispa* R. Br. (Parsley Fern ; Rock Brake)
*Pteris cretica* Linn. (Bracken)
*Asplenium Trichomanes* Linn. (Lady Fern)
*Aspidium Prescottianum* Hook. (Wood Fern)
*Nephrodium Brunonianum* Hook. (Buckler Fern)
*Polypodium clathratum* Clarke (Oak Fern ; Beech Fern)
　　　　*ebenipes* Hook.
*Botrychium Lunaria* Sw. (Moon Fern ; Flowering Fern)

# SUPPLEMENTARY LIST OF PLANTS COLLECTED BY R. L. HOLDSWORTH IN THE BHYUNDAR VALLEY AND UPPER GARHWAL IN 1931 AND OBSERVED OR NOT COLLECTED IN 1937

*Androsace globifera* Duby.
   *rotundifolia* Hardw.
*Aquilegia vulgaris* Hook.
*Arisaema flavum* Schott.
*Campanula argyrotricha* Wall.
   *colorata* Wall.
   *sylvatica* Wall.
*Caragana Gerardiana*
   *crassicaulis* Benth.
*Daphne oleoides* Schreb.
*Draba incompta* Stev.
*Gentiana Aprica*
   *Capitata*
*Gerbera lanuginosa* Benth.
*Inula grandiflora* Willd.
*Megacarpaea polyandra* Benth.
*Morina Persica* Linn.
*Paraquilegia microphylla* Drumm et Hutch.
*Pedicularis versicolor* Wahlb.
*Primula rotundifolia* Wall.
   *minutissima* Jacquem
   *reptans* Hook
   *sessilis* Royle
*Rhododendron barbatum* Wall.
*Saxifraga imbricata* Royle
*Senecio arnicoides* Wall.
*Strobilanthes alatus* Nees.
*Viburnum cotinifolium* D. Don.
*Viola serpens* Wall.

To KAMET
3 Miles

Plateau

MANA PEAK
23860

EAST

22000

21500

22892

21000

22481

Zaskar
Pass

Camp

20075

Plat

Camp
4

18992

2057

To MANA
and
BADRINATH

Camp

18000

19889

Camp

20353

20496

17000

Fluted
Peak
21516

N

BANKE

1600'

1600'

Miles

0                    2

NILGIRI   PARBA
21264

Bhyu

Ridge
Peak
Col
Ice-fall
Contour
Route

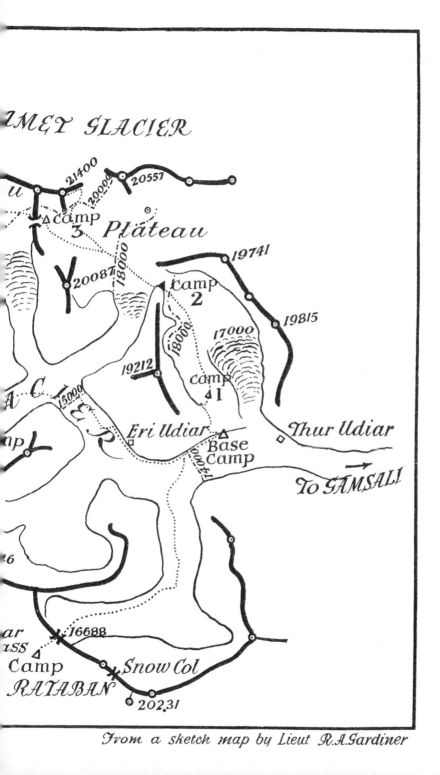

*From a sketch map by Lieut. R.A.Gardiner*

# INDEX

Wien, Dr. Karl, death of, 117

Willow-herb, species found, 117, 119

Wind-ripples, signification of, 269

Wind slab, conditions for, 269

Window-opening in railway carriages, 192

Wodehouse, P. G., 185

Wolves in Tibet, 85 *n.*

YAKS, and jhobus, grain carried by, 26

Yogis at Badrinath, 240

Young, W., and a " feeling " for the mountains, 270

ZASKAR PASS, 204, 209, 237, 239 ; ascent to, 280 ; height of, 211

Zaskar Range, 1, 30, 46, 62, 204